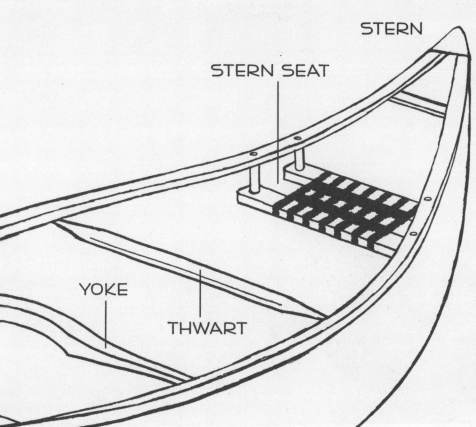

STERN

STERN SEAT

YOKE

THWART

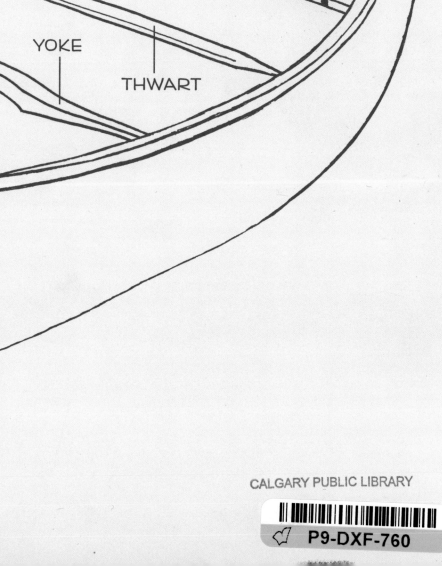

CANOE COUNTRY

ROY MacGREGOR

CANOE
COUNTRY

THE MAKING OF CANADA

RANDOM HOUSE CANADA

PUBLISHED BY RANDOM HOUSE CANADA
Copyright © 2015 Roy MacGregor

All rights reserved under International and Pan-American Copyright Conventions.
No part of this book may be reproduced in any form or by any electronic or
mechanical means, including information storage and retrieval systems, without
permission in writing from the publisher, except by a reviewer, who may quote brief
passages in a review. Published in 2015 by Random House Canada, a division of
Random House of Canada Limited, a Penguin Random House company. Distributed
in Canada by Random House of Canada Limited, Toronto.

www.penguinrandomhouse.ca

Random House Canada and colophon are registered trademarks.

Library and Archives Canada Cataloguing in Publication

MacGregor, Roy, 1948– , author
Canoe country : the making of Canada / Roy MacGregor.

Includes bibliographical references and index.
Issued in print and electronic formats.

ISBN 978-0-307-36141-7
eBook ISBN 978-0-307-361-43-1

1. Canoes and canoeing—Canada—History. 2. Canada—History.
I. Title.

GV776.15.A2M32 2015   797.1220971   C2015-902187-1

Book design by Andrew Roberts

Cover art: "Algonquin—Homage to Tom Thomson," © Ken Danby
Endpapers drawn by Andrew Roberts

Printed and bound in the United States of America

2 4 6 8 9 7 5 3 1

Penguin
Random House
RANDOM HOUSE CANADA

For Fisher, Sadie, Raphael, Hawkley and Noemie—
who will run their own rivers in life

CONTENTS

INTRODUCTION

It never occurred to me that my love affair with the canoe might one day lead to a death threat.

In the spring of 2007 I was coming to the end of a five-year, five-columns-a-week stint on the treasured page two of *The Globe and Mail*. The assignment—to tour this sprawling nation, writing about its people and places—had been the brainchild of then editor Edward Greenspon, as had been the title for the column, "This Country," and it was this unelected "office," surely, that led the CBC to ask that I serve as a juror for a contest the public broadcaster was launching to identify "The Seven Wonders of Canada."

The exercise began innocently. The idea had come out of a story meeting for CBC Radio's morning show *Sounds Like Canada*, and host Shelagh Rogers had invited listeners to send in their submissions for a national list of wonders. She and her producers expected a couple of thousand entries, at best, and were overwhelmed to receive more than 25,000. Clearly, the show had tapped into something.

Many of the nominations were obvious, such as Niagara Falls and the Rocky Mountains, but some others were delightfully eccentric and personal, such as "Mum's House in Scarborough." This nominator charmingly argued that the simple stucco home that her parents had come to from Holland in 1958, two weeks after their marriage, and where, a half century later, they still lived and patriotically flew the red maple leaf over the wrap-around porch, is a legitimate wonder. "It reminds us," Marilyn Arts Butcher wrote, "of where so many of us come from, and it is the physical fulfillment of a dream held by a young couple starting out a new life together in a country new to them."

How could the CBC resist?

The plan was to measure the nominations first by number of votes, then pare the nominations down to fifty or so before bringing in a panel of three judges to rank the top seven selections. Seemed simple enough. The two other judges asked to preside—no pay, but inside work and no heavy lifting—were Ra McGuire and Roberta Jamieson. Ra is leader of the legendary Canadian rock band Trooper, famous for such hits as "Raise a Little Hell" and "We're Here for a Good Time (Not a Long Time)." Ra came from British Columbia but knew the country intimately after more than thirty years of touring. Roberta, a former ombudsman of the Province of Ontario, is a Mohawk from Six Nations in southwest Ontario and head of the National Aboriginal Achievement Foundation.

The judging panel was far from perfect—no francophone, no easterner, all roughly the same age—but the three of us were about as familiar with the country as it is possible for any three citizens to be. The vastness of Canada verges on the incomprehensible: David Thompson, the great nineteenth-century explorer who travelled more than eighty thousand kilometres by canoe, foot and dogsled while mapping nearly four million square kilometres of North America, believed he had seen but a small percentage of the land mass that a decade after his death would become Canada. A small percentage indeed.

Throughout April and May the CBC knocked the master list down to fifty-two. The fifty-two included the fully expected—the Rockies, Niagara, Old Quebec City—but also familiar landmarks such as Gros Morne

National Park, Percé Rock, the Cypress Hills, the Northwest Passage, the Cabot Trail and Haida Gwaii. There were human creations as well: the CN Tower, the Vimy Memorial, the Rideau Canal, the Manitoba Legislative Building, the Stanley Cup and, of course, Mum's House in Scarborough. From that long list of fifty-two "wonders," listeners voted for their favourites. And this is when it really got wild. CBC received more than a *million* votes. At times the voting was so heavy that the computers doing the calculating crashed.

And then began the accusations of cheating . . .

The greatest vote-getter of all, much to the surprise of the CBC and other nominators, turned out to be the Sleeping Giant, a rock formation on a Lake Superior peninsula that, viewed from the harbour of Thunder Bay, looks uncannily like a giant in repose. The Giant tallied 177,305 votes to finish first overall—an impressive display of community involvement, considering that the population of the Thunder Bay area was then listed at 120,370.

The tally outraged the people of Niagara Falls, who had presumed—a bit arrogantly, a bit with cause—that their world-famous natural wonder would, of course, lead the pack. The famous falls, it turned out, had received less than half the number of votes (81,818) that had gone to the Giant, leading to accusations from Falls supporters that there was technological chicanery at work in the Lakehead. The people of Thunder Bay denied any nefarious plan, and eventually the "cheating" fuss died down.

The participating CBC programs, *Sounds Like Canada* (radio) and *The National* (television), announced that more than a million votes had been cast and a master list of fifty-two nominations was drawn up. The top seven according to the public vote were: (1) Sleeping Giant (177,305), (2) Niagara Falls (81,818), (3) Bay of Fundy (67,670), (4) Nahanni River (64,920), (5) northern lights (61,417), (6) Rocky Mountains (55,630) and (7) Cabot Trail (44,073). The three judges—the rock star, the Aboriginal leader and the journalist—would then come in to cull the top fifty-two down to fifteen and then to our own final seven. While the public's voting was to be a significant factor in the judges' determinations, it was not necessarily to be a deciding factor. The final decision on the Seven Wonders of Canada would be theirs alone to make. What had begun as a tiny radio project was now a full-blown television production with the three of us required on-set at CBC headquarters in Toronto.

With Peter Mansbridge hosting and Mark Kelley reporting on the action, Roberta, Ra and I fairly easily got the list of fifty-two down to fifteen—Fundy, Cabot, Cathedral Grove, Gros Morne, Haida Gwaii, Nahanni, Niagara, northern lights, Old Quebec, Pier 21, Prairie skies, Sleeping Giant, canoe, igloo, Rockies. As the first night of the program came to a close, with reporter and anchor talking about the beauty of Canadian "compromise," I made a crack about how we were likely to come up with a new phrase, "geographically correct," to stand with the country's current mania to be "politically correct." I had no idea at the moment how prescient that would prove to be. The next night, Peter Mansbridge announced, the nation would find out the final results for the Seven Wonders of Canada.

From the top fifty-two I had argued for the Stanley Cup and hockey, and lost. The "battle" I put up hadn't been impressive at all. I remember thinking I would need to champion something that otherwise might have a similar demise. I scanned down the final list and, frankly, could easily have voted for all fifteen of them. One, however, struck me as being easiest of all to dispense with. It had, after all, no actual *location* and it was becoming obvious that geographical correctness was going to have a say. And yet it struck me that this homeless nomination might, in many other ways, be most symbolic of all for Canada and Canadian history. It alone covered both history and geography and was, to me, the greatest wonder of a wonderful country.

The Canoe.

Introduction

"First God created a canoe," legendary paddler and outdoors film-maker Bill Mason liked to say, "then he created a country to go with it." Mason, in fact, once got into a passionate riverside debate with Pierre Trudeau over the choice of symbol on the Canadian flag, which had been introduced on February 15, 1965, nine months before the future prime minister of Canada was elected to office. Mason was convinced the Canadian government had erred in not choosing the canoe over the maple leaf.

Mason had a point. What could be more Canadian than the purely Canadian First-Nations invention that made Canada possible? The canoe *made* Canada. No canoe, no exploration of this second-largest country on earth. No canoe, no fur trade to open up the colony-then-country to commerce and settlement. No dugout, no birchbark canoe, no kayak, no umiak, then perhaps no survival for the various Aboriginal peoples who first inhabited this largely inhospitable and often frozen territory.

It is not by coincidence that the Mi'kmaq of the eastern shores tell of Glooscap coming to this land in a stone canoe, that the Ojibwa in the centre of the land have Nanabozho inventing the canoe on Manitoulin Island in the heart of the Great Lakes, that the late Haida sculptor Bill Reid's greatest works—*The Black Canoe* (located at the entrance to the Canadian embassy in Washington) and *The Jade Canoe* (at the Vancouver airport)—connect West Coast First Nations to their origins in Polynesia and Hawaii. It was the canoe that took Samuel de Champlain, Pierre-Esprit Radisson and his brother-in-law Médard Des Groseilliers, Alexander Mackenzie, David Thompson and countless other European explorers and adventurers into the interior. "Canada exists as it does today because of the canoe," says canoeist and Trent University history professor John Jennings. "In the United States it was the horse that determined the national boundaries; in Canada, the canoe."

The suggestion might be made that the canoe is but a historical artifact. Not so. Over the centuries, it has moved from tool to pastime to icon. The canoe stands well above most other unifying symbols. The red maple leaf on the flag, as Bill Mason pointed out to Pierre Trudeau on that long-ago canoe trip, is not found in much of the country, particularly the vast northern stands of black spruce and, obviously, anywhere above the treeline. The beaver, a symbol of the country by parliamentary decree, annoys a great many with its incessant damming and shoreline destruction. Mounties move in and out of favour. Polls continually show Canadians split on the monarchy. Peacekeeping missions take place within other borders. Hockey and lacrosse are the national sports; few play lacrosse, though, and hockey, in recent years, has met with rising public concern over the threat of injury in such a high-speed contact game.

But who would criticize the canoe? It requires no fuel beyond human muscle. It does not pollute. It makes no noise. It takes us to and from familiar places we love the best, introduces us to magical places we would not otherwise experience. When properly conducted, its passage through these fragile, special landscapes leaves no mark. There was even a time when a canoe was considered "baggage" on passenger trains travelling through the vast Canadian wilderness, no extra fee required.

Sometimes it takes an outside eye to give perspective. Ray Atherton, once United States ambassador to Canada, wrote an article in 1947 in which he argued,

> What the covered wagon has been to the United States, this and more the canoe has been to Canada—a symbol of the westward march of our civilization, a symbol of the spirit and courage of a great racial journey.
>
> But the story of the canoe is infinitely longer than the story of the covered wagon, beginning from the Indians in prehistoric times and continuing down to our own day.
>
> The story of the canoe is Canada's story, because Canada is a gigantic waterway, a complex system of lakes and rivers stretching from the Atlantic to the Rockies. . . .

Introduction

> In the canoe's wake the economy and the culture of Canada appeared. Starting from this walled city of Quebec, paddling up the St. Lawrence and a thousand other rivers, men in canoes have created Canada.

The canoe, says Janice Griffith, past general manager of the Canadian Canoe Museum in Peterborough, Ontario, is the perfect "metaphor for the Canadian character. It's not loud, pushy or brassy. It's quiet, adaptable and efficient, and it gets the job done."

The great stories of Canada's exploration—Champlain's voyage, Thompson's map-making, the Hudson's Bay Company and the Company of Adventurers—all were written by canoe. Great art of the country—Tom Thomson and the Group of Seven—was painted by canoe. Let the American silver dollar say, "In God We Trust." Ours had a canoe on it for largely the same reasons: trust and faith.

That canoe—birchbark, with a coureur de bois in the stern and an Aboriginal paddler in the bow—would be engraved on the ubiquitous "loonie" were it not for the Royal Canadian Mint trying to save $43.50. In the fall of 1986, the mint sent a local courier to the Winnipeg airport rather than the regular armed security service to collect dies for a new one-dollar coin. The dies never reached the plant. New dies were rushed to Winnipeg, these ones featuring the common loon. Curiously, almost immediately the Canadian dollar began a long dive in value that lasted a couple of decades.

On the plus side, *loonie* is a lot easier to say than *canoenie*.

The working canoe was a contemporary of the workhorse, the wagon and the steam engine, yet its popularity did not remain stuck in the nostalgic past with them. Rather than fading into the mists of time, or at least of a distant waterfall, the canoe only added to its iconic stature in the decades following the introduction of the outboard engine. When Marilyn Monroe was filming the 1954 Hollywood film *River of No Return* in Banff, she was photographed in the perfect Canadian setting: in a canoe with a Mountie standing alongside. The canoe became an advertising vehicle for beer and cigarettes in the 1950s. And the number of privately owned canoes kept growing, according to Statistics Canada, from 123,000 in 1970 to more than 600,000 by the early 1990s and, likely, in excess of a million today. Whereas the first summer catalogue produced by Eaton's in 1901 offered a lovely sixteen-foot canoe for twenty-five dollars, thirty-two dollars for the special varnish finish, canoes today of Kevlar or canvas can run well in excess of two thousand dollars. And yet the numbers continue to climb.

If yesterday the canoe's value was in furs, today its worth is incalculable. It is how millions find balance in lives seemingly overwhelmed by fuel and speed, cost and consumption. As the great American philosopher Henry David Thoreau once put it, "Everyone must believe in something. I believe I'll go canoeing."

It is this simplicity combined with effort that seems to attract so many. "Originality is unexplored territory," the American actor and canoeing enthusiast Alan Alda has argued. "You get there by carrying a canoe. You can't take a taxi. Be brave enough to live creatively. The creative is the place where no one else has ever been. You have to leave the city of your comfort and go into the wilderness of your intuition. You cannot get there by bus, only by hard work, risking and by not quite knowing what you are doing. What you will discover will be wonderful: yourself."

"What sets a canoeing expedition apart," Pierre Elliott Trudeau wrote in an essay a quarter century before he became Canada's fifteenth prime minister, "is that it purifies you more rapidly and inescapably than any other. Travel a thousand miles by train and you are a brute; pedal five hundred on a bicycle and you remain basically a bourgeois; paddle a hundred in a canoe and you are already a child of nature."

Long before Pierre Trudeau and long after him, Canadians have tried to put into words what it is about the canoe and its relationship to this country that so moves them.

Introduction

"No man can define the attraction and the disadvantages of heat, thirst, flies, long hours bent on a paddle, under rain or sunshine, hard carries over rough portages, all things inherent to such a trip made through unfrequented territories," Quebec adventure writer Raoul Clouthier wrote following a long paddle from Maniwaki, Quebec, to Grand Lake Victoria back in 1928. "What then urges one to go, knowing well what is in store for him? Perhaps the charm lies in magnificent sunrise and sunset scenes, or in contending with the forces of nature by one's own physical power. Or is it the soothing calm of the forest, the restful horizon of silvery lakes, the alluring noise of rapids and waterfalls? The question is hard to answer! One goes in spite of all, accepting in advance whatever may happen. He goes and returns satisfied, even if he only brings back memories of the beautiful panoramas he has had the privilege of admiring, memories of pleasant evenings spent around the camp fire, listening to the mysterious voices of the wild, memories of the freedom he has enjoyed, far from the tentacles of civilization."

In the late 1990s, Max Finkelstein, an Ottawa-based author who likes to say, "I'd be happy paddling a canoe in a ditch," set out to cross the country by canoe while retracing the 1793 trek by explorer Alexander Mackenzie. Mackenzie was the first European to reach the Pacific Ocean by way of land (and freshwater). Finkelstein needed three years to match the explorer's feat, as each paddling season he could take only a few months off work. Sometimes he travelled solo—from Ottawa to Cumberland House, Saskatchewan—and at times with company. With friend Chris Taggart, who also set out to paddle across Canada, Finkelstein left Bella Coola on the British Columbia coast, hiked over the Coast Range, paddled up the Fraser, down the Peace and reached Lake Athabasca. He completed his vast trip in the summer of 1999.

"That trip for me," Finkelstein said, "was a pilgrimage to being Canadian. To see the land from a canoe, to see the landscapes changing at the speed a canoe travels, to sleep on the land—it lets the land soak into you. I really feel Canadian now."

On the CBC's Seven Wonders website, it was possible to read what various nominators had to say in support of their chosen wonders. Those backing the canoe were often eloquent about what the canoe meant to them personally as well as to their country. One, Doug Barnes, was particularly convincing:

> Constructed with locally available materials, able to glide down the shallowest streams, light enough to be carried (portaged) overland to the next river, the canoe was the perfect vehicle to travel the North American interior. A vital part of the exploration of Canada, and the fur trade which followed. The large trader canoes were sufficiently seaworthy to travel the north shore of Lake Superior. The construction materials have changed, but the design of the canoe has remained unaltered for the last four hundred years. Our computer-assisted experts of the 21st century cannot improve it. The two things that make me feel the most Canadian are playing/watching hockey, and exploring the local waters in my canoe. There would still be a Canada without the CN Tower or Niagara Falls, but without the canoe, there wouldn't even be a Canada.

I grew up in and around Ontario's vast Algonquin Park, Canada's top canoeing destination. It has always fascinated me how the original inventors of the canoe had the foresight to design a craft that would fit perfectly, upside down, on cars that hadn't yet been imagined. Not only that, but they had such a sense of fashion that their invention fits like a dapper cap as car and canoe head up the narrowing highways toward certain adventure. I mean, think about it: What other vehicle on earth can you use as a hat when it rains, a shelter when it storms, or a table when it's time to eat? And what other country would define its people by their ability to make love in such a vehicle? Certainly the Germans don't do this with the Volkswagen Bug!

I love my canoe. Nothing in the material world has cost less to maintain and run; nothing has afforded me more opportunity to flee that world. In this age of fretting over our carbon footprint, how comforting is it to know that you not only don't require fuel but will not be spilling at the dock? For those who still follow the original art of canoe manufacturing, this is transportation that can be made and maintained forever with completely natural materials.

Given such wonderful tradition, then, it is only appropriate that while we have the National Gallery in Ottawa to hold Tom Thomson's *Jack Pine* and the Art Gallery of Ontario to show his *West Wind*, we also have the Canadian Canoe Museum in Peterborough to honour the craft that got him to such exquisite locations.

For the canoe is as much a part of the Canadian landscape as the trees, the rocks, the mountains, the rivers—and even the highways heading for essential escape.

How could I not defend such a wonder?

On one hand, the Seven Wonders of Canada was just a corny contest. Once the list of fifteen was whittled down to seven, it wasn't as if the world would notice or the Canadian government would designate them "Official Wonders." Schoolchildren would not be forced to memorize them. Also, the list would be totally subjective, given that the three judges—*and what, exactly, were their qualifications again?*—would select the seven regardless of how the public voting had gone. And yet . . . and yet. More than a million votes had poured in. *The National* was headlining the results on prime time television two nights running at a time when the news also contained the G8 nations gathering in Rostock, Germany; President Bush touring Europe; civil war in Sri Lanka; an attempted attack on the pope in the Vatican; and a Canadian hockey team with the first opportunity to bring the Stanley Cup home since the Montreal Canadiens in 1993. Corny or not, Canadians clearly felt passionately about this contest. Meaningless or not, it meant something to everyone who had a personal favourite.

We began by laying down our cards. Each of the final fifteen selections had been assigned a large card and we had to lay down our personal seven. Roberta opened with Pier 21, the igloo, Haida Gwaii, the Cabot Trail, the canoe (!), Niagara Falls and Prairie skies. Ra followed with Haida Gwaii, Niagara Falls, the Rockies, the igloo, (and then, so quietly I didn't quite hear, he added) the canoe, Old Quebec and the Bay of Fundy. I laid down my first card, the canoe, then added the Rockies, Niagara Falls, Old Quebec, the Nahanni, the Cabot Trail and Prairie skies, arguing that with the skies you get "two for one" in that we could also use this to cover off the northern lights.

We were already in the process of killing off.

It was remarkable how much in accordance we were. But it was also remarkable that this accordance spelled the end of the Sleeping Giant. This seemed grossly unfair and we were aware of the perception: the Giant had blown the competition away in the voting, only to get blown off by the judges. The Giant had more than twice as many votes as Niagara Falls, yet Niagara was being considered a *given* by the judges. (It was a given that we would hear about this. The following day, I was soon opening email as if each message was potentially a live grenade. I was told that if I dared show my face in Thunder Bay, I would be killed on arrival—a public "stoning" that I richly deserved for what I had done. It was not the only threat. I was accused of being anti-Northern Ontario—despite being born in Nipissing District and schooled in Sudbury. The dilemma was that, in a bizarre coincidence, I would soon be headed for Thunder Bay to attend, of all things, the Sleeping Giant Writers Festival, which I had committed to months before the CBC had even dreamed up the Seven Wonders contest. A few weeks later, I landed in Thunder Bay to be met by my cousin Liz as well as television cameras and a determined reporter who had most assuredly not come to ask what I planned to read that night. They, Cousin Liz included, wanted an explanation as much as I wanted an excuse.)

In a wild mathematical fluke, seven of the twenty-one cards laid down by the three judges overlapped—which of course should have meant the end of it and we could all go home. The seven cards were put up on a map of the country and, in an instant, we realized that my joke about being "geographically correct" was not so far off the mark. There was a massive gap in the North. To compensate, we added the igloo and then the Nahanni and, for the East, Roberta's first choice of Pier 21. It balanced, but now there were ten cards on the map. Three would have to go.

Here is where the complications set in. We all knew that there were *givens* here. How could we possibly leave Niagara Falls or the Rockies off any list of the Seven Wonders of Canada? We were already going to be criticized, but worse would be to be ridiculed. Those two wonders were a lock. In an effort to satisfy the map, we dropped the Cabot Trail for Pier 21. But we still had too many.

If we were going to be completely geographically correct, I knew the canoe was heading down the rapids. "The one that doesn't have a location and can be replaced would be the canoe," I said, "but I would be extremely against that. It was my number-one choice of them all."

Roberta asked me what, then, I was willing to give up. We debated some more and agreed to keep the igloo for the North and, unhappily, part with the Nahanni.

But there was still one too many. It seemed Prairie skies or the igloo might have to go. I have to confess that, for a moment, I buckled as a good Canadian citizen of compromise. The canoe could go, I supposed, because "it doesn't really belong anywhere—except in our minds." Before anyone could jump at such an ill-considered opening, however, I realized my error. "One last pitch, which I may not win," I hurriedly added. "If we were to take Haida Gwaii out and put the canoe back in, the canoe by its nature is as Aboriginal as you can get—and is the great Aboriginal gift to this land."

Much to my surprise, they agreed. We put the cards onto the map and nodded. Pier 21 in the East, Old Quebec City, Niagara Falls, the canoe, Prairie skies, the Rocky Mountains and, high above all the others, the igloo.

As Peter Mansbridge announced the final results, photographs of the seven went up on a screen behind him. And the first to be declared one of the Seven Wonders of Canada was . . . the canoe.

I very nearly betrayed the canoe by saying I was willing to give up on its choice as one of the great marvels of our country. I am glad for that change of heart for it would haunt me today if I had indeed given up. The connection has been long, deep and important to me. I owe the canoe.

There are a great many who have travelled more distance, braved wilder rapids, slogged over longer portages than I have in nearly six decades of paddling. I salute them and concede to anyone who wishes the bragging rights. But I have dumped in rapids, stumbled and fallen on portages, broken yokes and paddles, wondered where in hell we were and was once "shipwrecked" for three days in a freak blizzard while out in a freighter canoe on James Bay. Every canoeist, however, has his or her grand tales to tell, each one as treasured and as important as the next. It is the shared language of paddling.

I have been terrified while canoeing. Not by a bear or a wolf along the path, though we have encountered both, but by pure happenstance. We were coming down through the Barron Canyon on the eastern border of Algonquin Park when a freak thunderstorm hit. We were, at that moment, drifting along the Barron River, staring in awe at the high, high rocks of the canyon that rise virtually from the shoreline to the height of New York skyscrapers. Lightning struck nearby and when the thunder rolled into the granite canyon it simply exploded, the loudest I have ever heard. And then came the wind and the rain, the rain striking the river with such ferocity it seemed as if machine gunners were lined along the top of the canyon and spraying us with bullets. The rain hit so hard, the river water burst to the height of the gunwales.

We raced for an overhang and, instantly, found perfect shelter for all but our ears. Here the water was calm, the canoes steady. And I do not believe I have ever felt so safe, so happy and so stunningly impressed by the elements in all my life. An hour later the sun was out, the river calm, and two comical otters were entertaining our group with their antics and water gymnastics.

Such is the incredible power of nature. And there may be no better place to experience it than from a seat in the bow or stern of that great Wonder of Canada.

In the eight years since that moment the canoe was chosen, I have done a lot of paddling and a great deal of thinking about the canoe and its place in the national psyche. The canoe's historical import is well known—though perhaps not the astonishing story of the nearly four hundred Canadian voyageurs heading off to the Middle East in the 1880s to save General Charles "Chinese" Gordon from the Siege of Khartoum. Early commerce would have been impossible without the canoe; some would say today there is equivalent value in how it lets us get away, helps us find or rekindle romance, lets us heal and challenge ourselves. Once used to explore the land, the canoe is now used to explore ourselves.

In considering the prospects of a book on this Canadian treasure, it eventually occurred to me that the canoe is neither artifact nor symbol, but is in fact one of the great Canadian characters. What this calls out for is not so much a history of a water transportation vehicle as a "biography" of a significant national personality that was there at the very beginning and is, happily, as alive today as ever, even if serving much different purposes. These covers contain a canoe trip, if you will, that includes whitewater and flatwater, freshwater and saltwater, a journey with paddlers as diverse as David Thompson and Tom Thomson, Frances

Introduction

Anne Hopkins and Esther Keyser, Bill Mason and Pierre Trudeau, the canoe-building Commanda family of Kitigan Zibi, Blair Fraser and the paddling grandchildren he never knew—old voyageurs, new voyageurs and future voyageurs.

If the canoe is not on the Canadian flag, it is most certainly to be found in the Canadian imagination.

1

THE OLD RANGER'S CHESTNUT

MY MOTHER TAUGHT ME TO PADDLE.

Helen McCormick was born on August 5, 1915. It was a very hot and muggy day. We know that because her sister, Mary, who was three years old when Helen came into the world, remembered how their father set up a tent on the shore of the Algonquin Park lake where they lived so that his wife could go into labour surrounded by woollen blankets that had been soaked in the cool waters of Brule Lake and strung alongside her makeshift bed. In this rustic air-conditioned birthing unit, Bea McCormick produced the second of what would eventually be five children, three boys following the two girls.

Helen did not leave Brule Lake until 1932, when the family moved to Eganville, a small town in the Ottawa Valley, where the children finished their schooling. She returned to Algonquin Park several years later when Tom McCormick, now chief ranger, built a two-storey log home at Lake of Two Rivers. Over time, the Brule Lake home vanished back into the wilderness. Many, many years later still, when our mother would have to apply for a birth certificate in order to get a passport, there was nothing to mark where the old house or the tent had stood. Puzzled officials initially said the birthplace of Helen Geraldine McCormick might have to be listed as "45° 38' 0" North, 78° 49' 0" West," the geographical coordinates of Brule Lake.

Eventually, she was issued a passport declaring her birthplace as "Hunter Township, Nipissing District," placing her birth somewhere in a wild tract of land that had been surveyed long before the park's founding in 1893 and that included Brule Lake, McIntosh Lake, Misty Lake, Joe Lake and several dozen smaller bodies of water. There is nothing at the "45° 38' 0" North, 78° 49' 0" West" coordinates today but water and bush, the Precambrian Shield that forms the spine of Canada; but back in the 1890s the Grand Trunk Railway had been laid through the park on a track bed that can still be found in certain places, if remarkably overgrown. The railroad kept a small depot at Brule Lake for the steam engines to load up on lake water. There was also, around that time, a logging operation run by McLaughlin Brothers of Arnprior, a village north of the capital along the Ottawa River. It was at Arnprior that this wilderness railway, built by lumber baron J.R. Booth and originally known as the Ottawa, Arnprior & Parry Sound line, turned west and ran across the province to Depot Harbour, located on Lake Huron's Georgian Bay.

Brule Lake gradually became a small settlement. There was the station itself, the station agent's house and a bunkhouse and cookhouse for the men working for McLaughlin Brothers. Over time more buildings went up—a boarding house, a ranger's cabin, a handful of family homes, a store and post office and even a small school—but time and a later fire eventually wiped out all traces of the little community.

In 1907, my grandfather Tom McCormick, an eastern Ontario farm boy who had attended a small business college in Arnprior, was sent, at age twenty-three, to serve as McLaughlin's clerk at Brule Lake, where he kept the payroll and a running tally of the hardwood logs the skidders drew each winter from the surrounding hills. He was also in charge of supplies for the men and horses. In summer the tall and physically strong young man worked as a fire ranger and would soon leave lumbering to join the park staff and rise to the positions of chief fire ranger and, finally, chief ranger. Tom and Bea McCormick would live most of their lives in the park—Brule Lake, White Trout Lake, McIntosh Lake, Lake of

Two Rivers—and raise their five children (Mary, Helen, Roy, Irvine and Tom), four of whom were born at "45° 38' 0" North, 78° 49' 0" West," but only one in a tent.

It's unclear where Brule Lake got its name. It may have been the site of a forest fire—*pays brûlé*—but, given the lack of French names in adjoining lakes, may also have been named after Étienne Brûlé, commonly known as "the first coureur de bois." Certainly this is the explanation I prefer.

Brûlé was surely the most "native" of all the early explorers. He was only sixteen when he set sail from France with Samuel de Champlain in 1608. He was considered an "indentured servant" and referred to by Champlain as his "*garçon*" (boy), but soon after the founding of Quebec he took on a unique role as conduit between the French and the Aboriginal people the early Europeans encountered in this new land. Brûlé learned the habits and customs of the Hurons and often acted as interpreter for other explorers and traders. At one point, Champlain, now governor of New France, either sent the young man to live with the Hurons or else Brûlé fled on his own to escape being indentured forever. Whatever the case, Brûlé became fluent in the native language and took on the dress of the Hurons to the point that when Champlain met with the Hurons a year later he did not at first recognize his former servant.

Champlain referred to Brule in his journals as a "*sauvage*," but he let him remain with the Hurons for several years, during which time Brûlé is believed to have explored most of the Great Lakes area. Brûlé eventually returned to Quebec City, where he taught the Jesuit brothers the Huron language but soon fell out of favour with the Jesuits, who frowned on his native dress and his non-Christian "*sauvage*" ways. Champlain also turned on him, convinced that Brûlé was secretly helping the fur traders, who largely operated beyond the control of the New France government.

Champlain was probably correct in his suspicions. Brûlé was sent back to France, only to return as the guide for English invaders who in 1629 captured Quebec City. He was later captured by the Iroquois in battle and tortured before escaping back to the Huron village at Toanche, on the Penetanguishene peninsula at the south end of Georgian Bay. Brûlé clearly had trouble convincing those he dealt with to trust him, for his former Huron friends refused to believe his remarkable story of daring escape from the Iroquois. They decided he had to have been sent by their great enemy to spy on them. Instead of embracing their old comrade, they killed him and ate him.

Today, Étienne Brûlé is not remembered for his duplicity or his fate, but for being first among the Europeans to master the native way of travel, the canoe. It has always struck me as fortuitous that this lovely lake along the western edge of Algonquin Park might have been named for him and that this is where my mother and all of her siblings learned to paddle.

There were only two practical ways to get about in Algonquin Park: by train or by canoe. Early visitors combined the two forms of transportation, the trains happy to let the travellers and their canoes—considered "baggage"—off wherever they chose and to collect them wherever they waved a train down, having paddled one or more of the six major rivers—Petawawa, Madawaska, Opeongo, Oxtongue, Magnetawan, Amable du Fond—that have their headwaters in the park.

The park was a popular vacation destination even then. As a Grand Trunk Railway brochure put it in 1928,

> Deep within the heart of most men and women slumbers an instinct as old as humanity itself. It is the desire to renew contact with Nature, to live and to play in Nature's solitudes and recesses. It is the answer in men's soul to the lure of primeval spaces.
>
> In no other of Canada's famed playgrounds can man find more adequate answer to that desire than in Algonquin Park, vast forest and game preserve of 2721 square miles, gemmed with 1500 lakes of every conceivable size and shape, connected

by a labyrinth of rivers and streams all unmarred by the inroads of exploitation and promotion.

The train followed a schedule and cost money: roughly three cents a mile for a second-class seat in the early 1920s, or $2.20 for a one-way fare from Brule Lake to Scotia Junction, seventy-five miles to the west, which was where passengers could then disembark from the Grand Trunk train, which continued on to Depot Harbour, and connect to trains running north to North Bay and south to Toronto. As the most experienced park rangers were paid $850 in 1921, it is fair to say that frivolous trips were not taken by the McCormicks. They were hard-strapped, for the youngest child, Roy, had contracted polio after falling through the ice on Brule Lake and spent much of his childhood in Toronto's Hospital for Sick Children. He travelled more by train than the others, as he would often return with a Mr. Smedley, the hospital-appointed guardian, for special holidays. The other McCormick children would be sent, once a year when they reached school age, to the village of Kearney, on the western border of the park. Here they would bunk in with the Bice family—Ralph Bice was a park fishing guide in summer and a full-time trapper along the park boundary in winter—while taking their provincial school exams. The school year completed, they returned by train to Brule Lake. It was the only time each year when they rode the trains. To get anywhere else, they walked or paddled.

Canoeing was free, had no restrictions apart from water and portage, and followed no schedule but whim. Not all the family's paddling, however, was recreation. They paddled while fishing for the lake trout that, in summer, lay deep off the shoals of Brule Lake. They paddled to the rivers and creeks where the brook trout ran. Fishing then was more for sustenance than for fun, but they all enjoyed it. In 1926, the McCormicks purchased a small cabin on an island in McIntosh Lake, a slightly larger body of water just to the east of Brule Lake. Here there were no sounds from the logging operation, no trains, just a lovely clear lake spotted with islands.

When Bernard Wicksteed, a British journalist with the London *Daily Express*, came to write a feature on Canada shortly after the Second World War, he was mesmerized by McIntosh. "I suppose there are ten thousand lakes in Canada just as beautiful but this place is where I really lost my heart to the northern woodlands," he later wrote. "It was the last word in peace and restfulness. Whoever Mr. McIntosh was, he has a memorial as lovely as the Taj Mahal." The little lake, he said, "I shall remember until I die as one of the most beautiful spots on earth."

Another beauty of McIntosh Lake was that the McCormicks could paddle there from their grey clapboard, two-storey home on Brule, with only three portages, one quite short, and two tiny lakes, Ross and Clear (also known as Straight Shore Lake), along the way. Tom McCormick used four canoes to make the journey easier, keeping one at the end of each portage, then reversing the procedure on the return trip.

The island on which the family had their summer cabin was barely large enough to contain the building, an outhouse and a good dock. Because Tom McCormick worked as a fire ranger, he had a mortal fear of fires and had seen, all too often, what a careless campfire, a needless bonfire and even an unexpected lightning strike could do to dry summer bush. There were no water bombers and no roads for fire trucks. Fire rangers worked as fast as they could with hand-held pumps attached to rubberized backpacks.

To limit the possibility of accidental fire, Tom McCormick chose another small island nearby to be his "woodshed." He would float logs across from the mainland, split them on the island and pile the firewood in a small shelter. From the hills around McIntosh Lake he had his choice of hardwoods—maple, birch, beech—and from the lower lying areas came softer woods like white and red pine, hemlock, spruce and cedar for kindling. He split wood with precision and piled his work as if the cords and kindling were being laid out by plumb line and would later be checked by a surveyor. Some people square up their desks; he squared up his woodpiles.

The ranger, however, was often gone, with nothing predictable during fire season. He might be away for a week or two at a time, and the care of the young family and the cooking would be left to Bea, with whatever assistance the children, especially the two oldest, Mary and Helen, could provide. When at McIntosh during cool weather and high winds, they burned even more wood, sometimes requiring several trips a day to the island "shed" in order to heat the cabin and cook the food. Until the girls were old enough to handle this necessary chore, Bea paddled over herself, no matter what the weather—though she could not swim a stroke. She never dumped.

Bea McCormick was a woman of no small daring. She was born—as best one amateur family genealogist can determine—Bridget O'Dowd in the Ottawa Valley town of Renfrew to an unwed mother who would be passed off as an older sister. Later, they dropped the O and the Catholic Church would play no further role in the life of the Dowd "sisters," now four in number. She would marry in the Anglican Church and sign the registry "Bridget Dowd," soon also dropping the "Bridget" to become "Beatrice McCormick," devout Protestant in a part of the country where the division between Catholics and Protestants was wide and often rancorous.

She raised five children in the deep bush of Algonquin Park with no electricity, no running water, no central heating and a husband who was often off fighting bushfires in summer or patrolling for poachers in winter. In her later years, when she and Tom lived at Lake of Two Rivers, her young grandchildren walked outside one morning to see a huge black bear amble out of the bush and stand eyeing the log cabin. Bears were a concern in that part of Algonquin Park. Lake of Two Rivers was home to the park's largest campsite, the main garbage dump was less than a mile away and the dozens of black bears that gathered there for years had become a major attraction. The ranger not being home at the moment,

Bea took matters into her own hands, though the bear might have weighed 350 pounds and she barely weighed 100.

She grabbed two steel cooking pots from the kitchen table and, hammering the pots together, charged straight up the hill at the wandering bear. The bear turned and ran so fast it is a wonder his head didn't pass through his butt as his back legs churned in terror.

The McCormicks had few neighbours at Brule Lake, but one family, the Stringers, would many years later produce one of canoeing's great legends. Jack Stringer had been a barber in the Ottawa Valley and moved to the park to take a job as a fire ranger while still cutting hair on the side. Jack, known everywhere as "Pappy," and his wife, Kate, called "Mammy" by all, had sixteen children: John (known as "Jake"), William, Lila, Dan ("Mud"), Cyril ("Cy"), James, Earl ("Bolivar"), Albert ("Bert"), Wilmer ("Wam"), Catherine, Dellas, Stella ("Moon"), Omer ("Bung"), Mabel, Roy and Marion. Omer, or "Bung," would be known as the "King of Flatwater Canoeing." Like all his family, and all the McCormicks, Omer had been a fine paddler from a very early age. By fourteen, Bung was building his own canoes and guiding American fishermen and such famous Canadian landscape artists as A.Y. Jackson and Lawren Harris of the Group of Seven. A tiny man with hair like a beaver pelt, Bung reinvented many of the traditional styles of paddling. Some say he created the J-stroke, which is today the given way to control a canoe when paddling solo on flatwater. He eschewed the seats of the canoe and moved, instead, above the thwart so he would be kneeling almost in the middle of the boat. He gradually moved to the side, as well, so that he could lean over the water and use quick, easy strokes that propelled his canoe at an astonishing pace.

"Omer style" paddling—sometimes called "ballet paddling"—became popular in the park and eventually throughout the paddling world. He became the style's best proponent and number-one ambassador, an engaging little man who put on demonstrations where he would leap into his canoe much as the Lone Ranger would mount Silver, never tipping, and do such entertaining tricks as stand on his head in the canoe or walk, never tipping, around the entire canoe using just the gunwales. He would also stand on the gunwales and bounce the canoe through the water, the bow rising and slapping down hard with each piledriver thrust of his legs, while the tapered shape of the stern lifting from the water would thrust the canoe forward. Using this bizarre method of propulsion, he could hold his own in races without even having a paddle in his hands.

The Stringer family moved to Canoe Lake, a short distance east of Brule Lake along the Grand Trunk tracks, and by the 1930s the young man was teaching his techniques at Taylor Statten Camps on Canoe Lake, Camp Arowhon on nearby Teepee Lake and Camp Tanamakoon, a girls' camp on a small lake to the east. Omer and a partner, Lou Handler of Detroit, in 1936 opened their own camp, Tamakwa, on Tea Lake, a short paddle from Canoe Lake.

Omer Stringer led a fascinating life. He had next to no formal education yet was renowned for his ingenuity and ability to fix things. He had built his own radio by the age of twelve. When he enlisted in the Royal Canadian Air Force during the Second World War, he was soon tapped for intelligence work, served in India and Burma and was later seconded to the United States Air Force to provide intelligence on the Pacific front. Back in Canada, Omer met and married Edie Brooks, who was working in the Tamakwa office. As a veteran, he could qualify for education assistance and graduated in science from the University of Toronto, after which he became a high school teacher, continuing to spend each summer at Tamakwa with Edie and their growing family.

Michael Budman was ten years old when he left his Detroit home for a summer at Tamakwa. He was hockey crazed, a fan of the Red Wings and a promising young athlete in his own right. That summer he discovered paddling under the instruction of Omer Stringer and believes, to this day, that this new passion changed his life. By age twelve he had completed his "Voyageur" canoe badge. By nineteen he was an instructor at the camp, leading a group of eighteen on a thirteen-day expedition that took them up Canoe Lake and through a chain of small lakes and rivers until they reached the village of Kiosk, then back down the Petawawa River to Brent and the Barron Canyon.

"That was the best job I ever had," Budman says of his years at Tamakwa. "Tripping teaches you responsibility," he believes. "It gives you fitness and strength. But most of all it teaches you about teamwork. Teamwork is everything in life. People who don't get that I don't understand."

In the early 1970s, Budman teamed up with another Tamakwa camper from Michigan, Don Green, and together they founded the famous Roots clothing line. That team still holds today. Budman and Green moved permanently to Canada and Roots has grown to more than two hundred stores around the world selling their laid-back "rustic luxury" line of clothing, shoes and accessories. Several times they have outfitted Canada's Olympic teams with patriotic clothing that has, in turn, been exceptionally popular with the public.

In the early 1980s, the two young entrepreneurs formed a joint venture with Stringer that led to Beaver Canoe—*tamakwa* being an Ojibwa word for "beaver with wood." With yet another Tamakwa-connected partner, Howard Perlmutter, they set up a small enterprise in which Omer would build the first canoes—traditional style, cedar ribbing, canvas covered— entirely by hand. The company's bestselling canoe was, no surprise, called the "Omer Stringer Classic." A Beaver Canoe line of casual sweatshirts and T-shirts proved particularly popular with campers.

Long after the canoe company folded, Omer Stringer won a substantial lottery, but his fame in canoeing circles would remain the astonishing performances he put on with nothing but a canoe, a paddle and a small body of water. He died in the spring of 1988 at age seventy-five. His own beloved canoe—canvas painted red, with white stripes below the gunwales—hangs above the cafeteria tables in the Algonquin Park Visitor Centre.

Tourists who sit with their chips and gravy at those tables have no idea that a man would once perform handstands in that canoe, could get into it at a full run and leap without tipping over and could spin it like a top in the water with but a practised flip of the wrists. Some of them wear T-shirts and sweatshirts with the Beaver Canoe logo on them, the words *Built by Omer Stringer* emblazoned across their chest. Few, if any, would even recognize the name.

We grandchildren of Tom and Bea McCormick learned to canoe at Lake of Two Rivers, where in 1940 the chief ranger had built his magnificent log home on a long, high, pine-covered and rocky point with a southern exposure. Across the lake, running east and west along the south shore, the old railway beds stretched between Whitney and Cache Lake, the rails and ties long gone and the trails used in summer by blueberry and raspberry pickers.

From the high point on the north side of the lake, the old ranger could watch the morning sun rise over Spring Hill and in the evening set over the highlands heading toward Cache Lake. He built the home with his own hands and, with the help of a stonemason, added a beautiful granite and quartz fireplace—visitors swore they could see a bear's face in the way the white quartz had been laid in—along with three outer cabins and a cedar-log ice house. When he was finished, he took his carpenter's pencil and scribbled "Thomas McCormick, Sept. 10th, 1940" under a protected eave. He and Bea spent the entire year there until his retirement in 1954, at the age of seventy, and every spring, summer and fall until his death in 1962. Following Bea's death in 1968, the children sold the cottage to an American businessman from Rochester, New York. Less than a decade later, when there was panic among park cottagers about their leases not being renewed, the new owner tore the log home down, numbered the logs and hauled them away to re-erect the magnificent building in another part of the country. On one of our annual visits to the original Lake of Two Rivers site, our mother found the signed eave, wrapped it in a plastic bag and saved it as a priceless heirloom.

More than a century before Tom McCormick signed his work of art, the explorer David Thompson came paddling past that high rocky point in early October 1837. He was in search of a canal route from Georgian Bay to the Ottawa River and, at sixty-seven, had found the going hard for, ever since leaving Penetanguishene, he and his men had been travelling upstream. They had completed the Muskoka River, paddled up the Oxtongue River and past its several falls into the park area, where finally he made the Madawaska River, which flows in two separate branches into Lake of Two Rivers. Here he could at last write in his journal, "Current going with us, thank God."

Somewhere on the lake, Thompson came upon "a place of Indian resort" and was told by an old native man, Cha Unde, that they had been travelling the middle branch or proper Madawaska River and "that no white man had been on it." I like to think that the "Indian resort" that David Thompson came upon that day was the point Tom McCormick chose, though by the time he built his log home a century later, there were no native settlements to be found in the park.

Come summer, we grandchildren would travel to Lake of Two Rivers to live with the grandparents from the day after school let out until the day before school went back in. The MacGregors, parents and four children—Jim, Ann, Roy and Tom, the youngest—took over the sleeping cabins and the kitchen. Other cousins—Tom and Bea McCormick had fourteen grandchildren—regularly occupied the extra bedrooms in what was called the "Big House." For a child, it was heaven: diving into the deep, clear, cool waters off the high rocks to the west, wading and rafting off the low rocks to the east, catching crayfish, toads and frogs and minnows, fishing for bass off the shoals and for lake trout in the deep water. We had rafts and a flat-bottom rowing boat and a red canvas-covered cedar strip canoe. And we had the most essential of all summer advantages: time.

There were, however, strict rules, as might be expected from a ranger who seemed never out of uniform. Coal oil lamps were to be turned on and off by adults. The ranger's razor-sharp axe was to be used by the ranger alone. No one was allowed by the water when the gasoline-powered washing machine, which had to be used outside, was roaring through its long and throaty exhaust pipe. And there were specific swimming tests laid out by the ranger. Kids had to swim from the ramp to the boom of support logs on the inside of the huge floating dock before they were allowed to swim outside of the boom in deeper water. You had to swim in that deep water from the dock to the "duck rock" off the far end of the point and back before you were given permission to dive and swim from the high rocks in the very deep water on the opposite side of the point.

And then there was the canoe . . .

The ranger kept his Chestnut canoe in remarkable shape: freshly painted—red paint that glowed and flashed in the sunlight—and carefully "soaked" each spring before launching. He would "sink" both the wooden rowboat and the canoe by carefully piling heavy stones in them. The crafts would lie in the water for days, their wood swelling, and then the rocks were carefully removed so as not to scratch anything and the boat and canoe bailed out. The ribs would have become impenetrable—usually. If, on a rare spring, there was still a leak, he would break out the tar and melt it down and carefully track down the perforation and repair matters.

You had to swim well before you could use the canoe. And then you had to be taught the proper ways of paddling safely. There was an emergency landing strip on the far western edge of Lake of Two Rivers. The east wind would sweep across this barren field of grass and wild blueberries, gathering power, and could turn the glassy surface of Two Rivers to chop in an instant, from chop to whitecaps in a moment. The ranger had lost count of the number of canoeists—usually from the large campsite at the end of the lake, sometimes young summer campers well into their canoe trips—he had hauled out of the waves as they clung to their canoes. Calls for help on a windy afternoon were not as familiar as the loon's call in the evening, but they were a part of every summer's experience.

At the spot where the rocky point reached farthest into the lake, the ranger would stand by the flag he raised each morning and hauled down each night. While he worked the halyard—usually with a grandchild along to help fold the flag and ensure that the hem of his beloved Union Jack never, ever touched the ground—he would hail passing canoeists and advise them that they should rearrange their seating, hold the paddle differently—or get out of the water entirely.

Unfortunately, canoeists, for whatever reasons, do not take criticism well and he was usually ignored, sometimes having to head out in his rowboat to haul in the very ones who had dismissed his warnings.

This reluctance to heed advice is a phenomenon often noted among canoeists. The great American writer John McPhee, discussing the bark canoe in the 1970s, found this sensitivity widespread. "The look in their eyes showed a sense of insult," he wrote, "resting on the implication that every human being is born knowing how to use a canoe. The canoe itself apparently inspires such attitudes, because in form it is the most beautifully simple of all vehicles."

We grandchildren knew that you did as you were told at Lake of Two Rivers or you didn't do it, simple as that. And we did so happily, as Two Rivers was pure heaven for the many cousins who spent every day on the water or exploring in the woods—though it could be pure hell for our mother. Helen (MacGregor now) had the washing to take care of, hauling water out to the washing machine, hanging the sheets and clothes on the lines that ran to the back of the Big House. She had the meals to cook on a wood stove, the cleaning of the cabins and much of the Big House, and was the main safety patrol and lifeguard, caring for as many as ten youngsters at once, most of them under ten years of age. She herself had a mother with a powerful personality despite her tiny size; Bea McCormick was beloved as a grandmother but, to a daughter, could be judgmental and difficult to please.

Our mother needed her escape. And she often found her sanctuary in evenings on the water, paddling with one of her own four children and, more by example than by suggestion, teaching them the joys of being in a canoe on a calm evening, when your own silence is an invitation for the eerie, spine-tingling calls of the loon. If we learned not to scrape our paddles along the gunwales—something she insisted upon—we could even hear the soft kissing sound of a lake trout rising just enough to lick a bug off the water's surface. Nearer the shore, we could sometimes hear the sound a swallow's wing makes as it touches down with a quick tilt and flick of nothing more than a drop of lake water. We could hear the wind coming off the water into the arms of the white pines that stood high above the rocky point. And we could say nothing as much as we wished, as we were all aware that silence was her preferred method of communication while canoeing.

Some of my most treasured memories are of paddling together, her in the stern, steering, while the two of us travelled east down the length of the lake to where the mouth of the Madawaska pulled water away, the river twisting and turning through small swifts toward a small dam, where in David Thompson's day there had been strong rapids. If we paddled back west along the far shore, we would reach the area of the grass landing strip, the footings from the old McRae Lumber mill where our father had been working when our parents met. Here there were the two branches of the Madawaska as it entered the lake. Usually we would paddle awhile up one branch until the flow proved too strong to go on, and we would turn at the bottom of a small rapids and return to the larger lake.

Current going with us, thank God . . .

I recall nothing that was said on those evening paddles. Perhaps that's because nothing, or next to nothing, was said. But I do recall everything about the feel of that canoe slipping through the water as quietly as if we were gliding on air.

My father, a logger who spent his entire working life in Algonquin Park, gave me only two gifts in the forty-seven years I knew him. One was a .410 shotgun that I have not used for many years. The other was a canoe paddle, handcrafted out of cherry by his long-time Whitney friend Alex Cenzura. I still have, and use, the paddle, though it is now but one of far too many. Some people have a weakness for chocolates, for booze, for puppies. In our family, it's paddles.

I bought my first canoe in 1978 and should have named it "Otto." The first National Magazine Awards had been held that spring and a piece I had done for *The Canadian* magazine on the embattled federal minister of justice—"The Short, Unhappy Landing of Otto Lang"—had taken the University of Western Ontario's President's Medal as well as the gold medal for political writing. There was a thousand-dollar cash award and I used it to purchase a fifteen-foot, red cedar-and-canvas canoe from Albert Maw of Northland Canoes in Huntsville. My younger brother, Tom, had worked summers for Albert, lacquering and painting the lovely canoes Albert made by hand in a small shop near Fairy Lake. My canoe was numbered 3778—the thirty-seventh canoe Albert made in the year 1978—and cost $710. I still have it, in as fine shape as the day Albert helped me tie it onto the roof of my car. It is the singular material possession I treasure, the one keepsake I would enter a burning building—in this case, garage—to rescue.

"I used to think it was a major tragedy if anyone went through life never having owned a canoe," Bill Mason liked to say. "Now I believe it's only a minor tragedy."

I came late to canoe tripping. Never having attended summer camp, and never having lived any great distance from relatives in Algonquin Park, summer was a series of day trips if you went anywhere at all. We had relatives on Canoe Lake, Whitefish Lake, Galeairy Lake and Cache Lake, where cousins Tom and Jake Pigeon (the children of our mother's sister, Mary) were annual winners of the canoe races in the local regatta. But once the log home at Lake of Two Rivers was lost in the late 1960s— the grandparents having passed on, their children unable to agree on what to do, the grandchildren too young to step up—the only shelter available in Algonquin was a tent, and so the tripping began.

The Old Ranger's Chestnut

Very early in our marriage, my wife, Ellen, and I took a casual trek from Cache Lake through Lake of Two Rivers to Whitney with brother Tom and his then girlfriend, Wendy. We took our time, dawdling over four days, the highlight a wild and spectacular storm the night we camped, illegally, on the big island at the west end of Two Rivers. We loved every minute of it, even the soaking.

Over the years and decades to follow, we travelled over most routes in all sections of the park. Eventually we moved from the relative flatwater of Algonquin to some whitewater adventures, from the spectacular Dumoine River in Quebec to the historic voyageur and black robe route over the Mattawa River to the ice-cold and rolling Kootenay River in the British Columbia Rockies, where third daughter, Jocelyn, was working as a naturalist and a sometime canoeing and kayaking guide.

Like virtually everyone else I know who paddles, I use my canoe as my mother used hers: for escape. It calls me back to the places I love the best. This is a common claim and hardly original. Ken Danby, a hockey-playing friend and one of Canada's great painters, made it most elegantly before his death in 2007 at the relatively young age of sixty-seven—like Tom Thomson, he died in Algonquin Park, of a heart attack while tripping with his wife, Gillian, and friends in the North Tea Lake area. Ken had once made an exquisite poster for the park in which his painting of a canoe pulled up on a large, grey Canadian Shield rock is partnered with letter-perfect words: "The image of the canoe is synonymous with northern Ontario where I was born and spent my formative years. I titled this painting *True North* because the canoe's shape kept reminding me of a compass needle . . . almost as if it was guiding me home."

"Every so often a disappearance is in order," Colorado naturalist John A. Murray believes. "A vanishing. A checking out. An indeterminate period of unavailability. Each person, each sane person, maintains a refuge, or series of refuges, for this purpose. A place, or places, where they can, figuratively if not literally, suspend their membership in the human race."

At least once a year I find "a disappearance is in order." I want to be somewhere where phones don't ring, emails can't reach and the only deadline that matters is the day you finish your trip—and even that doesn't matter all that much. What truly matters is the sense of escape, the camaraderie of family and friends, the laughter, the challenge, the exercise, the relaxation, the routine and the mystery that lies around that next bend in the river.

There might be a moose feeding on water lilies in the shallows, a blue heron stalking frogs along the shore, an osprey climbing high over the trees with a twisting speckled trout in its talons. There might be an awe-inspiring stand of white pine, or an opening into a lake never before paddled. There might be a quickening to the current, a faint roar rising and the heart-catching sight of tumbling waters in the distance.

Knees down, paddle on.

2

SONGS ALONG THE DUMOINE

AH, SERENITY.

The river slides and swirls. The paddle gurgles slightly as it lifts at the end of a stroke, the sound close to a baby's gentle awakening, then turns and slips like a sharp knife through the water for the next slow, deep draw. A king-fisher swoops along the cedars closest to the shoreline as if hanging bunting for some late summer celebration. There is pickerelweed in dark purple bloom along the water's edge and arrowheads bending in the quieter current along the far shore, their sharply tapered leaves pointing downstream toward the next set of rapids ever so quietly rumbling in the distance.

It's not easy, however, to hear anything over Phil.

"*Duke!*" he shouts, the barked word echoing hard off the sheer granite cliff that rises back of the pickerelweed.

There is no need for an echo. He will supply his own.

"*Duke . . . Duke . . . Duke . . . Duke of Earl!*" Phil sings at the top of his lungs, the cliffs repeating each word like some Motown backup lacking only finger-snap accompaniment.

Duke . . . Duke . . .

Phil is difficult to explain, so let me just talk about him generally and leave the dot-connecting, if any is required, or should any appear, to the reader.

He is Phil Chester of Deep River, Ontario, which is, for him, a happily appropriate address. Phil is a retired high school teacher of English; unpublished novelist; published poet; accidental fabulist; father of four and grandfather of eight; lover of words, of philosophy, of all things to do with Grey Owl, of beer-league hockey in winter and slo-pitch ball in summer. He is also a river fanatic: former rafting and voyageur-canoe guide on the Ottawa River, paddler of an impressive list of the rivers the early explorers and the fur trade voyageurs paddled centuries earlier.

Phil also knows, by heart, every rock 'n' roll song that came out between 1962—the year of Gene Chandler's forever-stuck-in-your-head "Duke of Earl"—and Neil Young's mournful 1972 hit, "Heart of Gold." He knows every word to Donovan's "Catch the Wind" and can reach most of the falsetto notes in the Four Seasons' "Sherry" as well as the Temptations' "My Girl." Mungo Jerry and Bob Dylan are big with him, as are the Young Rascals (pre-Rascals). Yet nothing can move Phil to tears as easily as Gerry and the Pacemakers' version of Rodgers and Hammerstein's "You'll Never Walk Alone," which he likes to say is his creed as well as the official anthem of his beloved Liverpool Football Club.

> When you walk through the storm
> Hold your head up high
> And don't be afraid of the dark . . .

I have tried to point out to Phil that it is slightly inaccurate to include Young's 1972 song in a "Sixties" list, but Phil says, "It's okay—the Sixties were late getting to Canada." Looking back and realizing that my "Sixties" began in the summer of 1967—Montreal World's Fair, *The Graduate*, Scott McKenzie's "San Francisco"—and ran through Trudeaumania, two treks to Europe and North Africa, one by motorcycle, and two universities before landing my first full-time job and marrying in 1972—I have to admit he has a point there.

We met through a mutual friend, retired Pembroke teacher Bert Cain, who sadly passed away in the summer of 2014 after a valiant battle against cancer. Bert had been contacting me—his email handle was "riverdreams"—for several years about the Ottawa River and its many tributaries. Bert knew of my passion for the Ottawa Valley, as I had been born in Whitney, have relatives throughout the Ottawa and Madawaska valleys and even once wrote a novel, *The Last Season*, set in Wilno, the spectacular Upper Ottawa Valley site of the first Polish settlement in Canada—and, coincidentally, where Phil Chester once taught elementary school.

When Bert asked one time over our periodic lunches at Colonnade Pizza on Hazeldean Road in Kanata, his favourite fine-dining establishment, which of the various capillaries of whitewater that feed the mighty Ottawa I had run, I was embarrassed to answer, "None."

The fact of the matter is that despite half a century of dedicated paddling and enough canoe treks through Algonquin Park that people regularly ask me for route advice, I knew nothing, absolutely nothing, of whitewater canoeing apart from drifting down minor swifts and dealing with the odd ripple that would barely faze a ladybug riding a fall leaf. Algonquin Park, particularly in the middle, the western side and to the north, is almost uniformly flatwater: the scenery gorgeous, the threat of water almost exclusively found in the passing clouds.

Bert asked one day if I'd care to have a whitewater lesson. He was speaking to a person who has never taken a lesson in his life—not in golf, not in piano—a person who refuses even to read instructions before taking up the Allen key and, with a frightening mixture of curses and sweat, tackling an IKEA bookcase. But whitewater canoeing was something I'd always wanted to try, something I knew better than to thrust my red cedar-canvas canoe into without forethought, so I swallowed hard and said, "Yes . . . *please*."

A few weeks later found me, Bert, my son Gordon and his pal Jamie connecting on a gravel back road that brushed along the lower Petawawa, the most commanding of the many rivers that tumble out of the Algonquin

Park highlands into the Ottawa River watershed and make the Ottawa the world's third-largest river in terms of sheer volume. Bert had a canoe tied to his SUV but there was another vehicle there, a very small car, bearing a battered red canoe that looked several sizes too big for the roof.

And there was a man standing beside the little car and canoe. He wore what appeared to be an Australian cowboy hat, a red neckerchief, an old plaid shirt, ragged old pants held together with staples instead of stitches and tall, green-black lace-up footwear that he claimed were Vietnamese-army jungle boots.

"Phil Chester," he announced himself, smiling big, with a woodcarver's grip for a handshake.

And so began the lesson. On a sweeping curve of the Petawawa, with small Class I, and a few Class II, rapids down the middle and deeper, fast water swirling along the banks, we learned to eddy carefully into cross-currents along the shore, draw the canoes sideways, high brace and low brace to steady a rocking vessel and back ferry against the current to breach from one shore to the other. We learned to read currents and seek out the black tongues of fast-running, deepwater runs into the rapids. We talked about the differences between a haystack, a dangerous standing wave topped with whitewater, and a below-surface rock causing a high, even curl that a canoe can easily glide through. Perhaps most important, as well as most difficult, we learned to tell a hastily shouted *"RIGHT!"* from a near-screaming *"LEFT!"*

After we had "run" the sweeping curve multiple times, Phil said he was about to give us the most important lesson of all. We were holding the canoes tight to the shore in an eddy of quiet water while Phil walked out over the rolling stones. The water was deep enough there to splash over his ankle-high jungle boots. We thought he wanted us to walk the canoes out to him.

"Pull them up on shore!" he shouted over the roar of the water. "Leave 'em there and come stand here with me!"

Baffled, we did as told. Out over the slippery rocks we waded in our old sneakers until we reached Phil, standing like a breakwater just at the edge of the rapids.

"We're going down *without* the canoe this time," he announced.

We looked at each other, thinking he was joking.

"You're going to go over if you're going to do whitewater," he continued. "So you need to know what to do. Always have your life preserver on and done up properly. Always wear your helmet. Keep your feet in front of you and your bum to the bottom—and *follow me!*"

And with that, Phil turned and, with a deft kick upwards of his army boots, threw himself feet and bum first into the deeper, roaring whitewater. He disappeared, reappeared, bobbed and flew down the rapids on his back . . . laughing.

The three of us looked at each other, shrugged and leapt into the fast-moving water just as Phil had shown us. It was one of the strangest, most alarming-yet-exhilarating experiences imaginable: the water cold and very, very strong. Like a wild animal. Undeniable, the water simply tossed us down the rapids, our butts clipping the odd rounded rock and our feet like sights on a rifle as we aimed for the same route the laughing Phil had taken. Soon enough, we were laughing too.

We were now whitewater canoeists.

There have been many trips since that first introduction. And there have been times when the on-your-back, feet-first bounce down the rapids was necessary. Sometimes we make bad calls. The whitewater prayer— "God grant me the serenity to walk the portages I must, the courage to run the rapids I can and the wisdom to know the difference"—isn't always followed, but so be it. So be it. As some anonymous paddler—no one seems to remember who—once said, "The trick of running whitewater is not to try to rid your stomach of butterflies but to make them fly in formation."

In the summer of 2010, Phil talked me into running the Dumoine River with a group out of Lindsay, Ontario, that, somewhat alarmingly, call themselves the Crash Test Dummies. The "Dummies" include Phil's older brother Lorne; an Ontario court judge; three police officers, Scott Duffy, Harry Hughes and Lorne's daughter Kelly; Paul Burns, a Lindsay printer who has paddled and won the gruelling one-day North Bay to Mattawa race over one of the country's best-known fur trade routes; Terry Smith, a meditating librarian; an interloping journalist; and Phil.

There were four canoes: Lorne and Kelly, Harry and Scott, Paul and Terry, and Phil and me. We kept pace but were hardly the same, Harry and Scott moving fast by sheer strength and Paul and Terry effortlessly leading the pack at most times while the rest of us marvelled at Paul's effortlessly smooth strokes from the stern. Terry and Paul would switch sides every twenty-five strokes; Phil and I, both comfortable paddling from either side, switched never. We took turns doing the cooking, the two policemen grilling steaks over a fire, Phil digging a hole in the sand and placing hot rocks in it to cook vegetables carefully wrapped in foil. Harry, endlessly restive, would gather so much firewood at each campsite that we likely left a week's supply to whoever took it next. Harry's energy stood in stark contrast to Terry's calm, the paddling librarian sometimes found sitting cross-legged in the lotus position as he meditated on a rocky outcropping by the tumbling waters of the river we had come to paddle.

The Dumoine is one of the main rivers that drain Quebec's Laurentian Highlands down to the Ottawa (roughly opposite the Petawawa River, draining down from the Ontario side); others on the Quebec side include the Noire, the Coulonge and, just opposite Ottawa's Parliament Buildings, the Gatineau. The Dumoine is well known among canoeists for its challenges—nearly forty runnable rapids totalling about nine kilometres of good, often difficult, whitewater—and is revered for its scenery: lurching white pines, tall cliffs, spectacular vistas and superb campsites. Hydro-Québec would love to be able to dam the river and harness its power, just as Ontario Hydro has long coveted the rushing waters of the Petawawa. It would be a terrible shame if either dam, let alone both, ever came to pass.

One theory has the Dumoine named for the French military family the Le Moynes, as Sieur d'Iberville paddled up the Ottawa in 1697 with his seventeen-year-old brother, Jean-Baptiste Le Moyne, and several French soldiers on their way to attack the English trading forts along James Bay and Hudson Bay.

The Dumoine was a main route for the great timber drives that exploded in size during the Napoleonic Wars, from 1799 through 1815, as the Ottawa Valley became the main supply point for British ship masts and planking. Enormous rafts of timber would be assembled on the Ottawa for the long run to the St. Lawrence and on to Quebec City, where the timber would be milled and shipped to London.

It could be dangerous along the Ottawa, and even more dangerous on the tributaries. Thomas C. Keefer, a civil engineer, described life along these waterways in an 1854 speech in Montreal:

> There is scarcely a portage, a cleared point, jutting out into the river where you do not meet with wooden crosses, on which are crudely carved the initials of some poor unfortunate victim of the restless waters . . . In a prosperous year about ten thousand men are afloat on loose timber, or in frail canoes, and as many as eighty lives have been lost in a single spring . . . Some of the eddies in high water become whirlpools, tearing a bark canoe into shreds and engulfing every soul in it.

Only fools head down the Dumoine in "frail canoes," so we stopped at Valley Ventures in Deep River, Ontario, to rent some durable ABS Rolex river vessels and pick up some added supplies. While we were poking around the camping gear, the outfitting company's resident dog, Whiskey, broke into one of our packs and made off with a package of turkey and ham sandwich meat, leading to an unfortunately-not-caught-on-camera Keystone Cops episode as two beefy out-of-uniform policemen chased the dog and his pilfered treasure about the parking lot for a good ten minutes, eventually recovering most of the meat as well as a bit of their breath.

From there, a huge guy named Vern, with a white ponytail, an Alabama State baseball cap and a claim that he had once played in the Canadian Football League, drove our gear and a trailer full of the canoes to Driftwood Provincial Park, where we dropped off our own vehicles and got into the truck. Crammed in, we crossed the Ottawa at Rolphton, a ghost town that was once the site of Canada's first nuclear reactor. We took the Swisha Road—a local English interpretation of *Rapides-des-Joachims*—up some fifty kilometres of bad and twisting dirt roads, stopping only once, to check out an abandoned home deep in the Quebec bush, where, according to Vern, a trapper and his wife had raised six children. There were still mink traps under the steps of the rickety two-storey structure and shredded curtains on the bedroom windows. The perfect setting for a cheap horror flick. It would prove not to be the only occasion on this trip where dark thoughts came quickly to mind.

It was late in the day when we launched. We did not paddle far before making camp on a lovely rock outcropping with soft pine-needle carpeting and the sounds of the first impressive rapids in the near distance. In part, the reason for stopping early was social. I was the new guy and they wanted to have a quiet evening getting to know me and take quick measure of my skin. Was it thick enough for all the shots and cracks that are the culture of any closely knit group that shares adventure? It was clearly going to be a unique evening: steaks, fresh salad and, surprisingly, cold, cold beer, all carefully packed in ice and stored in soft plastic containers we would carry out. There was also wine—"clips," the Crash Test Dummies called them—in plastic bladders that would also be carried out once emptied. Eco-friendly wilderness gourmet.

We were enjoying the cold beer and the late afternoon sun when two canoes came into view, one very clearly manned by someone who knew what he was doing—the lone paddler kneeling, the canoe tilted off-centre, the paddle stroke smooth—and one being paddled by two men who looked about thirty years of age and also looked as if they had never before held a paddle nor sat in a canoe. It was quite comical to watch, the expert canoeist nursing—no, *herding*—the other canoe over to the far side and into a quiet eddy, where he told the two young men he would take both canoes down the rapids while they walked the long portage.

First, though, he crossed toward our camp. Perhaps it was to distance himself from the two novices before he permanently dispatched both of them in a rage; the closer he paddled, the more he came to resemble Rambo. He had a Tilley hat on that looked, curiously, as if it *had* passed through both portals of an elephant, as the Tilley Endurables company likes to claim is possible in its advertisements. He wore a tight military shirt, sleeves rolled up to reveal tattoos on sculpted biceps. He had a Guerrilla knife strapped across his chest within easy reach should he happen, say, to fall into the jaws of a rolling crocodile. Strapped to his right shoulder was a satellite phone, something we never carried but something it appeared he might like to use in the next few minutes: "Bradley Air Services? *GET ME THE HELL OUTTA HERE!*"

Phil read the moment perfectly. After pouring a fast beer out of the still cool beer bag, he carefully stepped down through the roots and rocks and onto the rough shoreline and had the beer out and ready just as "Rambo" pulled up.

His story was simple. A former soldier from the Petawawa base on the Ontario side of the Ottawa River—his membership in the controversial, and disbanded, elite Airborne unit was evident in one tattoo—he had decided to take up a post-military career as a wilderness guide. He had outfitted himself and advertised his services. The first call had come from a couple of city slickers who wanted to have their own whitewater *Deliverance* experience, minus the banjo music and violence. From the way their new guide spoke, they were pushing their luck on the violence.

He told us he had been completely conned. He had taken all the requisite courses. He had assembled all the right equipment. He was prepared for any emergency—but not this one. They had outright lied to him when he had grilled them over the telephone on their canoeing experience. They had clearly never done any whitewater; they had just as clearly never been anywhere near a canoe.

"I'm thinking of calling the plane back in," he said, tapping his satellite phone. "To hell with them—and no giving their money back."

We commiserated with him. Phil got him a second beer. They talked at length about the tricky spots on the Dumoine and how many whitewater runs the lying novices could avoid if they walked the portages while "Rambo" ran their canoe down the rapids separately, after running his own. It is, of course, more difficult for a single canoeist to run rapids than it is for a good pairing, but if the single has the expertise, it can certainly be done.

"I guess I've no choice but to give it a go," he said, shaking his head so the foam of the beer flicked off his upper lip. He grinned: "But I'd just as soon send them on ahead and then collect their bodies at the bottom."

Off he went after thanking Phil for the beer. We watched him paddle downstream until he came to the first dark tongue leading into the rapids, and in an instant he had slipped away. We could hear the two naive novices laughing as they walked, packless, down the portage, unaware of their good fortune that a highly trained killing machine didn't suddenly drop out of the pines and slit their throats to bring a quick end to the giggle they were having.

We never saw them again. Nor did we come across any floating bodies or freshly dug shallow graves.

What is it that makes people go into the wilderness by choice rather than necessity? There is no longer any fur trade to speak of; there is very little of this country that has not been explored. Yet humans, more often than not well-off enough to afford a good home with at least two working bathrooms, a laundry and a full kitchen including microwave oven, lucky to have one or two perfectly functional vehicles in the driveway and well able to afford a plane ticket to an all-inclusive resort where the meals are hot and the cold drinks there for the asking . . . these same humans will head off into the deep woods for a week or two or even longer, will fend off swarming blackflies and stormy weather, will grind themselves into the ground carrying impossible packs over difficult portages, will prepare their own meals over an open fire, will go days without bathing or a change of clothes, will drink filter-pumped warm water, sleep on the hard ground and, come morning, have to hang their sorry bottoms over a fallen log while holding an ever-diminishing, increasingly valuable roll of soggy toilet paper in one hand and swatting morning mosquitoes with the other.

And yet these same people will say the only thing that gets them through a Canadian winter is the dream of returning to this bug-infested alternative universe.

It was far back in the 1950s that the late historian W.L. Morton observed that the "alternate penetration of the wilderness and return to civilization is the basic rhythm of Canadian life." He pretty much nails it with this simple observation. I know countless people for whom the annual canoe trip is as much ritual as a New Year's resolution.

And far more often kept.

Personally, I treasure my annual "vanishings." Once or twice a year, we check out of our everyday lives. The matters of great import in that other life—career, contact, bills, appointments, duties, work and family problems—are replaced here by lifting and carrying and paddling, by striking and breaking camp, by gathering wood and setting fires and cooking and cleaning up, and often by the at-first-difficult task of doing absolutely nothing. "Looking for old pine nuts to burn, picking berries, and paddling a canoe are not only fulfilling in themselves," Sigurd Olson wrote, "they are an opportunity to participate in an act hallowed by forgotten generations."

There is a mysticism to canoeing that many writers have tried to capture, few so successfully as Olson and a young Alabaman named Harry Middleton, who might have gone on to stand with Olson and the few other giants of wilderness writing had he lived longer. Middleton was struggling as a writer—he had to take work as a garbage collector to make ends meet—and at only forty-four died after suffering an aneurysm while swimming with his children. He left behind, however, words that speak to everyone who has ever been captured by the magic of the canoe.

"Many a time," Middleton wrote, "have I merely closed my eyes at the end of yet another troublesome day and soaked my bruised psyche in wild water, rivers remembered and rivers imagined. Rivers course through my dreams, rivers cold and fast, rivers well-known and rivers nameless, rivers that seem like ribbons of blue water twisting through wide valleys, narrow rivers folded in layers of darkening shadows, rivers that have eroded down deep into a mountain's belly, sculpted the land, peeled back the planet's history exposing the texture of time itself. Rivers and sunlight, mountains and fish: they are always there, rising up out of exhaustion, a sudden rush of sound and motion, a Wagnerian assault of light and shadow, hissing water, pounding rapids, chilly mountain winds easing inexorably into a requiem of distant rapids, a fish's silent rise, the splash of blue-green water over the backs of wet black stones."

There is also the matter of a *frisson* of danger, and it is impossible to ignore this base animal instinct when discussing whitewater. A snippet of dialogue from 1951's *The African Queen*, starring Humphrey Bogart and Katharine Hepburn, says it all:

CHARLIE: *How'd you like it?*
ROSE: *Like it?*
CHARLIE: *Whitewater rapids!*
ROSE: *I never dreamed.*
CHARLIE: *I don't blame you for being scared, miss—not one little bit. Ain't no person in their right mind ain't scared of whitewater.*
ROSE: *I never dreamed that any mere physical experience could be so stimulating.*

For centuries that stimulating thrill had been a major attraction to whitewater canoeing. W.F. Butler, a nineteenth-century English officer and explorer, said, "It is difficult to find in life any event which so effectually condenses intense nervous sensation into the shortest possible space of time as does the work of shooting, or running, an immense rapid. There is no toil, no heartbreaking labour about it, but as much coolness, dexterity, and skill as man can throw into the work of hand, eye, and head; knowledge of when to strike and how to do it; knowledge of water and of rocks, and of the one hundred combinations which rock and water can assume."

Some people find in canoeing a sense of adventure that is missing from their other lives, even for those whose other lives hold more adventure than most others would wish. Craig Oliver has for decades been the main political correspondent for CTV News. He has reported on wars, natural disasters, assassinations, murders and political intrigue—but still needed canoeing to give him something his professional life lacked.

Oliver has an ocular condition that eventually put an end to his adventurous canoeing, but not before he had explored many of the most northern and more dangerous rivers in the country. Oliver and a core group of eight paddlers—expanding at various times to include a total of fifteen—called themselves the "Rideau Canal and Arctic Canoe Club" and, beginning in 1973, began annual, and expensive, treks into the Far North. Oliver took up paddling as a novice, a reporter sent to join an expedition along the Yukon River to Dawson in honour of the seventy-fifth anniversary of the gold rush's Trail of '98. He was hooked, and he soon hooked others, including the likes of television executives Tim Kotcheff and Denis Harvey, renowned art historian David Silcox, Toronto magazine editor John Macfarlane, and Liberal politicians Allan Rock and Paul Godfrey.

While they may have been "roughing it" at times in their canoes, they were living rather luxuriously when not kneeling down and heading into the whitewater. Their meals were extravagant and meticulously planned, complete with carefully matched wines. "In the early years," Oliver wrote in his 2011 memoir, "most of us were single, with good jobs that allowed for the expense of state-of-the-art gear and the cost of commercial flights to a jumping off point in the north, followed by private charters to some remote destination in the High Arctic."

In his accounts of those many trips north, Oliver talked of the necessity to leave vanity and ego behind, to get along and maintain even tempers no matter how great the tribulations or the simple annoyance of one paddler who would never be invited again. He wrote of bonding for life on such trips, of sharing the most private thoughts and over time forming a trust and loyalty that, for those paddlers who also found themselves involved in media and politics, became part of their work lives.

What kept them together was friendship. What drew them north each summer was the thrill. "There is a hanging moment of suspension at the top of a big chute or rapid," Oliver wrote. "The lead canoe team makes an irrevocable decision about whether to enter and what line to take, then contends with whatever faces it. The options can never be adequately judged from a far shore or a high point above the obstacle. At a distance, the forces are almost always underestimated. Modest standing waves become monsters at water level; ledges are deeper and rocks much wider at their base. In that blood-rushing moment of risk and excitement before the rapid, nothing else exists, no past and no future, only that instant of crazed exhilaration. And when it is over and safety reached, who would not succumb to feelings of triumph and relief? Or discover again a sense of balance with the natural world and joy in the camaraderie of sharing it with like-minded friends? John Godfrey once described any canoe trip as a legalized reversion to adolescence. Indeed, ours kept us young."

They were young and adventurous but never foolish. The Far North held many lessons of what could befall the unprepared. Perhaps the best known of all folly expeditions was the Moffatt expedition of 1955, which today stands as an example of what not to do when heading into the northern wilderness. Arthur Moffatt, a thirty-six-year-old film-maker and Dartmouth College graduate, talked five young Americans—two of them still teenagers—to join him on a paddle down the Dubawnt River, which runs through the Northwest Territories and Nunavut. The Dubawnt is considered a very difficult, even dangerous, river. Two of the five had limited experience; one had never paddled a canoe.

Ill-prepared and poorly supplied, the six paddlers ran into terrible weather and fought and argued their way along the nearly impossible journey. Short of food and faced with snowy weather, arguing their time was limited, they tried to make up time by running a long rapid without first scouting it. Two of the canoes went over. Moffatt froze to death on the banks while waiting for the others to be rescued.

Oliver and his paddling companions were never short of supplies—even the best wines—but they were also well stocked with common sense. If a rapid looked too difficult after scouting, they portaged. If a canoe went over, a rarity, others were always well positioned for a prompt and effective rescue. Common sense was a guiding principle.

Nor did Oliver ever get carried away with larger meanings to their adventures. They were not so much finding themselves as losing themselves for a brief period. He never pretended there was anything particularly profound about what his group was doing apart from momentary escape from reality.

"Those who go to the wilderness to discover themselves or God would do better to visit a therapist or a priest," he concluded. "I found no answers to the great perplexities of life in my years of wilderness adventures, but rather the joy of personal achievement."

It was a new day on the Dumoine River, the sun quickly burning the morning mist off the water and our group under way early. We had come down through the Bridge Rapids, shooting them after a quick scout had convinced us there was a safe route. Phil was in a grand mood, singing at the top of a voice that sometimes sounded like a full church choir, sometimes like the springs and shocks of Vern's old truck as it skipped and slammed along the washboard of the gravel road in. There were even moments where I could have sworn his throat was double-clutching.

> When you walk through a storm
> Hold your head up high
> And don't be afraid of the dark . . .

It was not the dark I was afraid of. In fast water you seek out the dark tongues, where the water runs deep and flat. Phil, the eternal Sixties hippie, becomes a polar opposite when rapids come into play. He moves as cautiously as whitetail deer, constantly checking everything for even the hint of danger. He scouts every rapid, memorizing the lines he wants to follow, pegging small landmarks—the big rock to the left, the haystack three-quarters of the way through, the sharp bend that conceals a fallen tree, a "sweeper," that points out into the water like a knight's lance—and he will sometimes walk the rocky shoreline to the very bottom of the run just so he knows the places where, if the canoe gets in trouble, it might slip into a safe eddy or, if worse comes to worse, where a safety line might be thrown from shore to haul in the downed canoeists.

His brother Lorne, the distinguished judge, takes exactly the opposite approach. Conservative off the water—he has even run for office under the Conservative banner—Lorne is close to an anarchist when paddling rivers. While Phil prefers the stern, with me paddling the bow and reacting to his instructions, Lorne paddles bow and has daughter Kelly, a strong paddler in her own right, in the stern. Lorne thinks scouting is a waste of time. Instead, as they near the rapids, he stands straight up in the canoe—a frightening sight in his oversized helmet, sunglasses, moustache, old paddling clothes and bright green garden knee pads—and intuitively chooses a route. It is this act of daring that earned him his nickname: "Riverhawk."

Each run begins with the same shout—"*Cut 'er down!*"—just as he enters the rapids. His stern paddler, Kelly, is expected to drive hard or ease up fast in response to his shouts as Lorne pries and draws and picks their way through the whitewater puzzle. It is daring and impressive, if not always successful. The "Riverhawk Hat Trick" is a phrase often used by the Crash Test Dummies to describe a spectacular Lorne Chester feat on Quebec's Ashuapmushuan River when he managed to dump at the top, middle and end of a single run down a long rapid.

Dumps invariably lead to excuses and, at times, disputes. Something obviously went wrong and, if there happen to be two paddlers, there is rarely one willing to take full blame. At one point Scott and Harry ground up onto a deadhead lying in wait just under the surface on a flat stretch of the Dumoine, the two stocky policemen arguing about whose fault it was—Harry for not scouting ahead from the bow, Scott for not steering away in time—but all of it ended in laughter as the two eventually wiggled free and away.

Paddlers work together or suffer the consequences, and tensions are hardly rare on long canoe trips. Such disputes tend to resolve out of necessity, but they can turn nasty. A young Eric Sevareid, the late, legendary CBS correspondent, set out on a marathon canoe trip in 1930, when he was only seventeen, that was to take him and a friend, nineteen-year-old Walter Port, from their home in Minneapolis all the way to Hudson Bay. They were ill-prepared for the immensity of such a challenge. Sevareid later confessed that, just before starting out he went cold to the very pit of his stomach, but young Port was stronger and full of confidence. By the time they reached the God's Lake area of Manitoba they were confused, cold, hungry, short on supplies and likely lost.

"Gradually our dispositions gave way under the strain," Sevareid later wrote of this teenage rift. "We became surly and irritable. The slightest mishap set our nerves jumping. At first all this went on only in our minds, but each knew the other's thoughts and it was only a matter of time before it came to words. Like children, we bickered. And then we came to blows. One cold morning as we prepared to load the canoe, a trifling incident occurred . . . we leaped at each other. Hitting and twisting violently as though we were fighting for our lives, we rolled over and over until we struck a tree trunk. The same thought must have come to each of us at the same moment and we were sane enough to recognize it: separation here in the wilderness would mean but one thing—death to both. Without speaking a word, we released our hold, staring at each other as if we had been having a bad dream."

Many years prior to this summer run, the Chester brothers had had a royal falling out at the very same Bridge Rapids we just successfully navigated. Back then, Phil thought the waters too wild to run; Lorne felt, and convinced the others, that it was worth risking for the thrill. Phil, convinced they would wrap a canoe on the rocks, dug in and refused to budge. The two brothers did not canoe together again for fifteen years. For the past many years, however, they have canoed happily together in groups, even if not in the same canoe. While this might be taken as preference, it is far more necessity, as the brothers are such superb whitewater canoeists that their talents are spread about. On the other hand, together the Chester brothers might tip on a flatwater paddle, so different is their take on the art of canoeing.

On this trip, Lorne was able to paddle with Kelly, and it was a joy to see them work together on the rapids, Lorne deciding the routes to take and Kelly providing the power from the stern as Lorne called for it as he picked his way down the chosen line. The two also had treasured moments away from the whitewater, Kelly—who competed in swimming while at Sudbury's Laurentian University—once slipping over the side of their canoe to swim and drift for more than an hour while Lorne paddled solo alongside of her. One evening by a falls, the rest of us stayed around the campfire, sipping our "clips" of wine, while father and daughter walked off and sat together on a log overlooking the river and had a long and quiet talk that ended with her reaching over with a hug of thanks.

With the two Chester brothers paddling with different partners, Lorne was left to his own preferences and Phil to his:

At the end of the storm
Is a golden sky
And the sweet silver song of a lark . . .

Later that day we were into a long stretch of flatwater headed toward the disturbingly named stretch of rapids known as "Canoe Eater." But that was a good hour or more away. The paddling on this warm, calm July day was easy, the current with us and the scenery spectacular. It was a quiet, restful time, perfect for looking about, singing, chatting, talking about everything from philosophy to pop music.

"The long, still water is the mental side of canoeing," Frederic Remington believed, "as the rapids is the life and movement."

That's correct: Frederic Remington, the famous artist and sculptor we associate with the Old West, the creator of such masterpieces as *The Cowboy*, *The Scout* and *The Broncho Buster*. Remington was a closet canoeist, living and working on a small upstate New York island in the St. Lawrence River and fanatical about catching the evening sunsets from his canoe.

Remington served as illustrator for an early publication of Henry Wadsworth Longfellow's *Song of Hiawatha*, painted native canoeists with uncanny accuracy and even wrote about canoeing, his long-still-water-is-the-mental-side-of-canoeing taken from an 1893 issue of *Harper's New Monthly Magazine* in which he described a trip down the Oswegatchie River, which runs from the Adirondacks to the St. Lawrence near Ogdensburg, New York.

Frederic Remington's passion for canoeing is a little-known side of the great artist. Canoe fanatics, however, invariably have another side—the career that allows them the leisure time to paddle and the where-withal to afford equipment and trips—and these are often at odds with the personality that takes over in a canoe. If Justice Lorne Chester showed up at court wearing his whitewater regalia complete with gardener's knee pads rather than his robes, the only thing that would rise at his entrance would be laughter. Brother Phil, on the other hand, is inseparable from his canoe personality. As a teacher, he often dressed as Mr. Canoehead, the strange Canadian superhero from the Frantics comedy group who had his aluminum canoe welded to his head by a bolt of lightning.

Phil enjoys nothing more than an opportunity, any opportunity, to expound on his own many philosophies of canoeing. Some are merely comical, for Phil Chester can be a great wit. Not long after Pierre Berton became famous in canoeing circles for claiming, "A true Canadian is one who can make love in a canoe without tipping," Phil improved on it by arguing, "Anyone can make love in a canoe—it's a Canadian *who knows enough to take out the centre thwart!*"

(It is perhaps indicative of how far the romantic notion of canoeing had come, given that more than a century earlier, writer Thomas C. Haliburton had his character Sam Slick say, "If I was a gal I'd always be courted in one, for you can't romp there, or you'd be upset. It's the safest place I know of.")

In an unpublished essay he entitled "Why Canoeists Are Disinclined to Play Golf (or The Missing Link)," Phil turns an imagined conversation with God into a dissertation on the merits of canoeing over golfing. God, it turns out, is addicted to golf, so much so that his blistered feet require soaking in a cool water hazard, which is how Phil the paddler happens to come across his Creator. The prophets, apparently, are split on whether God is playing fair if he scores a hole-in-one on every hole played, which would, of course, be a simple matter for him.

God's dilemma has been compounded by the fact that to create this heavenly golf course, they have had to destroy the natural beauty of the wetlands and creek and landscape that, of course, God himself had once created and declared himself well satisfied with. Even the bugs, for that matter.

It is an eclectic essay with a vast cast: Moses, Aristotle, Socrates, Homer, Plato, Descartes, Nietzsche and Marshall McLuhan are all fully-paid-up members of this exclusive golf club. When God dared protest the destruction of this perfect bit of nature, they removed him from the board of directors. Phil talks God into trying a new pastime—canoeing—and though he turns out to be a bit of a lily-dipper, he quickly takes to it and seems to like it.

"Canoeing," Phil tells God at one point, "works in tandem with nature and you're not likely to break your paddle in half. If you did, you wouldn't get home. Canoeing goes with the flow. It sails with the wind, and is constantly seeking equilibrium. The beam points toward a simpler, healthier and happier lifestyle it seems to me. It's a re-creation, which appeals to me as you might suspect. It's not a competition, and the action to propel the canoe is a gentle forward dipping motion like this."

Following Phil's instructions, God soon shows the bow stroke of an expert. "He was starting to feel like his old Self again. Calm. Laid back. Justified in His own house." Finally, after hours of conversation about everything from carbon footprints to that first golf swing on the moon, God declares in favour of canoeing:

> Everything that is natural on a golf course has a negative connotation. You're constantly being penalized if you go into the "rough." I happen to like long grass, sedges and wildflowers. Sand and water become "traps," "bunkers" and "hazards." According to USGA Rule 18, Section 1, Parts (a) and (b), geese, deer, squirrels, etc., are deemed "outside agencies." Burrowing animals like rabbits, moles, gophers and, yes, salamanders, come under "abnormal ground conditions." Bear scat, moose poop, dung, dead animals, etc., are termed "loose impediments." Clearly, the accepted jargon of the sport has no genuine regard for the life force without which it could not operate or function, namely, the Earth.

There are his comical essays and his mischievous essays, but there is also a most serious "still side" and "mental side" to Phil Chester that he pours into the many essays he has written, some of which have been published. For the collection *Canexus: The Canoe in Canadian Culture*, which appeared in 1988, he penned a piece in which he bemoans the fact that virtually all the literature concerning the canoe is "children's stories": "There has never been a major, serious work of fiction ever written in this country about a mode of transportation which has so obviously played a key role in our economic, social and political development."

In an essay he called "The Unified Stream Theory of the Canoe," Phil ties Einstein's unified field theory to paddling. He argues that the principles of "grounding," "centering," "balancing" and "pace" are the primary forces in canoeing, just as Albert Einstein believed there were primary forces in nature that explained all. Drawing extensively on literature and with reference to troubled lives as divergent as Hamlet, Terry Fox and professional hockey player Theo Fleury, and including his own past demons, he argues that by demanding balance, a centre, grounding and sensible pace, the canoe can take you to a place of healing that will be marked on no map but the one inside your head.

He wrote, "The romantic image of an empty canoe—the vessel without decks—beached on the shoreline or tethered to a branch at the head of a rapid invites us to consider a different way of connecting with the world, the natural world, the world of painted turtles and peeping frogs, blackflies, starry nights, misty mornings, scudding clouds. To sleep on the ground, to rest with your back against a giant white pine by the water's edge; to listen to the sounds of nature in tranquility and just be. A *human being* for a change and *not* a human having or a human doing as we so often allow ourselves to be."

It is a remarkable and revealing essay on himself, in the end, one that lays the demons and troubles out in plain sight—death of a friend, end of a relationship, triple bypass surgery, alienation from family, being "cut" (with good reason, he says) from the Crash Test Dummies' annual canoe trip—and how the canoe was what came and rescued him at age fifty-eight from those demons:

> The poet T.S. Eliot wrote about "the still point of the turning world." For me, that still point has always been the yoke hole of the centre thwart. This is such a liberating feeling. The canoe has the power to transport us "into the mystic" as Van Morrison sang. The steady, loyal and reliable canoe helps us to align our inner universe with the outer one. That is no small achievement. I trust the canoe. The canoe is, for me, the central informing power of my life.
>
> Whenever I find life getting a bit stormy, when balancing the in-going and out-going forces of nature is tricky, I will find myself standing in the middle of my living room with that key-hole yoke around my neck. Sort of like eddying out during the descent of a rapid . . .

When I asked Phil if I might mention his many essays on canoeing, his message back to me was simple and straightforward: "You could hard boil the whole gall-darn philosophical and psychological aspect of canoe-ing down to four words: 'Keep an even keel.'"

We failed to do this at Canoe Eater. We spent a long time scouting the rapids, convinced that the water level was such that a quick buck down the right hand side would work so long as we avoided several large rocks near the bottom where you could choose to go either left, and slip through a narrow gap, or else go right and run fast along the shore, where, we were certain, the water was deep enough that we'd get through with minimal scraping and bouncing.

The alternative was an easy portage of two hundred yards, which we were considering as we stood on a jumble of suitcase-size rocks along the shoreline, carefully tracing the line we might follow. It was not, it turned out, the line Riverhawk would take. As we were standing there trying to be sensible, careful, cautious and smart, Lorne and Kelly's red canoe came into view, Lorne standing on the bow like Leonardo DiCaprio in *Titanic*, "Jack" about to spread his arms and shout, *"I AM KING OF THE WORLD!"* while "Rose" (Kate Winslet) stands back of him, watching with total admiration.

In truth, Kelly Chester watched her helmeted, aviator-glassed, garden-protector-kneed father with benign amusement, well used to his disdain for scouting rapids. The ultimate freelancer, he would make it up as he went. If they went over, no worries: Kelly, after all, was a champion swimmer.

From his standing vantage point, Lorne chose the far side, quickly kneeling and prying the bow over into a dark tongue that seemed to pull them like a giant slingshot down into the churning waters. They danced, slammed, slipped, twisted, shot free and bounced through Canoe Eater, deftly turning to the left at the bottom into quieter water, swirls, and small, harmless whirlpools.

Phil watched Lorne making it up as he and Kelly pounded through the whitewater, Phil's face split between disdain and admiration for the older brother.

"Let's do it," Phil suddenly said.

We walked and hobbled over the rocks to our canoe. We tightened up our life jackets, strapped on our helmets, knelt with our knees spread wide and ferried back to get a direct run at the closest tongue. Phil was sticking to the route he'd so carefully and thoughtfully mapped out on the side opposite to what his river-gambler brother had chosen.

"Hard!" Phil shouted from behind.

I dug in at the bow, pumping hard as we entered the tongue and dipped down into the first roaring whitewater of this mechanical bull of a rapids.

We splashed hard off a haystack, then lurched right. The roar of the water was more like being on a runway than a river. Phil was in full volume—no longer singing—and I was having some trouble sorting out the instructions.

"Keep to the right of that rock!"

"There's a hydraulic straight ahead! Left! Left! LEFT!"

"Careful! Careful! NOW–HARD PADDLE!"

"Right! Right! RIIIGGGHHHTTTTTTT!"

Okay, so sometimes I do not know my left from my right. I have had trouble driving in England. I throw right but bat left. I play hockey left-handed but play golf right-handed. I blame all my problems on my older brother Jim, who was once given a right-handed five iron and taught himself to golf with it, then handed the five iron on to me.

Phil maintains I dug in hard, left, when he was shouting—no, *scream-ing*—right. I maintain that he was yelling too much, Canoe Eater was roaring too much, and my personal hard drive had reached capacity about halfway through.

No matter, we were over and, as James Raffan says in his hilarious Maxims for Happy Paddling, "Don't argue in rapids." (He also says "Duct tape can save a marriage," "WD-40 on a worm attracts fish," "Grey Owl paddled on both sides" and "Change your underwear.")

Looking back, I am astonished at how slow it all went. We were in very fast water. We were paddling hard. And yet slowly, ever so slowly, the canoe hit on the flat rock Phil wanted to avoid, rode up it like a stalled car being ramped onto a flatbed, and stopped. Yes, *stopped*. Stopped dead. For just a moment, but very much long enough for the two of us to ponder the nature of the universe and where, in fact, we fit into it. There was no "creaking" sound but there should have been. We stopped, we turned as the water cuffed the stern hard and, a moment later, we began this long, slow, fully aware fall from grace, and the canoe.

The shock of the water is a constant. No matter how often you might have dumped a canoe, either deliberately or by accident, in flatwater or whitewater; no matter whether the water is ice cold from the mountains or bathtub warm from the August sun; no matter whether it happens in an instant or happens, as it did on Canoe Eater, over what felt like a matter of several decades, it shocks.

I remember hoping my feet would slip out from under the seat. How they did I have no idea, but instantly I realized I was free of the canoe, under water, and the roar was silenced. I could feel the water—cool and very physical—tossing me about as I fought to gain the surface. I came up to see a jumble of yellow and red dry bags floating past our overturned canoe.

"On your back!" Phil shouted. "Feet first!"

I was already there, floating along like a kid in a carnival ride as I bounced, Slinky-like, down the "stairs" of Canoe Eater and into a wide swirling pool at the bottom, where, so thoughtfully, the centrifugal force of the circling current, deposited me and Phil and one pack, in a quiet eddy where we could stand on the jumble of small rocks below.

I prepared myself for a blast from Phil. I got it—though hardly the one I had anticipated:

> It's a beautiful mornin', ahhh,
> I think I'll go outside a while,
> An jus' smile.

It was beautiful indeed that morning—as it was every morning that we were on the Dumoine. When Phil wasn't singing hits from the Sixties, he was talking—perhaps it might be better to say "lecturing"—about his life-long passion: the Canadian wilderness writer known as Grey Owl.

While studying at Carleton University many years earlier, Phil had chosen Grey Owl as his topic for an honours English thesis: "Knight Errant of the Canadian Wilderness." He had so immersed himself in the famous Canadian woodsman and author that he had, in some ways, *become* Grey Owl. To educate eastern Ontario students about the conservation messages of the late world-famous writer, Phil had read everything written on Grey Owl and was particularly enthralled with Donald B. Smith's *From the Land of Shadows*, for which Phil had been a principal reader and early adviser. He had memorized passages from Grey Owl's many books, had buckskin regalia similar to Grey Owl's made for him by Peggy Commanda Dick of Golden Lake First Nation and had mounted a "show" that was such a hit with Canadian students that England's Grey Owl Society had invited him to bring it to British schools. Queen Elizabeth herself had written a letter of appreciation after his successful visit to schools in South East England.

I thought I was quite familiar with the story of Grey Owl, who was never the "full-blooded red Indian" the 1930s promotional posters promised as he toured Europe and the United States on fabulously successful speaking tours. He was, rather, a full-blooded Englishman named Archibald Stansfeld Frumage, later changed to Belaney. He came to Canada and reinvented himself entirely, learning to trap and living in the wilderness of Northern Ontario and, later, northern Saskatchewan. He claimed to be the illegitimate child of a Scots adventurer and an Apache woman. He dyed his hair black, used henna to redden his skin and supposedly flattened his nose by pressing hard and rolling a spoon back and forth across it. He wore a headdress picked up in a souvenir shop, performed "Apache" war dances while singing pure gibberish—and became, for many years, by far the most famous *Canadian* in the entire world.

It was only following Belaney's death in 1938—from pneumonia, but likely directly linked to his alcoholism—that the *North Bay Nugget* exposed the hoax. The little newspaper had been sitting on the story for years. What astonished me even more than the paper holding such a scoop was that the fraud wasn't immediately recognized by anyone who picked up one of Grey Owl's many books. *Pilgrims of the Wild*, published in 1935, is chock full of language that would ring false in backwoods Canada and could only have come from a British grammar school upbringing. He talks of "rampikes." He says someone has the "speed and endurance of a greyhound." He speaks disparagingly of "belowstairs snobbery."

And yet, when you go back over the sections that are not about his leaving trapping behind and, with his half-Mohawk wife, Anahareo, raising beaver kits in their cabin on Ajawaan Lake in Saskatchewan's Prince

Albert National Park, Belaney seems almost to be baiting readers to challenge him on this point. At one point, he says, "My precise and stilted English was, like a stiff and ceremonious suit of Sunday best, something to be taken out of the closet and worn on occasion, and its use ended, returned to the limbo of unneeded things." Later on, in speaking of his increasing fame, the author slams critics who seemed scandalized that "an uncultured bushwhacker of acknowledged Indian blood should so step out of character and become articulate . . . They seemed to take it as a personal affront that there were in existence beings who, without benefit of education, had common knowledge of many things not taught in halls of learning . . . "

Yet he was not challenged. His books sold around the world. He appeared in films. His lecture tours were sold out. He gave a royal command performance, delighting little Princess Elizabeth and ending the evening by patting King George VI on the back and saying, "I'll be seeing you, brother." When he was finally exposed in death, the backlash was as strong as the embrace had been—a backlash that has largely continued down through the years. In her essay collection *Strange Things*, Margaret Atwood wrote of "The Grey Owl Syndrome" that strikes so many native wannabes eager to follow the lead of this shape-changing Englishman.

Phil Chester took that personally. He figured he was among the intended targets and it stung. He argued that there is a long tradition of one-man shows on authors—Hal Holbrook playing Mark Twain on stage being but one example—and he had always deliberately ended his Grey Owl performances by stripping off the native paraphernalia to ensure the students understood that he was just Phil Chester, teacher, and not someone thinking he was the second coming of Grey Owl.

Phil deeply resented the continuing attacks on Grey Owl over the years. He found M.T. Kelly's short story "Case History," in Kelly's collection *Breath Dances Between Them*, offensive in its reference to this "tall, twisted imperial phoney, a Brit who 'seeded' native women, then abandoned the children, a violent psychopath only concerned with himself, his reactions to the country, his feelings." Belaney, Phil felt, was profoundly misunderstood in death and his message lost.

In the late 1990s, when Sir Richard Attenborough came to the Ottawa area to film *Grey Owl*, Phil offered his services as a Grey Owl expert. He even went on-set one day in the Gatineau Hills and met briefly with the film's star, Pierce Brosnan. But Attenborough did not take him up on the offer.

Attenborough had already enlisted wilderness expert Hap Wilson, who spent many futile days trying to teach Brosnan to paddle properly. Perhaps it was because of Brosnan's inability to master simple paddling techniques that Attenborough, the director, elected to have no whitewater in the film, though it would have contributed significantly to the visual impact. Grey Owl was also a great advocate of rapids-running. In *Pilgrims of the Wild* he had spoken of "the feel of the funnel at the thigh; the sound of flying spray in the face." And in *The Men of the Last Frontier* he had written admiringly of the "'white water men' to whom the thunderous roar of the rapids and the smell of spray flying in the face are as the intoxication of strong drink."

The film proved unconvincing in the extreme—the poetic and well-spoken Belaney played by Brosnan as a man of few words and simplistic messages, the relationship between Brosnan and French-Canadian actress Annie Galipeau without chemistry. Attenborough's $42-million wilderness extravaganza would go down in history as one of the great film flops of all time. None of this, however, had any effect on the admiration felt for the original Grey Owl by either Phil Chester or Hap Wilson.

"Beyond the fact that he was a failed father, husband, and lover," Wilson wrote in *Grey Owl and Me*, "and lied to the world about who he was, there is the greater truth in all of this: Archie Belaney, by whatever influences, brought the message of conservation to the world. From a purely Machiavellian perspective, *the end does justify the means*."

"Despite what his critics say, Canada is a better place for Grey Owl having lighted here," Phil Chester believes. "He drew the world's attention to the plight of wild animals, wild spaces and Aboriginal people in our country and he gave real impetus to the development of our national parks system."

Phil also feels that the controversy over Grey Owl's identity and intentions clouded another great achievement of Belaney, who came from Hastings, England, and made himself into one of the most accomplished wilderness persons Canada has ever known.

Grey Owl/Archie Belaney was, in Phil's opinion, "a pioneer conservationist who, over his entire adult life, helped to effect laws to protect our forests, rivers, lakes and the earth itself from wanton, indiscriminate exploitation." He says that Grey Owl gave Canada's fledgling national parks system important attention during the Depression years, "putting our parks on the global map." He was a patriot who fought for Canada in the Great War and fought for nature the remainder of his life.

"Whatever else Grey Owl was or pretended to be," Phil wrote in a recent letter to the Canadian Canoe Museum in Peterborough, "whatever others have said or written about him (and his detractors are legion) he was first and foremost a canoeman, probably the most confounding and enigmatic *Canadian* canoeman who ever lived, and as a skilled canoeman who wrote Canadian wilderness classics, he deserves his spot of sunlight in the Canadian Canoe Museum."

He has yet to receive a reply.

The one quote Phil most often uses in talking about Grey Owl is something Grey Owl never put in his books or in his lectures but late in his life happened to say to his secretary, Betty Somervell, out of the blue: "Down the avenue of trees I see a spot of sunlight and I am trying so hard to get there."

To Phil, this simple sentence encompasses Archie Belaney's struggles with his own demons as well as with the world he was trying to change.

Phil has first-hand knowledge of these same demons and has spent decades reaching his own "spot of sunlight," where he stands today.

A metaphor for life; a metaphor for all long portages.

Grey Owl saw the wilderness river as "a living thing." In 1938, not long before his death, he wrote, "It sometimes seems as if it was watching us, like some huge half-sleeping serpent that observes us dreamily, lying there secure in his consciousness of power while we . . . play perilously on his back."

We certainly played on the back of the Dumoine, but never really perilously. There was never any question that we would be portaging around Grand Chute, a violent, dramatic drop surrounded by massive granite cliffs that even driftwood would balk at chancing.

We camped just above the falls and, in the middle of the night, a wicked summer storm rolled in, the rain pelting our tents and the thunder echoing along the gorge in what sounded like, and felt like, continuous shelling. At one point the lightning sizzled and crackled and cracked so close that Phil and I made plans to scoot through the downpour and hide under a rock ledge until it passed.

But then, in an instant, it was gone—it left as hurriedly as it arrived, both times unannounced. The only remaining sounds were the roar of the falls downstream and the light tapping of raindrops that worked down through the pines and onto our tent. (Phil claims to have fallen asleep to the sounds of me whimpering, but, if so, it was only because the storm was like a lullaby compared to his snoring.)

The portage around Grand Chute—you take it or you die—is about fifteen hundred metres over some pretty choppy ground. You put in at a calm pool and are instantly into rapids, though small ones.

From here on, the Dumoine is a water dance. We shot the Red Pine Rapids, a long series of difficult water that required a few scouting stops—for us, not Lorne and Kelly—and then passed under a five-hundred-foot wall of granite known as Bald Eagle Cliff. On through the gentle rapids of the Three Sisters—three giant rocks that stand as guardians in the river—and on to Ryan's Chute, where at one point three dozen pairs of hobnail boots were nailed to trees as a makeshift memorial to those who died here driving logs down to the Ottawa River. We shot Drowned Rapids without incident and then had a long, leisurely paddle out to the mouth of the river and our crossing point to Driftwood Provincial Park, where the vehicles had been left.

Phil pointed out that it was only mid-morning and the wind had yet to come up, so he suggested a wide, sweeping arc to the northwest across the Ottawa that would negate the high winds and current that might otherwise push us far downstream, missing our intended landing site at the Ontario park. We were barely cleared of the mouth when we felt the wind rising and the swells begin to grow. Soon we were riding so high on the crests and dropping so low in the troughs that the four canoes seemed to be toys on the water, bobbing up and down, in sight and then out of sight. We took on water but not much, Phil carefully working the high upstream arc across the Ottawa so that we rode the swells as much as possible, only rarely slamming into the rolling tubes of water. I was a bit concerned; he not at all:

> *I've been to Hollywood*
> *I've been to Redwood*
> *I crossed the ocean . . .*

It was a long paddle and, given that Phil was in full voice and not talking, a time for reflection. The images were fresh: the haunting sense of ghost children playing on the porch of the abandoned trapper's home; the belly laughs caused by Scott's wicked, trickster-ish sense of humour; the awe felt while paddling under Bald Eagle Cliff; the storm that bowled up the gorge at Grand Chute; dunking at Canoe Eater; and, of course, Lorne's Stilton cheese.

The cheese ritual was a complete surprise to me. It dated from the late 1970s and was actually born on this very river, the Dumoine. The Chester brothers were accompanied by, among others, an English friend, Les, who toted a backpack that emitted a strong smell. "Like a small animal had died inside," Phil claimed. On the last night of the trip, as they camped just above Ryan's Chute, Les brought out his hidden treasure—a pack of nearly liquefied Stilton cheese—and placed it on the blade of a wooden paddle with a knife for cutting and then, from the same pack, produced a bottle of tawny port to drink with the cheese.

The Chesters turned the event into a tradition, the "Ode-R of Stilton" ceremony, in which the cheese is joined by a silver spoon that once belonged to their mother and a poem, written by Phil, is recited by a person wearing a Scottish bonnet:

Stilton! Brave Stilton!
Blue blood of Arthur's seat
Fair Albion's sweet ambrosia

Thou which runneth by the white waters
We canoemen trumpet and salute you!

Your flakey crust and creamy coat
Your smell of rotten river feet
We spoon you, mites and maggots round.

Thus do we un-clip the tawny port and sup
Stilton! Thou keep'st our peckers up!

Such rituals are not unique to the Crash Test Dummies but are, oddly, virtually standard fare among those who regularly trip together. Most groups have a sacred hat, a Scotch or Jameson Irish Whiskey ritual, wine in the evenings, moonlight skinny-dipping, a "polar bear dip" in cold mountain water, group photographs at the beginning and end. Perhaps the Dummies take it a bit further than others, though, as "posterior trumpeting is encouraged" during and after the cheese ceremony, as is "silly walking"—though the port may contribute to that to a certain degree.

Phil Chester also has a very private ritual he keeps to. On any river he runs, he leaves tobacco as thanks to the First Nations who travelled these routes, who gave Canada the canoe and who to this day, in such places as the Petawawa and Dumoine, still have unsettled land claims over the territory. A non-smoker, he nonetheless carries tobacco with him on every trip and, at some point along the paddle, will wander off to hold a quiet, private ceremony where he gives thanks for being allowed the privilege of travelling these traditional routes. The Dumoine holds a special place in his heart, as well as in his future, and he has tried to express those feelings in a poem:

La Rivière Dumoine

She brings me eternal summer
touches me at the sacred core of Being—
tamarack, water lilies, pickle weed
misty mornings, heavy rain
the spot of sunlight at the end of the hard portage trail.

Yes, my keel has traced her many faces—
Lac Brulart, Laforge, Manitou, Benoit—
twisting and turning
a ribbon of the finest silk;
the fancy bow at *La Grande Chute*
makes me pause to picnic and kneel in awe
of her cascading beauty.

Songs along the Dumoine

The Seine, the Nile, the Thames
have not this numinous power over me.
La Rivière Dumoine draws me forever longingly to herself
leaving her blaze mark upon my soul.
And I must follow the allure of her holy curves
dreaming to awaken in her kind and loving embrace.

The river is a Spirit Woman

Pilgrim, do not presume to ask for her regal hand,
for she is wild in her natural course; a breaker of hulls
    and hearts,
the ruffles of her boreal dress,
the neck-lasses of starlight sparkle
upon the ineffable finery of her trousseau.

Her bouquet of charms—rollicking haystack waves, drop pools
fierce eddies and bluing swifts
inspire the soft discourse of moonlit water
and her many tongues, smooth and dark as obsidian,
Invite me to the Dance and I enter the deep water of Mystery.

Enchanted, cast under her meandering spell,
the potpourri of woodland flowers and wood smoke intoxicates—
The Queen of Rivers draws back the veil.

At *Des Épingles Rouges* I rest my head upon her bosom
and beneath a great white pine:
there, by a most ancient medicine granite rock,
I leave tobacco—someday my ashes—
for the Creator and all my Relations.

—Phil Chester

3

THE TWO ICONS

IT WAS OCTOBER 2, 2000, one of those early fall days where the light seems to have been rinsed before it falls on soft brown fields and brings out the bright red and orange of hardwood hills. The sky was filled with arrows of geese pointing south as Via Rail Train 638 slowly made its way from the nation's capital to Montreal. It was a short train, unscheduled until required by necessity, only a single engine and four cars, the last of which carried the remains of Joseph Philippe Pierre Yves Elliott Trudeau, the fifteenth prime minister of Canada.

There was a coach for the casket—curtains drawn open so it could be seen from both sides—a coach for the family and close friends, a coach for RCMP pallbearers and officials, and a coach for the media—where I sat staring out at a country staring back.

Because the natural reflex of Ottawa is to manage information, those dealing with the very few media allowed on board had determined well beforehand what the storyline would be. One by one, Trudeau colleagues—former finance minister Marc Lalonde now, Senator Jacques Hébert next—would be trotted out and sat at a table, and we were expected to gather around and take notes while they reminisced about their sadly departed leader and friend, the man who had been prime minister twice, from 1968 to 1979 and from 1980 to 1984, Pierre Trudeau, dead just weeks before his eighty-first birthday.

A nice gesture, but personal recollections by colleagues wasn't the story this day. Perhaps on the day news broke of his death it was, but not now. The story that mattered, and told so very much more, was unfolding on the other side of the clear, clean windows of Via 638. It first became apparent when the train, just leaving the outskirts of Ottawa, moved past the Ottawa-Carleton Transpo repair shops. The mechanics had laid down tools and come out, as a group, to stand by the fence and watch the train roll by at what one official had called "a respectful pace." The mechanics stood as if they were in a choir, all dressed in dark blue coveralls, each with his blackened hands folded neatly in front as if in a recital.

They were but the first signal that the real story that day was not about the past but about the present, not about Trudeau's life but his death. As the train pulled through small outlying villages, it passed by volunteer fire brigades, uniformed peewee hockey teams, Cubs, Girl Guides, cadets . . . all forming impromptu honour guards for the funeral train. In weather that felt left over from summer, people gathered, some standing, some in cars, some sitting in folding lawn chairs at rail crossings to watch in silence as the train passed. Sometimes they applauded, sometimes they stood at attention. Men working on a culvert along a back road stopped what they were doing, hard hats respectfully removed, while the train moved by, one of the men standing in the hole they had been digging, with only his head visible. A farmer stopped disking a field, stepped down from his tractor, took off a sweat-darkened cap and stood with his hand over his heart. At the golf course near Casselman, a foursome on the green stopped their putting and removed their golf caps.

It was hard to say exactly what was causing this. The uniformed youngsters who stood at attention at each little station would not even have been alive when Pierre Trudeau was last in office. Those who had voted him into office the first time had also voted him out once and, had he lingered on past 1984, would likely have voted him out again. Perhaps they were not only saying farewell to a significant force—a leader who, as the CBC's

Gordon Donaldson put it, had burst onto the Canadian political scene like "a stone through a stained-glass window"—but paying homage to a lost time when everyone was young and everything seemed possible.

At Alexandria, near the Ontario-Quebec border, Via 638 dramatically slowed down as it pulled into the small town. The train jerked and lost speed abruptly at one point, staggering those of us standing. A conductor on our coach seemed concerned, mystified. We could now see that the crowd, which seemed to have grown larger with each passing village or town, was now massive. People were lined six to eight deep along the tracks leading into the station, where the crowd was huge. Scouts and Guides and Legion members—their chests out, medals flashing in the sunlight—were having to stutter-step closer just to maintain their prime positions at the front.

There was a strange, eerie, squeaking sound. I thought, given the conductor's clear concern, that it must be the brakes of the train, or the wheels. Perhaps we would have to change one of the coaches. Perhaps even the engine.

But the strange sound was none of that. It was the sound of human skin—the hands of Alexandria—on steel. The people had pressed so close to the moving train that they were reaching out to touch it as it passed through their town. I do not believe I have ever heard anything that caused such chills to dance up and down my spine.

Nor that day did I see anything that more eloquently evoked the simple values of a very complicated man than a woman standing sentry at a lonely railway crossing. As Via 638 passed by at a much quicker speed than it crept through Alexandria, she held up a cherry paddle with a rainbow-coloured voyageur sash tied around its handle.

No explanation required.

And none was required later that day when the remains of the former prime minister were taken to Notre-Dame Basilica. The coffin was draped with the Canadian flag and something very special was leaned against it.

A single canoe paddle.

The Two Icons

There are fourteen statues on Parliament Hill. These include two queens, Victoria and Elizabeth II. There is a statue of five women who fought for the right to vote. There is a statue to honour two men who fought for responsible government, Robert Baldwin and Louis-Hippolyte LaFontaine. There are statues for two Fathers of Confederation who were killed: Thomas D'Arcy McGee, assassinated near Parliament Hill in 1868, and George Brown, the founder of the *Globe* newspaper, who was shot by a disgruntled employee in 1880. There is even a statue to the bell that survived the 1916 Centre Block fire.

Six prime ministers are honoured: Sir John A. Macdonald, Alexander Mackenzie, Sir Wilfrid Laurier, William Lyon Mackenzie King, John Diefenbaker and Lester Pearson. A statue was created for a seventh, Arthur Meighen, who, like Trudeau, was twice prime minister, but it was considered so ugly (former prime minister John Diefenbaker called it "the greatest monstrosity ever produced—a mixture of Ichabod Crane and Daddy-Long-Legs") that the Meighen statue was hidden away for years in a vault below Wellington Street and eventually taken to his hometown of St. Marys, Ontario, where it stands today.

Not surprisingly, shortly after the death of Pierre Trudeau there were calls for a statue to honour the man who had served as his nation's leader for sixteen years, reformed the justice system, led Canada through its greatest unity crisis, promoted bilingualism and repatriated the Constitution.

There was ample room on Parliament Hill, both in front of and behind the Centre Block. But how to portray him? Signing the new Canadian Constitution seated beside the Queen? Pirouetting behind the Queen's back at Buckingham Palace? There was certainly no lack of familiar images.

But a committee struck specially to honour Pierre Trudeau had other ideas. They chose a location away from Parliament Hill, some fourteen kilometres upstream along the Ottawa River. There, in a lovely small park where the river widens dramatically, with the Gatineau Hills rising across the water to the east, they would build a statue that would commemorate the fifteenth prime minister as he liked to see himself: in buckskin, reclining on a rock of the Canadian Shield, a paddle by his side.

"It's perfect," Justin Trudeau said one chill day in December 2001, when the son came to the chosen spot in Andrew Haydon Park.

The bronzed statue—still not in place by 2015—would show the late prime minister far from politics, "looking," said Terrence Bell of the committee, "for all the world like he's about to set off on another canoe trip."

Pierre Trudeau, curiously, was once far better known for his thoughts on the great outdoors than whether the government had any business in the bedrooms of the nation.

In 1944, when he was just twenty-five years old, Trudeau published an essay in *Jeunesse Étudiante Catholique*, the publication of a students' Christian movement founded in France in the late 1920s that spread around the world. Translated into English, Trudeau's essay, "Exhaustion and Fulfillment: The Ascetic in a Canoe," eventually found its way into English Canada when former *Maclean's* magazine editor Borden Spears selected it to appear in a 1970 collection called *Wilderness Canada*. The essay eventually rose to the status of wilderness prayer for canoeists.

Trudeau begins by claiming, "I would not know how to instill a taste for adventure in those who have not acquired it." He accepts, though there is a rather disparaging tone, the joys of paddling a calm pond in a city park and the delights of an overnight paddle, portage, tent and return—but what he wishes to glorify is the "canoeing expedition" that involves time, challenge, physical endurance and ingenuity.

"It involves a starting rather than a parting," the young student wrote about the true canoeing experience. "Although it assumes the breaking of ties, its purpose is not to destroy the past, but to lay a foundation for the future. From now on, every living act will be built on this step, which will serve as a base long after the return of the expedition . . . and until the next one.

"What is essential at the beginning is the resolve to reach the saturation point. Ideally, the trip should end only when the members are making no further progress within themselves."

There is a bit of the braggart here, but a twenty-five-year-old deserves at least a bit of grace. He writes of paddling for days, even months, on end. He talks about having to paddle more than a thousand miles from Montreal to Hudson Bay with a friend (they did reach James Bay). He boasts of requiring only the bare necessities—canoe and paddle, blanket and knife, salt pork and flour, fishing rod and rifle—to survive such a trip, almost as if he were fancying himself in some Western movie.

And yet the words that follow are as evocative, and truthful, as any that have ever been written or spoken about the joys of a canoe trip. His contention that once you set out on a canoe trip "you are already a child of nature" has been quoted hundreds of times and will be quoted thousands more when canoeing enthusiasts attempt to explain the elusive draw of an enterprise where you work hard, struggle, sweat, have no access to showers, sit on blocks of wood or stones, carry heavy loads over difficult terrain, sometimes flip over, are often cold and wet—and love every moment of it.

Trudeau was introduced to the canoe at Taylor Statten Camps in Algonquin Park. He was only fifteen years old when his father, Charles, a wealthy Montreal businessman, died suddenly after contracting pneumonia on a trip to Florida to visit the spring training facilities of his minor league baseball team. His mother, Grace, would have welcomed the distractions that Ahmek, the boys' camp, offered her grieving teenager. Young Pierre threw himself into boxing, the theatre—where he played a villainous Black Bart—and, most of all, canoeing. It is hardly surprising that much of the essay he would soon write had to do with the therapeutic values of paddling and the endless busyness of a canoe trip.

"How does the trip affect your personality?" he wrote. "Allow me to make a fine distinction, and I would say that you return not so much a man who reasons more, but a more reasonable man. For, throughout this time, your mind has learned to exercise itself in the working conditions which nature intended. Its primordial role has been to sustain the body in the struggle against a powerful universe."

The excursions from the Canoe Lake summer camp changed him dramatically. It taught him a love of the country that could never have been found while sitting in the stands in Montreal, watching his father's Royals play baseball. He would not know it through studies, through books or even through imagining. He had to experience it first-hand. "I know a man whose school could never teach him patriotism," he wrote, "but who acquired that virtue when he felt in his bones the vastness of his land, and the greatness of those who founded it."

The love of paddling that he discovered in Algonquin Park served him for life. It also had significant effect on the formation of the personality that would so fascinate and agitate his country in later years. In 1956, when poet and constitutional expert F.R. Scott let it be known in Montreal circles that he was headed into the Canadian North come summer to better know his country, a young lawyer named Trudeau asked if he might come along. Scott agreed and they headed off into what the poet would later call "a huge nowhere."

It was while on the Peace River that Scott saw something in Trudeau that the country would eventually see. They were standing at the head of rapids that run, virtually continually, for some twenty-seven kilometres along the Peace River. Suddenly, young Trudeau began wading into the churning waters.

"I'm going in!" he shouted back to Scott.

"Here!" the much older Scott protested. "Don't be silly—you can't go into that!"

"Oh, I'm going in," Trudeau shot back.

And he did, wading out into the water where it was picking up speed, bracing himself against the current and smiling in the face of foolishness. We know he was smiling, because Scott took a photograph of the moment and later penned a telling poem:

Pierre, suddenly challenged,
Stripped and walked into the rapids,
Firming his feet against rock.
Standing white, in white water,
Leaning south of the current
To stem the downward rush,
A man testing his strength
Against the strength of his country.

In 1960, Trudeau and two pals from Montreal concocted a mad scheme to paddle from Key West, Florida, to Cuba—this was two years before the Cuban Missile Crisis—and were swamped about fifty kilometres off shore and had to be towed back by a shrimp boat. It was a humiliation, but it did nothing to quell his love of the canoe and paddle.

After being elected to Parliament in 1965 and moving to Ottawa, Trudeau fell in with a group of experienced paddlers led by Eric Morse, national director of the Canadian Clubs, and, the following year, travelled with Morse's group to the Northwest Territories to paddle the Coppermine River. The following spring he went down the Petawawa with, among others, Blair Fraser, the Ottawa editor of *Maclean's* magazine. Trudeau flipped and survived fine. A year later Fraser capsized and was lost.

There is film footage from the 1966 trip down the Coppermine and the 1967 paddle down the Petawawa. The films were taken by Jim Bayly and are grainy, a bit jumpy, but they show in colour the incredible beauty of both rivers. They also show, in quick scans around the campfire and shots of walking a portage and boarding a float plane, a Pierre Trudeau few ever got to know. He seems so small and slight compared to the other men. He seems shy and a bit standoffish. But he is always smiling.

There can be no doubt that Trudeau loved canoeing but, equally, there can be little doubt a man so acutely aware of image felt the canoe connection was a welcome personal brand. Paddling had political currency in this country so dependent on the native means of travel for its very being. "The canoe also carried a subliminal message," his close friend Alastair Gillespie believed. "The symbolism was right. What could be more Canadian? It represents the very essence of our existence, of discovery, of improvisation, the response to enormous challenges."

Once Trudeau became prime minister, the northern canoe trips he had come to love proved difficult. At his rustic cabin in the Laurentians, where he could rarely get to, he still kept the little cedar-and-canvas canoe in which he'd taken his first trips. He called the beloved canoe "*Ça ira*," for "It'll get there." For whitewater dalliance he owned a Prospector—the design of choice for most serious trippers—and when he was prime minister he had been given a birchbark canoe that now sits in the Canadian Canoe Museum in Peterborough, Ontario.

When he did get out onto the water, he stuck for the most part to rivers near Ottawa, such as the Gatineau, on the Quebec side of the Ottawa River, and the Petawawa. He made sure that his three boys—Justin, Alexandre (Sacha) and Michel—all learned to paddle, even if it was only on brief excursions when he could get away for a quiet day with them at Harrington Lake, the prime minister's official summer residence.

"Maybe my most indelible canoe memory from that cottage was one of the rites of passage for the Trudeau boys," Justin wrote in a 2012 article for *Cottage Life* magazine. "When we hit five or six years old, our dad would put us into the canoe and we'd shoot the rapids on the stream that went down into Meech Lake. There's a little dam there, and in the spring they'd open the dam, and there would be a huge V and a standing wave. With much trepidation, we'd sit in the front and go down the drop. I look back on it now and laugh, because my father was sterning, and there was nothing I could do from the bow to aim it right—but it was very, very important for us to do it. To get into the bow of a canoe with my father for the first time, to be the bowman for the first time, and to go down this big, scary rapid."

It was as prime minister that Trudeau commissioned the Canadian Wild River Survey. Teams of canoeists spread out across the country to inventory Canada's rivers. It led, ultimately, to the creation of the Canadian Heritage Rivers System. Just as significantly, scores of young students who found summer work doing that original inventory became river disciples, many of them familiar and admired names in the wilderness canoeing community.

His contribution to the *idea* of canoeing was essential. The activity had drifted in and out of popularity since the birchbark canoe largely vanished, but Pierre Trudeau made canoeing wild rivers *cool*. Those who travelled with him considered it an honour. "The pleasure of tripping with this energetic, thoughtful, fascinating, generous and confident paddler was a privilege given to a very few," said Ted Johnson, who served as executive assistant to the prime minister.

Following his defeat at the hands of Joe Clark's Progressive Conservatives in early June of 1979, Trudeau set off with seven friends to canoe the Hanbury and Thelon rivers. Some of his fellow travellers were old friends, like *La Presse* columnist Jean Pelletier, and some were old canoeing companions such as Craig Oliver and David Silcox. Trudeau seemed to them to be almost relieved to be out of power. At one point, when a bush plane buzzed their campsite, he shouted out that the Clark government had fallen and they were coming to get him to take over again.

Later, in his 1993 *Memoirs*, he wrote, "I think a lot of people want to go back to the basics sometimes, to find their bearings. For me a good way to do that is to get into nature by canoe—to take myself as far away as possible from everyday life, from its complications and from the artificial wants created by civilization. Canoeing forces you to make a distinction between your needs and your wants. When you are canoeing, you have to deal with your needs: survival, food, sleep, protection from the weather. These are all things that you tend to take for granted when you are living in so-called civilization, with its constant pressure to do this or that for social reasons created by others, or to satisfy artificial wants created by advertising. Canoeing gets you back close to nature, using a method of travel that does not even call for roads or paths. You are following nature's road; you are choosing the road less travelled by, as Robert Frost once wrote in another context, and that makes all the difference. You discover a sort of simplifying of your values, a distinction between values artificially created and those that are necessary to your spiritual and human development."

When it came to the photograph for the jacket of the book, the choices were myriad: the formally dressed Trudeau signing the Constitution, the dapper young prime minister in his otter coat, the "gunslinger" at centre stage during his final campaign or . . . what he chose as an illustration to grace the cover.

An informal shot of himself in his buckskin jacket, his paddling clothes.

In the days before obsessive security and black SUV convoys whisking the prime minister between the official residence at 24 Sussex and the summer residence in the Gatineau Hills, newly elected Pierre Trudeau was known to take solitary walks down the road from Harrington Lake to the far end of Meech Lake. Here, where several people lived year-round along the narrow road that snaked along the shoreline, he was struck one evening by the warm sounds of a particular house that seemed to welcome the world.

Curious, he knocked on the door. A small girl answered. Her name was Becky. She called out to her parents, Bill and Joyce, to come to the door and it was here, by accident, that two canoeing icons, Pierre Trudeau and Bill Mason, first met. Both small, wiry, both given to covering up shyness and social awkwardness with bravado or even shock, they hit it off immediately and remained friendly for life.

And yet they were so very different. Trudeau was French, born into privilege, highly educated and trained by the Jesuits in both belief and control of one's emotions; Mason was English, son of a lowly and unhappy office clerk, comparably uneducated, leaning toward Christian fundamentalism and openly, often wildly, emotional.

Many years later, the little girl who answered the door at Meech Lake—Becky Mason, now a recognized canoe expert in her own right—tried to explain what it was that drew this intensely private man of high office to a man whose only office was the wild and who believed in sharing every-thing with everyone.

"I think Pierre Trudeau really enjoyed my dad because my dad had this naïveté," Becky said in the summer of 2014. "It's not quite the right word, but he had this amazing quality of living so intensely and enjoying the simple things in life. He was just so *passionate* about it. And I think Pierre Trudeau loved my dad's passion for just the craft of the canoe and where it could take you.

"I really think it's what my husband [Reid McLachlan] once said about Pierre: 'He didn't feel threatened' by my dad. They never talked politics at all. Ever. It was a totally different relationship, and Pierre Trudeau valued it, he *treasured* it. It was like a touchstone for him. He would invite my dad to 24 Sussex with all his broomball friends and they'd have a big dinner about broomball. And Pierre Trudeau loved it, loved it. It was really special."

Becky believes that in her father Trudeau found something he needed: a playmate. Bill Mason's enthusiasm for absolutely everything was some-thing the usually reserved Trudeau could only marvel at. Mason's spon-taneity was a trait Trudeau—who had even practised his famous "spontaneous" pirouette behind the Queen—did not possess but may have wished he could tap into.

"He had to act like Pierre Trudeau himself," Becky says. "No one could act otherwise with my dad. My dad was a humble guy, but he brought out qualities in people that they quested after. I think that has something to do with it. My dad had this lovely quality that brought the best out of people. He taught people how to live using their whole soul. He revived them. He was like an egg beater with his enthusiasms. He would stop everything and say, 'Let's go play,' and he'd play flat out for two hours and then go back to work.

"I think Pierre Trudeau really appreciated that. . . . We'd go down to Harrington Lake and we would go for tea and we would inevitably go in the canoes and play."

Famous for his shy looks, Trudeau was never shy around the Masons. Nor was he pretentious: Becky never once saw him paddling in the buckskin jacket that became a key part of his iconic image. And while others who met Trudeau one-on-one would often describe him as cold, incapable of small talk, and relatively humourless, laughter—even silliness—was a constant when he was around the Masons. With them, he could shift from a formal state dinner one night to cramming into the small Mason cabin the next, sitting on the floor with a plate of food in his lap just like everyone else who happened to drop in or be invited by Bill and Joyce.

"They were good friends," remembers Becky, "but my dad was careful with him, careful not to go to areas where he didn't have any knowledge. Their relationship was a lovely relationship, really. My dad was a little curious as to why Trudeau wanted to come by and play broomball with us, but everyone just treated him like a normal person.

"We never talked to any reporters ever about any relationship. My dad made it very clear early on that this was a special relationship we had and we didn't want to ruin it. It could have turned into a bit of a circus."

It certainly would have if the national media had known about the day when, thanks to Bill Mason's spontaneous enthusiasms, the Mounties lost the prime minister.

It happened on a spring day in the late 1970s. Bill Mason noted that the water levels were well up from the spring flush, and the Picanoc River up near Kazabazua, in western Quebec, would be ideal for the first run of the season. He rounded up his kids, Paul and Becky, contacted old friend Terry Orlick, a well-known sports psychologist who teaches at the University of Ottawa, and then, almost naively, put a call in to the prime minister to see if he was interested. Pierre Trudeau was. Not only would he come, but he'd bring his two older sons, Justin and Sacha.

Prime ministerial security requires that the RCMP accompany the sitting prime minister wherever he or she might travel. In the instance of canoeing, this had already proved problematic, as the Mounties sent to accompany Trudeau on a previous whitewater run had flipped their canoe barely outside the launch site. A compromise was reached for the Picanoc: the RCMP assignment would accompany Trudeau and his children to the launch and see them off safely, then drive downstream to meet them at the chosen rendezvous point where the day trip would end.

It was a great day to be on the water. The paddlers shot rapids and later stopped to picnic and do a little skinny-dipping in the cold spring water. They warmed up with tea that Bill prepared. Bill noticed that their little spot by the side of the rushing Picanoc was surrounded by maple trees and he stared up at them for a long time before turning to Trudeau. He looked the prime minister straight in the eyes.

"Pierre," he said, "you made a big mistake with the flag."

Trudeau was caught off guard. The new Canadian flag had been brought in by Prime Minister Lester B. Pearson and introduced on February 15, 1965, nearly nine months before Trudeau was elected to office.

"You should have put a canoe on the flag," Bill continued, "not a maple leaf."

The others sat listening and giggling as the debate raged, Trudeau defending the flag his Liberal Party had brought in, Mason attacking the chosen symbol. "It was so funny to watch and listen to that interaction sitting in front of a campfire on a rock in the middle of nowhere," remembers Terry Orlick. "Bill was adamant about the canoe being the best symbol for Canada and how it had carved out the history of the country."

The picnic and "The Second Great Canadian Flag Debate" over, the paddlers returned to the water and continued on through smooth paddling and some whitewater play. In late afternoon they reached the bridge over the Picanoc where they had agreed to pull the canoes off the water and link up again with the security detail. Only there was no RCMP in sight.

No security for the prime minister and his boys, and a weather threat to all, as it had clouded over and rain was beginning to pelt down upon the little group.

Not at all amused, Trudeau led the wet and weary paddlers over to a nearby rundown cottage, where he knocked impatiently at the door.

An older francophone couple answered and, flabbergasted to see the country's prime minister at the door, hastily invited the group into a room where there were not enough chairs to go around, but at least there was a telephone.

Trudeau immediately called the Mounties, using code names—he was "Maple 1," Justin "Maple 3" and Sacha "Maple 4"—to let them know he was where he was and to ask, in some pique, just where the hell were they. Turned out the RCMP cruiser had got bogged down in mud and was stuck fast. Not only that, but once freed, they had travelled to the wrong bridge and were themselves lost.

Bill Mason offered to hitchhike back to the village of Gracefield and lead the RCMP to the correct spot. Trudeau agreed and Bill set out. While the group waited patiently in the crammed room, a sound other than grumbling began to be heard, one that Becky Mason would never forget.

"Through the paper-thin walls, from the other room came the unmistakable sounds of an amorous couple enjoying themselves very thoroughly . . .

"I still chuckle about our prime minister being so near a bedroom of the nation that day!"

Bill Mason was ten years younger than Pierre Trudeau. He was born into modest means in Winnipeg in the spring of 1929, less than six months before the Wall Street stock market crash. He was a tiny, sickly baby who would, despite regular battles with asthma, grow into a tiny, strong man.

According to James Raffan's fabulous biography of Mason, *Fire in the Bones*, the Masons survived the Depression rather effortlessly, as Bill's namesake father, an Englishman from Birmingham, England, had permanent employment with the Great-West Life Assurance Company. The senior William Mason was far from enthusiastic about his work but did appreciate the steady income at a time when jobs were hard to come by. Sadie Mason ran a frugal home, making the family comparatively well off in such hard times. They even had an escape from the city heat come summer. Sadie's parents, the Fairs, rented a cottage on Lake Winnipeg and later purchased their own at Grand Beach, and it was here, at the summer home of his maternal grandparents, where young "Billy" first became entranced with the ancient form of transportation that would, essentially, become his life.

Back in Winnipeg during the long Manitoba winters, Bill Mason played hockey on the outdoor rinks. He was a vigorous, competitive player, but his diminutive size meant he could never be a star. He had a gift for art and soon applied it to design. When he was thirteen he built his own boat, which resembled something not quite canoe, not quite kayak. No matter, the youngster had become infatuated with the stories of the voyageurs, and now, in his own mind anyway, he was one himself.

At fifteen he went off to Manitoba Pioneer Camp, received badges for his canoeing and swimming and camp craft, and finally felt like he had found something he could indeed star at. "Even before going to camp," he later wrote in a camp newsletter, "I was obsessed with a love for the canoe—a love which has never diminished."

The camp used Calvin Rutstrum's *Way of the Wilderness* as a manual for the young adventurers. The book had originally been intended as a wilderness guide for Camp Lincoln, in Minnesota, where the Indiana native had worked for most of a decade. The manual gave instructions on everything from finding food in the wild to paddling a canoe and surviving winter weather. The booklet was then published in hardcover in 1946 and became an instant hit, establishing Rutstrum as a writer in the ranks of Henry David Thoreau, John Muir and Sigurd Olson.

In explaining his great passion for the wilderness—year after year he would take off on summer adventures, even if it required quitting good jobs—Rutstrum later told American writer Jim Dale Vickery, "I had a commitment to happiness. We need the joy of living optimally, where every natural force is playing on one's being, as multi-colored spotlights play on the actor who is exuberant with the joy of assuming his role. That exquisite pleasure of being an integral part of the natural universe, of being in its spotlight, makes one ecstatic about just living." Rutstrum's priorities in life were a perfect match for the priorities of a young Bill Mason.

James Raffan's biography came out eight years after Mason's death from cancer in 1988. He was only fifty-nine when he died yet had accomplished so much that Michael Peake, editor of the Canadian wilderness journal *Che-Mun*, felt Mason could be fairly called "the patron saint of Canadian canoeing." Mason's film work for the National Film Board (NFB), his books and his thousands of presentations across North America had made him the most famous modern canoeist known: his thick grey, then white, hair and beard giving him the look of a leprechaun, his clipped Central-Canadian rural speech patterns, his jaunty caps and constant "lumberjack" shirts created an image not easily forgotten. His prowess with a paddle and the skills he and Joyce passed on to their children, Paul and Becky, made the Masons the "First Family of Canoeing."

Mason was eccentric, beyond doubt. He would lard Biblical passages into his voice-over commentaries—Grandmother Mason had been extremely devout—and, as might be expected of one so dedicated to the canoe, he was a fervent traditionalist. Viewers of his fantastic *Path of the Paddle* films on whitewater methods are often struck by the fact that the canoe that he and Paul work through the tumbling waters and jagged rocks of the Petawawa River is wooden, whereas most paddlers of such testing waters travel in far more resilient vessels. Paul estimated they ran the Petawawa in that canoe thirty-five times during the filming of the series.

"The more he went down the Petawawa, the more he loved it," says Becky Mason. She believes if she and her father had the opportunity for one more paddle in life, it would be here, down the spectacular Petawawa River.

Bill's favourite canoe was a Chestnut Prospector, a red cedar-and-canvas model that became his brand even more so than the buckskin jacket became Pierre Trudeau's signature look. Let others use the banged-up and banged-out aluminum canoes, the rugged ABS canoes or the ultralight

Kevlar canoes of more modern eras. Same for his tent and equipment. The sight of Bill Mason making camp would suggest an outdoorsman from roughly the same era as one of his great outdoor heroes, painter Tom Thomson. Thomson, however, died in 1917, more than half a century before Bill Mason began filming his adventures in the wilderness.

Beginning in the 1950s, Mason put his inner child, his love of the canoe and his ambitions as a filmmaker together in the making of *Paddle to the Sea*. The inspiration began with a children's book his mother had ordered from the Eaton's catalogue when Bill was still a child. The story had captured his imagination: a small doll falling into a stream and eventually working its way all the way to the ocean. It took fifteen years to film but ended up getting an Oscar nomination in 1968 for best animated film.

For someone renowned for his playful—some would say reckless—enthusiasm, Bill Mason was also capable of enormous stretches of total focus on his work. When he was out in his little workshop splicing film and writing voice-overs, the Mason children learned to interrupt him at their peril.

"He really begrudged any time given to anybody when he was in a creative mode," Becky recalls. "He would hardly sleep or eat for three days sometimes, and he would make a film. If somebody came up to the house and knocked on the door, we'd know not to let them go out to the studio and just say hello. He would be diverted and become quite miserable about it.

"It was a bit worrisome how focused he could be. Everything would be falling down around him and not impact him. My mom was a little alarmed at times. He would be taking care of the kids and there would be just mayhem around him. He was the greatest dad in the world and he cared for us very much, but it was this focus that allowed him to accomplish so much in his life."

Mason's creative reputation would rest in his work for the NFB, but some of his best work took place in the Masons' Meech Lake living room and church basements and small theatres where he would present an endlessly polished slide show he tagged "God Revealed." It featured music, historical and literary quotes, magnificent shots of canoes and wilderness and, of course, Bill Mason's distinctive, almost childlike voice. When Raffan was researching his book on the famous canoeist, he came across scribbled notes for the show.

"This is voyageur country," Mason's voice-over would tell the crowds mesmerized by his wilderness shots. "Only 150 years ago, voyageurs manned birchbark canoes along these same waterways. Sounds are the same. Inhabitants are the same. Mile-thick glaciers carved out the lakes.

"Professor Arthur Lower expressed himself thus: 'Only those who have had the experience can know what a sense of physical and spiritual excitement comes to one who turns his face away from men towards the unknown. In his small way, he is doing what the great explorers have done before him and his elation recaptures theirs.' Wilderness is time-less. Blessed is the wilderness."

And at this point, Grandmother Mason would come through, as the slide show became half-adventure, half-sermon, with preacher William Mason at the pulpit:

"Life. Is it merely a sentimental delusion, a 'pathetic fallacy,' to think that one sees in the animal a capacity for joy which man himself is tend-ing to lose? We have invented exercise, recreation, pleasure, amusement and the rest. To 'have fun' is a desire often expressed by those who live in this age of anxiety, and most of us have at times actually 'had fun.' But recreation, pleasure, amusement, fun and all the rest are poor substitutes for joy; and joy, I am convinced, has its roots in something from which civilization tends to cut us off. . . .

"Cried the angel in Revelations: 'Hurt not the earth, neither the sea, nor the trees.' For nature is part of the glorious fullness of God's creation no less than man."

Bill Mason never ventured far from such thinking. His first profes-sional film, *Wilderness Treasure*, was produced for the Inter-Varsity Christian Fellowship in 1959 and later distributed by the NFB. It is the story of a canoe trip but also of another journey, according to the narration: "There are many treasures in the wilderness for those who learn to look and listen, but the deeper treasures need an understanding that only the Creator himself can give. We've turned from the book of Nature to the book of the written word of God and then back again with an ever deeper appreciation of the one who wrote them both."

Mason was hardly new in linking nature to God and back again to nature. A century earlier there had been "muscular Christianity"—a personal commitment by young men to piety and physical well-being—which preached a connection between athletic testing and faith in God and country. After United States president Theodore Roosevelt visited Yellowstone Park with famed naturalist John Burroughs around the turn of the last century, the most "physical" of all American presidents declared that "no nation facing the unhealthy softening and relaxation of fibre that tends to accompany civilization can afford to neglect anything that will develop hardihood, resolution, and the scorn of discomfort and danger."

So much of recreational canoeing dates from the European sojourns of John MacGregor (no relation that I am aware of), a London barrister who visited Canada in the late 1850s, fell in love with canoeing and took his new passion back to Great Britain. He built a vessel—more kayak than canoe, really—that he christened the "Rob Roy" and in 1865 set off on a three-month, one-thousand-mile trek through France, Switzerland and Germany. The book MacGregor published the following year, *A Thousand Miles in the Rob Roy Canoe*, was pivotal in popularizing the canoe in Europe.

"It cannot be concealed that continual physical enjoyment . . . is a dangerous luxury if it be not properly used," wrote MacGregor. "When I thought of the hospitals of London, of the herds of squalid poor in fetid alleys, of the palefaced ragged boys, and the vice, sadness, pain, and poverty we are sent to do battle with, if we be true Christian soldiers, I could not help asking: 'Am I right in thus enjoying such comfort, such scenery, and such health?'"

In some of the earliest writings on recreational canoeing, it seems almost as if trippers are carrying wooden crosses down the portages, not canoes. "It is one of the supreme joys of life to be thoroughly fit," believed Ralph Connor, Canada's bestselling novelist at the turn of the last century. Connor was, in fact, Charles Gordon, a Presbyterian minister.

"Being as God meant you to be," Connor/Gordon argued, could be accomplished as much by canoe tripping as by prayer. As he put it in his autobiography: "It was worth all the agony of knees, ankles and toes, all the hotbox of the shoulder blade, all the staggering backbreak of the portage, all the long weariness of the unending swing of the paddle, worth all just to be fit. Ready to meet with a spring everything and anything the hour may bring you. To wake and be willing to spring from your spruce bed ready for your morning dive, ready for sowbelly and blackstrap and flapjack with a fish, if you are lucky, ten minutes from the hook to the pan, ready for the swift smooth technique of camp-breaking and canoe-packing."

This tendency to connect religion and canoeing still exists—there are many Christian summer camps offering excellent tripping programs—but muscular Christianity long ago faded out of fashion except for isolated incidents. Perhaps the most infamous was involving St. John's Cathedral Boys' School in Selkirk, Manitoba, and Claremont, Ontario. The NFB's *The New Boys* captures the Selkirk group's initiation trip in 1973, when first-year students were sent off on a torturous, five-hundred-kilometre, two-week trip that sorely tested the boys—the schools claimed that "only by confronting the wilderness does a boy become a man"—and left them drained, cold and wet. Adult leaders pushed the youngsters to and beyond their limits to "test" them, the cruel trip bizarrely bracketed by chapel services before and after.

Five years later a similar expedition, this from the St. John's School of Ontario, met disaster on Lake Temiskaming when thirteen paddlers, a dozen of them young boys, perished while attempting what the coroner would call "an exaggerated and pointless challenge." With four leaders, the youths set out to paddle to James Bay on a three-week trek, beginning in good weather. By the end of the first day, however, all four of their war canoes had turned over in high waves and the twelve boys and one leader perished from hypothermia.

Unbelievably, the school had the more than a dozen survivors carry on "for the challenge." Apparently, the parents were fine with this, one telling journalist Robert Collins that "God can bring good out of it."

Even decades before, religion had gradually become less spoken of in wilderness conversations and "spiritualism" had taken over. In an article in *Outing* magazine published in 1901, Leslie Peabody wrote, "It is only a canoe that can give you these noiseless intimate hours when you listen to the breathing of the world and become part of the vibrating mystery." For many wilderness canoeists, those words are as meaningful today as they were more than a century ago.

There was actually a movement in various parts of the United States in the 1930s to ban canoes everywhere but calm artificial lakes in parks. As canoeists became more adventurous, accidents began taking a toll that alarmed people. The movement found little traction in Canada, fortunately, and over the years canoe trips organized by summer camps became regarded as both safe and beneficial for young people.

Queen's University School of Religion professor Bill James has written extensively on the canoe trip as religious quest. James had canoed at summer camps when he was growing up but had not paddled for several years while working on a doctoral thesis about the epic hero in English literature. When he purchased a canoe and took up the activity once again, he began to view canoeing differently, becoming increasingly convinced that there was a clear resemblance between a trip and the heroic quests he had studied.

During a 1975 trip into Algonquin Park, James and his canoeing companions became lost in a twisting, splitting creek that eventually ended in a dead end of swamp. The paddlers had seemed to know what they were doing and, coincidentally, a stranger who had been following them for an hour, convinced they knew the way, finally paddled close and asked if any of the party had read *The Lord of the Rings*.

"The sympathy was immediate," James later recalled in an essay. "Like Frodo and his questing companions we had lost our way, been deflected from our goal, expended much time and energy uselessly, and now had to go back and begin again.

"That episode was the beginning of my conscious reflection on the similarities between the quest, as I had become acquainted with that theme in literature, and my experience of the canoe trip. All of the ingredients were there: the departure from the known, the voyage into the unknown, and the return to civilization; the obstacles of high winds, rough waters, brutal portages, dissension, and long dreary rainy days; the unexpected pleasures of new vistas, of wildlife seen, of achievements and minor triumphs, and the joy of one's companions; the sense of participation in a primitive reality, or the re-enactment of an archetypal event, the sloughing off of the inessential and the experience of renewal."

He began asking others about their canoe trips and studying the journals of explorers and literature of the nineteenth and twentieth centuries that involved canoeing, as well as more recent magazine accounts of trips. Some of the archetypes are obvious: a journey; a test; choices to make; a beginning, middle and end, the destination. In religious terms, the journey is a pilgrimage.

The amount of material James covered is prodigious, from the explorers to historian W.L. Morton, from literary scholar Northrop Frye to magazine journalist Blair Fraser. In the work of popular outdoor writers like John and Janet Foster, he found the therapeutic benefits to canoeing, the healing effect of solitude, when they wrote, "Every year it is just as cold. But there is pure magic in that first moment as you push away from shore. The canoe seems to hang suspended above the dark water, momentarily floating in space, quietly separating from the land that has held you throughout the winter months. And now the noise and tumult and vibrations of the city 200 miles away begin to fade."

In the journals of Susanna Moodie, who despised the country she had come to with her soldier husband, James found the canoe was what calmed her rage and softened her attitude to the country she referred to as a "prison-house." Out on the water during evenings with her husband, she claimed to have felt "a magic spell upon our spirits."

After one calm day on the waters, Moodie wrote, "Every object was new to us. We felt as if we were the first discoverers of every beautiful flower and stately tree that attracted our attention, and we gave names to fantastic rocks and fairy isles."

To James, she could well have been describing the Garden of Eden.

Each, obviously, must find his or her own explanation for the delight they find in canoeing. All that is certain is there is more to it than paddling and portaging, making camp and striking camp, departure and arrival. Perhaps it takes a poet to say it most simply, so let us turn to the pages of Canada's Douglas LePan, Governor-General's Literary Award winner in both fiction and poetry. In a poem called "Canoe Trip," LePan required but a half dozen words to say it all:

. . . here are crooked nerves made straight.

Bill Mason never lived to hear the term "nature deficit disorder," but he would have embraced the concept if not the fancy phrasing. Becky Mason believes her father was "ahead of his time" in noting that, to an alarming degree, outdoor play was vanishing from modern society.

The "disorder" was coined by Richard Louv in *Last Child in the Woods*, the book he published in 2005. Louv argues that the outdoors experience has a health value far beyond anything previously claimed by the likes of Lord Baden-Powell and Ernest Thompson Seton. Being in the outdoors has obvious benefits, but *not* being there also has an effect—and not a pretty one. Louv connects a vast range of behavioural problems among the young to nature deprivation. He argues that there is a direct line connecting attention disorders, depression and, of course, child obesity to a lack of experience in the natural world. Better, he says, to have children in the sorts of "forest kindergartens" found in parts of Europe; better to have a hands-off approach rather than a hands-on; better to let children range free and discover for themselves. Much as Bill and Joyce raised Paul and Becky.

Bill Mason did not just pass on the art of paddling to his children; he gave them—more by example than by lecture—essential lessons for life in teaching them canoe expertise and love of the wilderness.

"The canoe is really important to me," Becky Mason says today, "and I am letting it be an aide to my life. I'm treating it like a cradle and it is taking me to places I would not otherwise be able to go. Sometimes with the current, sometimes very admirably against the current."

Pierre Trudeau would appreciate such an attitude, as he himself so often went against the current or, at the least, challenged the current. But he was also a good team player, which the Masons appreciated. He was not prime minister on their trips or any other of the trips he took. "Pierre took his turn like everyone else with the camp chores," fellow paddler Tim Kotcheff recalled after a northern trek with Trudeau. "He was by far the best dish-washer, fire-maker and camp organizer. He put some of us to shame. . . . Not only was he fit, he turned out to be one of the best canoeists and sternsmen in the group. If anyone succumbed to the elements, it wouldn't be Pierre."

Trudeau continued to paddle even after he had returned to office for a four-year run following the surprising fall of the Clark government within a year. He did not, however, undertake any of the more strenuous trips. In the fall of 1998 his and Margaret Trudeau's youngest son, Michel, was killed in an avalanche while skiing in British Columbia's Kokanee Glacier Provincial Park. He was only twenty-three; his body was never recovered.

"Pierre was never the same again," says Ted Johnson. Johnson was part of Trudeau's very last trip down the Petawawa River. "Within a couple of years," Johnson remembered, "we lost him."

Pierre Trudeau died when he was almost eighty-one. Bill Mason was not yet sixty when he passed away. Mason had played hockey and skied all through the winter of 1987–88, but when spring came and he began loading the red Prospector on top of the old Toyota to check out the spring runs, friends and family began to notice a change. He had difficulty paddling the length of Canoe Lake in Algonquin Park. He couldn't keep food down. He did not look good.

Bill was in hospital in Ottawa for tests when Paul's wedding date (to Judy Seaman) arrived in mid-June, and Bill signed himself out for the rehearsal and Saturday wedding. He did his amusing "canoe waltz" at the reception, grabbing a canoe from outside, hoisting it over his head portage-style and moving inside for a hilarious, and nearly dangerous, jig around the dance floor.

"He was so excited about my brother being married," remembers Becky. "He didn't do it for optics. He did it because he was so happy. People just ducked out of the way. That was my dad. Whenever he did things people thought it was great.

"He shouldn't have been able to pick it up. He was just so sick. It was unbelievable, but that's the way my dad was. It really was 'fire in the bones.' When he got a fire in his bones in any instance, he was just so happy—and it surpassed all physical limitations."

In the next short while doctors would discover a cancer had spread to a point where surgery was pointless. Bill asked if he could go canoeing. With the help of friend Wally Schaber, he put together one final great trip—the Nahanni—for a dozen family and friends.

There were rivers still to be run, films to be shot and paintings left undone when Bill Mason passed on. He had finished his sixth, and final, canoeing film, *Waterwalker*, but it had been a difficult creative birth, complete with fallings-out with fellow filmmakers at the NFB and complaints about its structure. "*Waterwalker* was a mess," James Raffan wrote in his biography of Mason. The filmmaker "had never been challenged in this way in his life." The film was completed in 1984 and was nominated for a Genie Award for best documentary feature, but it was not Bill Mason's best.

Mason went off on a short solo canoe trip on the White River, many believed to lick his wounds over the falling out at the NFB and criticisms of what would be his final film. Becky Mason says they were wrong, that her father was "happy as a clam and just wanted to go canoeing. In my opinion, he was such a happy fellow all the time. There were no regrets."

Nor should there have been. His earlier films had been great successes, including an Oscar nomination for *Paddle to the Sea*. His *Path of the Paddle: An Illustrated Guide to the Art of Canoeing* was considered the bible by most trippers. He left behind a great body of work. "As such," Raffan wrote, "Bill Mason, perhaps even more in death than when he was alive, and more than any other person affiliated with the canoe, was and is synonymous with the canoe in Canadian culture."

His films and books brought fame, and with fame came change. "My dad loved to canoe," says Becky Mason. "And he loved to share his love of this perfect craft that allowed him to access places he couldn't otherwise get to. But he wanted to share that with everybody. What happened is he started sharing it and as he became more and more well known in later years, people would be coming up to us when we were canoeing in our special places. Lots of people. They wanted a piece of him. They wanted to touch him. They wanted to hear a story. It was a bit hard to handle."

A quarter century after the death of her father, however, Becky has learned to appreciate the recognition that came to Bill Mason. In 2010 and again in 2011 she and her husband, Reid, did two six-week tours of Europe, doing talks on canoeing and giving demonstrations and lessons. Worried about a possible lack of interest in this North American passion, Becky sent off letters to various canoe clubs, asking if they thought she would be able to fill her paddling lessons. The response was overwhelming.

"It was because they'd grown up watching his films," she says. "We went to Milano, Italy, to a rented beach house on a lake and eighty people showed up for lessons. The only English word they knew was *Prospector*. When we went down to the water there were thirty or so Prospector canoes on the beach. I said, 'There are other canoes, you know,' and they said, 'No. Prospectors . . . Bill Mason . . . Prospectors.'

"People ask me, 'Is it hard to be Bill Mason's daughter?' Well, no—it's a continuation."

Bill Mason's words will live on so long as there is a canoe, a paddle and a body of water to be found. Some of his sayings and thoughts are as timeless as the vehicle itself:

> When you look at the face of Canada and study the geography carefully, you come away with the feeling that God could have designed the canoe first and then set about to conceive a land in which it could flourish.
>
> The first thing you must learn about canoeing is that the canoe is not a lifeless, inanimate object; it feels very much alive, alive with the life of the river. Life is transmitted to the canoe by currents of air and the water upon which it rides. The behaviour and temperament of the canoe is dependent upon the elements: from the slightest breeze to a raging storm, from the smallest ripple to a towering wave, or from a meandering stream to a thundering rapid.

Mason had been working on a book that would be about his paintings and canoeing but had never got past the mock-up stage. The family was able to take the text he had completed, his paintings and the design he had wished and, seven years after his death, *Canoescapes* was published.

In a 1999 article, Becky talked about the project and quoted him from the book that he'd been unable to complete: "I have always believed that the Canadian canoe is one of the greatest achievements of mankind. There is nothing so aesthetically pleasing and yet so functional and versatile. It is as much a part of our land as the rocks, trees, lakes and rivers. Most of my enjoyment and creative endeavours in the Canadian wilderness have been from a canoe."

Becky wrote of her father's deep love of portaging, a necessity that many canoeists deplore. He saw it differently: a change of pace, different scenery from both directions, a chance to get deeper into the wild. Again, she quoted from the text he left behind:

> The price you must pay for a spectacular waterfall is a long and arduous portage but I wouldn't want it any other way. . . . The part I like best about portaging is the walk back for the second load. You see things you would never see while staggering under a ninety-pound pack or eighty-pound canoe. . . . On a river journey by canoe, doing a portage properly and enjoying the scenery along the way is just as important as paddling the canoe. Not that you would catch me portaging a rapid that was runnable, unless it was to carry the canoe back up to run it again. If it weren't for rapids, falls and their accompanying portages, there would be no wilderness, no place to hear the cry of the loon. Let's keep our portages wild, the wilder the better.

The last book Bill Mason held in his hands was *Song of the Paddle*, his study of canoeing and camping. It was launched eleven days before his passing at Meech Lake on October 29, 1988. Among the various speakers at the launch was a friend who—perhaps apocryphally—claimed to have been watching a hockey match on CBC one Saturday night when, during a break in the action, the camera settled on Pierre Trudeau sitting in the stands with a white-bearded man.

The friend's young son, a lover of hockey and canoe tripping—but obviously not of politics—had a question.

"Who's that guy sitting beside Bill Mason?"

The author gets away for a little weekend research.

The icon: Tom Thomson's painting "The Canoe."

Sisters Helen and Mary McCormick, paddling happily on Brule Lake.

My mother,
Helen McCormick.

The ranger Tom McCormick and his Chestnut.

My grandparents Tom and Bea McCormick.

The cottage on Lake of Two Rivers.

Phil Chester, philosopher, poet, singer, paddler.

The Riverhawk is up! Lorne Chester considers the coming rapids.

Filmmaker and canoeing legend Bill Mason and family.

Mason's friend Pierre Trudeau keeps the tradition alive, with his son Justin.

The Mahdi,
besieger of Khartoum.

"General Gordon's Last Stand"
depicted with liberties by George
William Joy.

The Nile Expedition
gathers in Ottawa.

4

THE NILE EXPEDITION

FOR A SENSE OF WHAT THIS COUNTRY was like for the original voyageurs, paddle the Mattawa River. Not much more than forty kilometres
downstream from Trout Lake, on the edge of the Northern Ontario
city of North Bay, you'll find the small town of Mattawa—Ojibwa for
"meeting of the waters"—at the confluence of the Mattawa and Upper
Ottawa rivers. It's not a difficult paddle. There are but a dozen portage
decisions, only four of which are must-takes, and eight rapids that can
be run or skipped, depending on water levels and whitewater compe-
tence. It can be a very relaxing three or four days, though manic
paddlers do it in less than a day during the annual North Bay to
Mattawa canoe race.

But none of that is the point.

The point is that here you can get a small sense of what life on a
Canadian river was once like. Forget the odd cottage and the outboard
motors on certain stretches, ignore the ultralight camping equipment
and vacuum-packed dried foods we carry and let your imagination drift
back centuries to a time before . . . Deep Woods Off.

Étienne Brûlé, possible namesake of the lake where my mother was
born, is considered the first white man to paddle these tea-coloured
waters. Brûlé paddled up the Mattawa, portaging from Trout Lake to

Lake Nipissing and down the French River in 1610 with a group of Algonquins. The second is believed to have been a Recollet missionary called Joseph Le Caron, who had been brought over to New France by Champlain to turn the Huron "heathens," with whom the French were trading, into good Christians. He came in late spring, foolish man, and recorded the experience in his diary.

"If I had not kept my face wrapped in cloth," the good brother wrote, "I am almost sure they would have blinded me, so pestiferous and poisonous are the bites of these little demons. They make one look like a leper, hideous to behold. I confess this is the worst martyrdom I suffered in this country: hunger, thirst, weariness and fever are nothing to it. These little beasts not only persecute you all day but at night they get into your eyes and mouth, crawl under your clothes . . . "

There is a portage along this route that the voyageurs called Mauvais de Musique—bad music—but there are far worse to be encountered along the Mattawa. Alexander Mackenzie, the Scottish explorer who beat Lewis and Clark across the North American continent by a full decade, believed the Talon Portage was the "worst" he had encountered in all his years of exploration. Bad, yes—dangerously slippery when wet, difficult climbs up craggy granite bluffs, awkward descents through twisting, rock-strewn paths—but at its comparatively short length of 275 paces, mercifully short. There is even a bronze plaque at the start of this portage to commemorate the honour of being the "worst" of what must have been thousands of such whitewater bypasses. "Many men," Mackenzie wrote in his 1794 journal of the whitewater the portage skirted, "have been crushed to death by canoes."

Some 215 years after Mackenzie grumbled about the impossible whitewater, we had come to paddle this little-changed river highway that had taken the first Europeans into the gut of Canada. Mackenzie had taken the Talon Portage, as did Pierre-Esprit Radisson, Médard Chouart Des Groseilliers, Peter Pond, Sieur de La Salle, Sieur de La Vérendrye, Martin Frobisher, Father Jean de Brébeuf and dozens of other names from the storied list of explorers, traders, missionaries and adventurers—all of whom surely complained about it.

It was the Talon Portage where I witnessed, first-hand, what difficult terrain and overexertion can do to someone on an ostensibly relaxing canoe trip. We had our minds set on a campsite a few hours downstream—a lovely spot with a small waterfall chuckling behind a flat sand beach perfect for pitching tents.

It appeared that the party behind us on the portage—the only other paddlers we had seen since setting out—must have been hoping for this same charming campsite, for they seemed determined somehow to pass us. I was slowly making my way up the rocky, craggy, difficult trail—think of the Rocky Mountains as a playground structure—when from behind came a heavy-breathing, sweating man with a rented canoe on his shoulders and a large pack worn in reverse the way you might carry a baby, so that its weight would be balanced forward off his stomach. He seemed desperate to pass and I was happy to oblige, having stepped to the side in order to rest our canoe on a rock while I caught my own breath. His was uncatchable.

He said not a word as he grunted past. He climbed, rocks breaking loose and scattering, and tried to mount the steep hill as if it were steps of a ladder. I stood, watching, as he raised his back straight to see where the next rise was, and was still watching as, in super slow motion, the canoe tipped up, up, up and over, falling straight back over his head and crashing down the rocks to below, where it came to rest in a hawthorn bush.

Had he not let go, he, too, might have been "crushed to death by canoes"—with the rapids not even within sight.

I helped him retrieve his scratched-but-not-bashed vessel and even helped him a bit to get it up the hill to the crest, from which he took off with barely a grunt of gratitude. Happily, we never again saw him or the unhappy young family that scurried after him. Even more delightfully, the campsite we wrongly thought he was racing us for turned out to be empty when we got to it, and we passed a lovely night sleeping to the lullaby of gently falling water.

Seeing that man struggle so foolishly up the high rocks at Talon Portage made me think of all those voyageurs who would have passed through exactly the same path, carrying in both directions. In heading out, their main weight was supplies; in returning, it would have been furs. While this large, strong man required two trips to make the portage, these much smaller, slimmer voyageurs would have scoffed at his efforts and, surely, would have howled at his fall.

The true voyageurs were rarely taller than five foot six. Their endurance was legendary: they paddled at a rate of forty to sixty strokes per minute, thirty thousand strokes a day. On land, they covered 150 portages between Montreal and distant Fort Chipewyan in the northeast of what is now Alberta. Every hour, they stopped briefly for a pipe break and stopped, as well, for breakfast and lunch. The average voyageur, it is believed, needed five thousand calories a day and, with no time to fish or hunt, much of what they carried in both directions would have been their own kitchen supplies. In good conditions, they might cover 130 kilometres a day, four or five times what good paddlers consider a fair workout on a summer trek.

And as legend goes they loved it. American Indian agent Thomas L. McKenney noted in 1826 that "a Canadian, if born to be a labourer, deems himself very unfortunate if he should chance to grow over five feet five, or six inches—and if he shall reach five feet ten or eleven, it forever excludes him from the privilege of becoming a voyageur. There is no room for the legs of such people, in these canoes. But if he shall stop growing at about five feet four inches, and be gifted with a good voice, and lungs that never tire, he is considered as having been born under a most favourable star."

There are several versions of a quote attributed to a voyageur on Lake Winnipeg in 1825. "I could carry, paddle, walk and sing with any man I ever saw," the old voyageur apparently claimed. "I have been twenty-four years a canoe man, and forty-one years in service; no portage was ever too long for me, fifty songs could I sing. I have saved the lives of ten voyageurs, have had twelve wives and six running dogs. I spent all of my money in pleasure. Were I young again, I would spend my life the same way over. There is no life so happy as a voyageur's life!"

They were not, of course, all the same or paid the same. The most senior of the men would usually serve as the guide, choosing the routes, deciding the rapids and acting as a sort of "foreman" when it came to controlling and paying the others. Three paddlers were considered special, the *avant* in the bow, the *gouvernail* steering from the stern and a man in the middle who set the pace and was usually the strongest paddler and best in the rapids. Their greater roles naturally worked out to higher wages, often double what the others were making.

The voyageur needed muscular legs as well as the strong shoulders and arms required for hard paddling and carrying. A "piece" was considered a ninety-pound pack of fur, merchandise or supplies. Men were expected to carry two pieces, one on his back with a tumpline across the forehead for support, one on his chest. Some carried more, though it strains credulity to swallow Alexander Mackenzie's claim that he had seen men carry seven pieces—630 pounds—at one time over long portages without so much as a stop for breath.

The men also had to carry the canoes. The *canot de maître*, at thirty-six feet long and weighing upwards of six hundred pounds, was usually carried upside down by four men, two at the bow and two at the stern. The smaller *canot du nord*, twenty-five feet long and three hundred pounds or more, could be carried right side up by two men, one at each end.

On portages, each paddler was responsible for six pieces, whether equipment, supplies or furs, as well as his personal gear. Walking bent to support and balance the load, they would set off in a shuffle down the trails. Usually it would require three loads over and two trips back, meaning that for every kilometre of portage they actually travelled five kilometres of trail, three of those trips requiring them to carry heavy loads on their backs.

Two academics at Lakehead University in Thunder Bay set out to examine such amazing claims. Dr. Norm LaVoie, a professor in the School of Kinesiology, and Dr. Ron Lappage, an expert in sports history, selected two wrestlers and two taller and larger hockey players—all four, incredibly fit athletes—and had them carry similar loads on treadmills to test their oxygen capabilities. The MaxVO$_2$ measures the rate of oxygen consumption during incremental exercise and is considered an excellent indication of the individual's aerobic fitness. An extremely fit individual might work at 70 per cent MaxVO$_2$, while only elite modern athletes would be able to perform as high as 85 per cent MaxVO$_2$.

After completing their experiments, the two researchers concluded, "It would appear that the voyageurs would require the ability to work at greater than 85 per cent of their MaxVO$_2$ to complete some sections of a portage without undue fatigue."

So here you have these squat, short, elite athletes scurrying along portages with their heads tilted toward the ground by dint of the weights on their backs and the requirement to keep that tumpline tight. They were French and Scots and Metis, largely uneducated and mostly illiterate. What did they think about as they sweated their way in one direction? What did they see as they ambled back, their spines now allowed to straighten, their necks free to turn from side to side and take in such beauties and wonders as are still found along a river like the snaking, sometimes tumbling Mattawa?

There were certainly things to see while they were paddling. At the north end of Trout Lake, where many begin the run, archaeologists have found remnants of ancient worshipping ruins—stone platforms and stairways, serpent mounds and petroglyphs—that predate Stonehenge by two millennia.

Not far from Lake Talon—so named after the first *Intendant* of New France, Jean Talon, 1626-1694, an early "social engineer" who once brought a thousand orphan girls across the ocean to marry his wife-less settlers—there is a rock formation known as "Dog Face" that is convincing enough to have been featured in *Ripley's Believe It or Not* back in the 1950s. At Pimisi Bay there is another rock—mammoth, with a high flat back—where native people would leave offerings in order to give them safe passage over the rapids to come.

And farther downstream, near breathtaking Paresseux Falls, is the mysterious Porte de L'Enfer—Gate of Hell.

It is a deep hole carved out of the embankment, the hole surrounded by dark red and crumbling rock—hematite, an iron oxide that area natives once used for rock paintings—and, when we passed a few summers back, there was a thick, torn rope that looked as if it had once been used to hang someone but had snapped from the weight.

"In the side of a hill on the north side of the river," recorded Alexander Henry, who passed by in the summer of 1861, "there is a curious cave, concerning which marvelous tales are related by the voyageurs."

Some of the fur trade paddlers believed that the red earth surrounding the dark cave was, in fact, dried blood. And some of the more imaginative of them further thought that deep in the darkness of the Gate of Hell lived a monster who ate the bodies of voyageurs who were lost in the rapids or snatched those who failed to pay attention as they scurried along the portages with their heads down.

The original voyageurs may not have been able to read or write, but they were certainly not without their stories.

And no story could possibly be more remarkable—even unbelievable— than the Canadian voyageurs' Nile Expedition of 1884–85.

Our family does not know who he was, though he is said to have been a part of us all. It's a bit embarrassing, really, but Canada is filled with people who did not come over with the Pilgrims, very ordinary people who did not lead expeditions, hold high office or even have accommodations above steerage on the voyage across the Atlantic. Their departures may have been noted by whatever relatives remained to see them off, but their arrivals were, sadly, more noticed if they landed dead than alive. Their family trees have broken and missing branches, unexpected thorns, hidden roots and, frankly, no record at all of when many of the family leaves bloomed and eventually fell.

Duncan MacGregor, Helen's husband and father of four, of whom I am the third born, was a logger all his life. He walked to the winter camboose camps, cut and drew timber that was then floated down the tributary rivers to the mills along the Ottawa River. Duncan eventually rose to be the head lumber scaler for McRae Lumber Company in the small Ontario village of Whitney. He worked in camps all through Algonquin Park and the Madawaska Valley, which runs west off the larger Ottawa Valley. He was still working at seventy-three when a logging truck skidded on the ice, caught him in its locked wheels and crashed him into a snowbank at the bottom of a long decline. It broke his pelvis, and the men at the mill, not sure what to do, put him in the back of a pickup and bounced him, in sub-zero weather, forty kilometres up the road to the Barry's Bay hospital, from which they transferred him to hospital in Peterborough and then on to St. Michael's Hospital in Toronto. The doctors operated on his pelvis but said he likely wouldn't walk again.

However, the doctors seriously underestimated the draw of the Empire Hotel beverage room, three blocks from where Duncan took up forced retirement with our mother in the small north Muskoka town of Huntsville. He spent the next fifteen years conducting his own physiotherapy, taking his daily stroll down to the beverage room for beer and the corner store for tobacco, papers—both the ones you read and the ones you roll—and his weekly lottery ticket. He was nearly eighty-eight when he died in the late spring of 1995.

Duncan loved to read history. He had an enormous grasp of world history from the Middle Ages on, knew all about the British Empire, could recite Tennyson's "The Charge of the Light Brigade" ("Into the valley of Death / Rode the six hundred . . . ") and was particularly taken with the tragic tale of "Chinese Gordon" and the Siege of Khartoum.

He had good reason for liking that famous story. A relative of ours, he often said, had been one of the Canadian "voyageurs" who, in 1884, left their logging jobs in the Ottawa Valley and went off to rescue General Charles Gordon by, strange as it may seem, paddling canoes up the difficult and often treacherous Nile River.

We all should have listened more closely, or at least written down whatever details were given. Dunc's family were the McGregors (later spelled "MacGregor") on his father's side, Keenans on his mother's. The Keenans—Scots by way of County Antrim in Ireland—settled in the Ottawa Valley in the late 1820s. John Keenan, born in 1831, was a licensed square timber raft pilot who would "drive" the timber from the Bonnechere River to Quebec City.

But nowhere can we find any reference to a Keenan heading for the Sudan to rescue Gordon. And no McGregor or MacGregor. My younger brother, Tom, believes the relative our father had in mind was named Jack Carson and came from Round Lake Centre, just south of Algonquin Park's eastern boundary. (Clearly, Tom listened more carefully than I did.) While I could never establish the branch that might have linked the Carsons to either of our two families, I did find Carsons listed in the 1851 Canada East census. They were living in McNab Township of Renfrew County, as Ottawa Valley as it is possible to be. James Carson, listed as a labourer (likely farm work), was head of the family of ten, including a son named John.

John—known as "Jack"—Carson was recorded as ten years old in 1851, which would make him approximately forty-three years old when the Canadian Expeditionary Force left Ottawa for the Nile River in the summer of 1884.

Is this the "Jack Carson" our father talked about with such pride? The task of finding a definitive list of those who signed up proved immediately difficult. Many of the men who went to save Gordon could not even spell their names when they agreed to the terms of their engagement.

Back in the 1970s, when former diplomat and former federal cabinet minister Roy MacLaren was researching *Canadians on the Nile, 1882–1898*, his fascinating book on Canada's most unusual military adventure, he found the closest he would come to a complete list in the appendix of historian C.P. Stacey's *Records of the Nile Voyageurs, 1884–85*, published by the Champlain Society in the late 1950s. But that list held no Carson.

Could Jack Carson of Round Lake Centre still have been among the nearly four hundred French, English and Metis loggers, raftsmen and canoeists who set out to save Gordon—and not be listed as a participant?

"If Stacey's is not a definitive list," MacLaren told me in 2014, "then the answer is yes."

According to Anthony P. Michel, an Ottawa historian who works for the Department of Canadian Heritage and has spent years researching a book on the Nile voyageurs, it is pretty much impossible to say precisely who left Canada for the mission. "There was an official 'nominal roll,'" Michel found, "but it should be understood to be approximate at best. The men signed up in rushed circumstances, some jumped on board and some left before the boat left Canada. When they did the first roll call after leaving Canada, they found out that the list was not at all accurate. There are subsequent lists in newspapers of returning contingents. There are revised pay books. There is also a medal roll. They don't all line up. The paperwork for the entire episode was a mess, and part of this was due to the complete novelty of the thing, both for the officers in charge of the contingent and the officials in Ottawa reporting on it."

The answer, then, on Jack Carson is neither yes nor no—but possibly.

The year 1884 seems no more remarkable than the average relatively quiet, low-conflict year when you stare at a long list of historical world events. France gave the Statue of Liberty to America. Mark Twain published Adventures of Huckleberry Finn. Gold was discovered in Transvaal. Brahms completed his Symphony no. 3 in F Major. Grover Cleveland was elected president of the United States of America. Canada is not even mentioned.

But there, in a small note for January 18, 1884: "General Charles Gordon departs London for Khartoum." Again on February 18: "General Charles Gordon arrives in Khartoum." And then, on March 13: "The Siege of Khartoum begins."

Khartoum today is the capital of the Republic of Sudan and a metropolis of some five million, but in the nineteenth century it was an outpost for the Egyptian army. Its strategic location—the White Nile River flowing north from Lake Victoria, the Blue Nile coming west from Ethiopia and the confluence of the two flowing north toward Egypt and the Mediterranean Sea—soon made the settlement a key trading centre for both goods and slaves. Egypt and its key ally, Great Britain, considered control of Khartoum critical; other forces unfriendly to the British Empire wanted to take that control away. A clash was inevitable.

By mid-March of 1884 the Siege of Khartoum was under way—troops loyal to the revolutionary Mahdi attacking, soldiers in the Anglo-Egyptian garrison defending. The new Dominion of Canada, just sixteen years old, was about to find itself directly involved in world affairs for the very first time.

The story of the Nile Expedition is complicated, confusing and, ultimately, catastrophic. It came at the end of the great British Empire—many historians, in fact, date this disastrous military excursion as the end of British Imperialism—and involved high adventure, genocide, murder, racism, extremism on both sides and no end of military bumbling.

And canoes.

Sometime between 1840 and 1844—different books give different dates—a Sudanese boat-builder named Ahmed had a child he and his unnamed wife called Mohammed. The child was born with a mole on his cheek and, when his adult teeth came in, there was a significant V-shaped gap between his upper incisors. Islamic teaching had always maintained that these mildly unusual physical attributes would be a sign of the long-anticipated appearance of the Muslim "Mahdi," or messiah, and that he would make his full presence known in year 1300 of the Muslim calendar—which is roughly year 1883 Anno Domini of the Christian calendar.

Eventually, the young Mahdi-in-waiting went off into the desert on retreat and emerged announcing that he was indeed the chosen one. God had spoken directly to him, telling him that anyone who "doubts my mission does not believe in God or his prophets."

That no one challenged young Mohammed on the trick construction of this statement—*what of those who believed in God and believed Mohammed was suffering from sunstroke?*—may have had to do with promises the Mahdi was making. Die for the jihad he was pledging against all who suppressed the Sudanese, he told them, and they'd be joined by forty thousand angels.

It was only a matter of time before his many followers began claiming they had actually seen the Mahdi's angels hovering overhead in case one of the faithful should perish. When some ten thousand of his men were killed or wounded in a botched early bid to capture a provincial capital, he told them that the loss had been sent by God to test their commitment and zeal—and they bought it.

The Mahdi was as strident in his day as any Taliban leader might be today. He forbade his followers to drink or smoke or conduct any degrading sins of the flesh. He outlawed hand-clapping and crying at funerals. "Clothe your women in a decent way," he ordered, "and let them be careful not to speak to unknown persons." At the same time, he made sure that the most beautiful girl slaves be sent to his personal harem.

No one protested. In fact, so convinced were his followers that he was channeling the thoughts and wishes of God that they would drink his bathwater in the hopes of curing whatever sickness might be ailing them.

The Suez Canal had opened in 1869 after a decade of continuous and difficult construction. The canal was, for its time, the greatest engineering feat ever undertaken: more than 160 kilometres of deepwater passage through Egypt, connecting the Red Sea to the Mediterranean Sea without a single lock. It cut the journey from England to India in half and instantly became a key trade route. Great Britain had never supported the construction and its use of slave labour, but well understood the advantages of such a shortcut. Despite these misgivings, London was not concerned about its access to the canal, given Britain's strong and lengthy links with Egypt.

The Brits, however, failed to take into consideration the increasingly troublesome Sudanese, controlled at the time by their British-backed Eyptian neighbours to the immediate north. Now marshalling under their charismatic new leader, the insurgents were winning battles against Egyptian forces and turning from spear to artillery with weapons taken from poorly commanded and trained Egyptian troops composed mostly of conscripts.

After numerous Egyptian failures to calm the area, British prime minister William Gladstone, now serving his second go-round as PM, grew increasingly annoyed with the situation. With mounting problems at home—the growing unrest in Ireland just one of many—Gladstone had come to the conclusion that bolstering Egypt's control of the Sudan was not worth the effort, so inept had Egyptian efforts proved at putting down the rebels. Because of the importance the canal now brought to the region, he couldn't just turn his back on the mounting conflict (as he surely preferred) but had to ensure, somehow, that safe passage would continue for British trade.

"The insecurity of the Canal is a symptom only," Gladstone told the House of Commons, "and the seat of the disease is the interior of Egypt, in its disturbed and anarchical condition."

The Sudanese were giving the British headaches and the Egyptians themselves were increasingly a concern. "Egypt for the Egyptians" had become a popular cry and, in a June 11, 1882, riot in Alexandria, an enraged mob had bludgeoned fifty Europeans to death. The British, Gladstone declared, would restore authority in Egypt and, in turn, keep the Sudanese at bay.

The Mahdi was gaining power and influence steadily. He was readying an attack on Khartoum, now grown to become the most important centre in the region, and once Khartoum fell he believed he would control all the Sudan. It seemed only a matter of time. He bragged he would soon take Egypt and from there would move on to take Turkey and then cross the isthmus to attack and ultimately rule all of Europe. Not since the Crusades had Brits become so nervous about the Middle East. They wanted Gladstone to find a solution, and the obvious solution, the people and the press argued, was to send the one man they all believed could save the Empire. "Chinese Gordon for the Sudan!" became the cry.

Charles George Gordon, born to a military family in 1833, was considered the essence of the heroic defender of the Empire. He had served with distinction in the religiously fuelled Crimean War against Russia and performed well when sent to China during the bloody Taiping Rebellion. But he was also a loose cannon. His own father called him a "powder keg" and he was renowned for temper tantrums. He slapped servants, once stabbed his fork into a waiter's hand and grew so frustrated with a young cadet's performance that he beat him soundly before throwing him through a window. A heavy-drinking chain smoker, Gordon was short at five feet five, with hypnotic blue eyes and a great love of the Bible (he once spent a whole year searching for Christ's grave). He was visibly uncomfortable in the presence of women and kept the company of several young boys he referred to as his "kings."

But the people loved him. As he had previously served in the Sudan without any problems, Gordon seemed the perfect answer to this troublesome Mahdi and his followers, who were derisively referred to by the

Brits as "dervishes" and "fuzzy wuzzies." The people wanted Gordon; Gladstone wanted quiet, even if retreat were required; but Gordon himself wasn't sure that he was the right man for the job.

"I own to having been very insubordinate to Her Majesty's Government and its officials, but it is in my nature and I cannot help it," he wrote in his journal. "I know that if *I* was chief, I would never employ *myself*, for I am incorrigible."

Gladstone eventually caved to the pressure and sent Gordon off to take over the defence of Khartoum. There, he found fifty thousand civilians poorly protected by seven thousand soldiers, almost all of them Egyptian or Sudanese. He was so warmly welcomed that women lined up just so he could touch their sick children. They called him "Saviour"—rather ironically, given that the Mahdi was also claiming to be one—and a confident, cocky Gordon quickly reported back that Khartoum, despite the obvious threat outside its gates, was "as safe as Kensington Park."

The British press of the day had sent him off as a hero, claiming that he would defy the Muslim fanatic, but it quickly became clear that the Mahdi's forces were rising to a size and strength at which they would eventually overwhelm the barricades and Khartoum would be lost. The Queen herself expressed concern for Gordon's safety. The media shifted from declaring certain victory to demanding that the Gladstone government intervene to rescue their hero. "We absolutely refuse to believe that the Government means to abandon Gordon," editorialized *The Times*.

It is important to understand the climate of the day. This, remember, was the era of "muscular Christianity" in the English-speaking world. The white man's "burden" was to rule and civilize (and Christianize) the rest of humanity. *Tom Brown's School Days* was studied in schools, the story of a great and lasting friendship between two healthy young men who exercise and pray regularly, who play sports with determination and gentlemanly conduct, who learn such values that they can then carry on into civic and military duty. The Crimean War had been as much about poetry and sacrifice (Florence Nightingale, "The Charge of the

Light Brigade," etc.) as it had been new warfare and stunning loss of life. War correspondents were the Indiana Joneses of the day. Adventure and romance were central ingredients to all H. Rider Haggard and Rudyard Kipling wrote. And Chinese Gordon held all these values in one stout British heart.

Nothing would do but to rescue Gordon. *But how?*

And this is where the Canadians and the canoe came in.

The Brits turned to the "very model of a modern Major-General," as Gilbert and Sullivan had put it in *The Pirates of Penzance*, their musical that had recently run for more than three hundred successful performances at London's Opera Comique. The "very model" was in this case Garnet Joseph Wolseley, 1st Viscount Wolseley and later field marshal. He and Gordon had become friends during the Crimean campaign and Wolseley considered Gordon the epitome of the "Christian hero."

The Irish-born Wolseley had survived a hellish Burma campaign and had lost an eye in the Crimea. His courage was brazen and unchallenged. One oft-repeated account had him standing beside other soldiers when a sapper had his head blown off with such force that the dead man's jawbone became imbedded in another soldier's face. Splattered with blood, Wolseley had stared at the carnage as impassively as if it were merely a curiosity.

Wolseley's main man—a cornerstone of his "ring"—was Brigadier General Redvers Buller, a member of the King's Royal Rifle Corps. Buller had won the Victoria Cross for his actions in South Africa a few years earlier and was a beefy man with little neck and far too much temper, known for what was called his "berserk appetite for killing savages." Taking on the dervishes in the Sudan held great appeal to him.

Wolseley had earlier been sent to the British colony in North America. He arrived in the Canadas, Lower and Upper, in late 1861 and was still there in the summer of 1870 when the Red River Rebellion had taken place. It was only three years after Confederation and would be the first true test of the new Dominion of Canada.

To put down the uprising, and to give chase to the troublemaking Metis leader, Louis Riel, Wolseley had led an expedition, with Buller a key part of it, to assert colonial authority at Fort Garry, Manitoba. Faced with the difficult problem of how to get soldiers who were used to marching over open fields through some eight hundred kilometres of wilderness, swamp and fast-flowing rivers, it had been Wolseley's ingenious suggestion that they use voyageurs to take the soldiers in by canoe.

Led by some four hundred expert canoeists, many from the Iroquois village of Caughnawaga near Montreal, Wolseley and his men completed the difficult trip and routed the troublemakers. (Riel fled to the United States but would make a dramatic return fifteen years later, be captured and later be hanged as a traitor.) Wolseley returned to a hero's welcome in Montreal. He would never forget the thrill of racing to Fort Garry over treacherous rapids and difficult portages. "The falls, the rapids, the whirlpools, the great rushing angry waters, and the many hair-breadth escapes its navigation involved, are indelibly stamped upon my memory," he wrote of his time on the Winnipeg River. "We had one or two boats wrecked, but no life was lost. The pleasurable excitement of danger is always a pleasant experience, but the enthralling delight of feeling your frail canoe or boat bound under you, as it were down a steep incline of wilding rushing waters into what looks like a boiling, steaming cauldron of bubbling and confused waters, exceeds most of the other maddening delights that man can dream of."

The urgency of getting to Khartoum was pressing. Gordon had sent his aide, a Colonel J.D.H. Stewart, off with messages about help, but the colonel's steamer had grounded on a rock in the Nile waters and all aboard, including Stewart, were murdered by supporters of the Mahdi. Gordon was now alone in Khartoum, his fate almost certainly doomed.

Wolseley was floating his scheme—mad or inspired—to reach Khartoum the same way he had reached and, all believed, had saved Fort Garry: by canoe. He felt he could get soldiers from Cairo to Khartoum faster by water than by land, even if so much of it would

involve the soldiers fighting their way upstream. The overland journey, by camel, would be extremely difficult, for the rescue mission
would be under almost constant threat from tribesmen and the
Mahdi's followers. It was also deemed to take longer than travelling
by water and, significantly, British soldiers had historically had little
to no luck mastering the art of long-distance riding on the cantanker-
ous desert animals.

"I would propose," Wolseley told his superiors in London, "to send all
the dismounted portion of the force up the Nile to Khartoum in boats,
as we sent the little expeditionary force from Lake Superior to Fort Garry
on the Red River in 1870."

New vessels—large enough to hold troops and with sailing capabilities
as well as able to be guided through the Nile's treacherous whitewater—
would have to be built in a hurry. "A more wicked waste of money was
never perpetrated," railed the *Army and Navy Gazette* of September 13,
1884. The publication attacked the War Office for allowing Wolseley to
proceed with his mad idea to build "that unfloatable flotilla for the Nile.
Burn them for firewood! . . . Make matches of them—do anything with
them! Put men in them, and try and send them up the Nile cataracts—
never, we beg of you!"

Wolseley was not to be dissuaded. The key, he believed, was in having
men with river expertise to get the vessels and soldiers past the difficult
cataracts and to Khartoum in time. And he knew where to find such
men. Wolseley fired off a formal request to Lord Lansdowne, the
Governor General of Canada, asking for three hundred voyageurs that
he could take to Egypt. Wolseley was hoping that they could be found in
the same places—the Caughnawaga and St. Regis reserves, the Manitoba
rivermen—that had supplied such able canoeists for the Red River mission. He said they would be away for half a year, would be paid forty
dollars a month (foremen would get seventy-five dollars) and would be
clothed and fed at the British government's expense. He wanted them to
set sail for England by early fall.

Prime Minister John A. Macdonald, sensitive to growing criticism of British imperialism, okayed the mission so long as it was made clear to the men and public that they were signing on with the British government, would be paid by the British government, and that the expedition had nothing official to do with Canada.

Much, however, had changed since Wolseley had led his men to Fort Garry fourteen years earlier. Voyageurs were rare enough in 1870 but virtually unknown in 1884. People and trade now crossed the Dominion by rail, not canoe. Yet the pay was so good that the call for volunteers was quickly answered by woodsmen from the Ottawa Valley, most of whom were idle, or doing farm work, in the summer months. These men had experience on the spring log runs down the various tributaries of the Ottawa River and understood the precarious nature of rapids. Many were experienced in canoe travel. The men who now possessed the great river skills of yesterday's voyageurs tended to be raftsmen who worked the annual log drives along larger rivers like the Ottawa and the St. Lawrence. Lord Lansdowne described these unique men of the lumber trade as "excessively hardy and unequalled in their knowledge of river navigation."

Such men—loggers, river runners, raftsmen, some farmers—were recruited by brokers in Ottawa, where 171 men signed up. Caughnawaga sent fifty-six, and others came from such places as Peterborough, Trois-Rivières and Sherbrooke. Wolseley had recalled the good Manitoba Metis who had served him so well and ninety-one were recruited in Winnipeg, though many turned out to be bored bank tellers and office clerks anxious for a little adventure but with no experience whatsoever in either river travel or battle.

Wolseley had dearly hoped for more natives, whom he hugely admired for their river skills. Lansdowne, however, was advised at one point that "the white man would be more desirable for the task in question than the red man." Lansdowne appeared convinced, as he then wrote to Lord Derby at the Colonial Office in London, saying, "The freighting business formerly carried on by these [native] people has greatly declined of late."

Wolseley's best bet, Lansdowne felt, lay not in the few dozen natives who signed on, but in the Ottawa Valley and Montreal area raftsmen. "I am assured," he wrote, "by the most competent authorities that there is every reason for preferring a force composed of white men or partly of white men and partly of Indians to one composed exclusively of Indians and Halfbreeds." At most, he suggested, there might be "a sprinkling of Indians and Halfbreeds."

Lansdowne had his military secretary seek out a suitable commander for the volunteers and an invitation was sent out to Frederick C. Denison, a Toronto politician who, as a young man, had served as Wolseley's orderly during the Red River campaign and had found whitewater travel exciting and exhilarating. The adventure to save Gordon appealed enormously to him and he readily agreed, though he balked at the inclusion of the Winnipeg contingent, as he believed, correctly, they had nothing to offer. Lansdowne's military secretary overruled him, however, and soon they had 389 volunteers approved for the expedition.

There is a photograph of about two hundred of them standing in front of the Peace Tower on Parliament Hill. It is a formal portrait and, given the times, no one is smiling. The men are well dressed, most with some sort of tie and jacket, all with various types of hats: caps, derbies, stetsons, even a top hat. A youngster at the very back of the assemblage is standing on the wall, one hand wrapped around a street lamp. He is likely also going. They ranged from teenagers to men in their sixties.

Perhaps one of them is Jack Carson.

The adventure began even before the volunteers boarded the train that would take them to Montreal. They marched behind the band of the Governor General's foot guards—one of the songs played was "Home, Sweet Home"—while people cheered them as if they were trained soldiers heading off to war rather than a bunch of never-trained bushmen, most of whom had no idea where they were going or why. Many, if not most, were illiterate. They had not only read nothing of Gordon's predicament, they did not know his name, had never heard of a thing called a "Mahdi" and couldn't have placed Sudan on a map of the world—if they'd ever seen a map of the world. They attended a dinner held for them that night before catching the early train and, next morning, two of the foremen had to stay behind to round up drunks for the next train.

The men gathered in Montreal on September 13, 1884, where they boarded the *Ocean King*, stopping first at Quebec City, where Lord Lansdowne, then staying at the Citadel so his family might enjoy the late summer weather, wished them well but also passed on a delicate word of caution. "Remember," the Governor General told them in his posh English accent, "that you carry with you the reputation of your own country, and that when you return next year you must bring that reputation back with you without blot or blemish."

As it turned out, they couldn't even leave Canada without blot or blemish. There were incidents of drunkenness and of women trying to smuggle bottles of whisky on board the *Ocean King* in the hours following Lansdowne's cautioning. Not surprisingly, the men began drinking as soon as they disembarked in Sydney, Nova Scotia, while the ship took on coal. One drunk stumbled into a schoolhouse, made an incoherent speech to the children, hit on the teacher and then knocked out the policeman who came to get him out of the school and back to the ship. Three of the men never returned to the ship, meaning 386 actually left Canadian shores.

The trip across the Atlantic to Gibraltar must have been a nightmare. Most were terribly hungover the first few days. They were seasick and homesick and completely at sea themselves as to what they were expected to do once they got to wherever they were going. Incredibly, they had only *two* canoes with them, both birchbark, but one was tagged for Wolseley as a gift.

While Wolseley's master plan had been inspired by canoes and voyageurs, the reality was that voyageurs were virtually non-existent by this time and his notion of Canadian canoes navigating the Nile was naive.

The eventual "canoe" design the British settled on, with strong input from the Canadian experts, would be not quite the canoe, not quite the flat-bottom boat that river navigators used in such difficult crossings as the Lachine Rapids near Montreal, different again from the James Bay freighters and the York boats used in the Far North fur trade. They would be uniquely designed for the task at hand, but the Canadian ability to master whitewater rivers, learned in the traditional canoe, would be pivotal to any success the British expedition might find. It was the skills of the canoeists who'd gotten his men to Fort Garry fourteen years earlier that Wolseley coveted, not necessarily their boats.

The Nile vessels were already under construction in Britain when the Canadians began crossing the Atlantic. While the Canadian canoe had clearly been the inspiration, the British design would more resemble a modified whaling boat—though the second birchbark canoe on board would eventually be used for quick and discreet "scouting" missions once the group reached the Nile.

The new Nile vessels had to be large enough to carry a dozen soldiers, their equipment and supplies, light enough to be carried over portages, and sleek and manoeuvrable enough to handle rapids in both directions. The expert canoeists and rafters—the vast majority Canadians but with a sprinkling of Africans with knowledge of the Nile—would determine which rapids might be run downstream, while some of the lesser rapids could be breached upstream by poling and ropes. The new vessels had to have strong oars for the soldiers to wield under the direction of the Canadian river canoeing experts, keels for steering clear of rocks and sails for those times when the river was wide enough and the wind favourable enough to catch.

If the vessels that moved the soldiers did not look much like the Canadian canoe, the guides scouting the rapids, choosing the lines to run and guiding the vessels from stern and bow certainly looked like Canadian whitewater experts—for that is precisely what a small but critical group of the volunteers were.

The building of the Nile "fleet" was alone a remarkable story. Shipyards around the English coast were set to work on the design. Nearly fifty yards built eight hundred vessels at a unit cost of £275. They had ten weeks in which to complete the commission—and they met their target in time to have steamers unload them all in Alexandria by October 18.

Meanwhile, the Canadian ship was on its way and packed with supplies, including 1.6 million tins of bully beef, thirty thousand gallons of rum and one thousand bottles of champagne, which well-off Victorians like Wolseley considered a great comfort for the sick. There were books for the recruits to read but few could take advantage. Instead, they held singsongs and thought about the drink that awaited them once they landed at Gibraltar. There they flocked to the bars, ended up in fights, and those who did not return drunk did not return at all. The captain gave them a stern lecture on the joys of abstention, though it obviously fell on deaf ears.

The British, it appears, were quickly learning what the French had long known about those who plied the rivers of the fur trade. Father Pierre François Xavier de Charlevoix, a Jesuit priest considered the first historian of New France, had warned as far back as the 1740s that the voyageurs' love of personal freedom was considered sacred by the coureurs de bois. "It is alleged they make bad servants," Charlevoix had written. Nor were they cut out to be soldiers taking orders.

So worried were the Brits about their boatload of reckless, drunken Canadian bushmen that when the ship reached Alexandria, the next stop, an armed guard was sent aboard to ensure no one disembarked. From Alexandria it was on to Wadi Halfa, a 550-mile trek along quiet waters where the men crowded the decks and stared in amazement at the sights—particularly the nearly naked women washing clothes along the shore. Having come from a culture where men might not even see their wives undressed, the Canadians were both delighted and in shock.

Wolseley met them at Wadi Halfa—known as "Bloody Halfway" to the British soldiers—and later wrote in his journal: "a rough-looking lot, but I hope I shall get plenty of work out of them."

Their work would now begin. At "Bloody Halfway" they took to the smaller boats, many of the British soldiers rowing for the first time. Half a dozen would row while a "voyageur" sat in each bow, reading the currents, watching for rocks and shouting warnings back to the helmsman, who was also a "voyageur." Not surprisingly, many of the volunteers from Manitoba hadn't the foggiest notion how to navigate a river. They were, for the most part, a disaster. Perhaps the *Winnipeg Sun* was sympathizing, or reacting to letters home from some of the more-educated men, when it wrote that the boatmen were "a grade of soldier only a few degrees higher than the army mule."

The contingent used the second birchbark canoe to scout ahead of the larger boats, choosing the routes to follow and deciding where and when it was necessary to stop poling the boats up difficult passages—some too shallow, some too turbulent—and start carrying them. Some of the more able Canadians were posted at various cataracts to organize the boats and oversee the difficult task of towing the fully loaded boats against the current, often with as many as three dozen men on a rope.

The Canadians were apparently content with this work. In the evenings, they'd have their rum rations and pipes, and they passed their little idle time exploring, pranking each other and, in some cases, trying to master the riding of intransigent camels. When they worked, however, the majority of them worked like the loggers and rivermen they had been back home.

"Nothing less than the level-headedness and surpassing skills of the voyageurs could have guided us," a Sergeant Gordon of the Black Watch wrote in one report. "Many were the hairbreadth escapes from death; for once cast overboard would have meant doom sealed; not only a watery grave but even if we could float, a zigzag journey thereto with bangs and slams against rocks, a course over which one would have no more control than an insect."

"If you had seen us Canadians," Louis Duguay of Trois-Rivières wrote home to his family, "you would have been really proud of it. . . . It was extraordinary to see the rapidity with which the expedition travels since the *Canadiens* have arrived."

It was extremely difficult and dangerous travel. Nine boats were lost and another thirteen damaged. Five of the Canadians drowned in the rapids. Three others died of disease. They found the going slow and frustrating and began to long for home. Many had planned all along to be back in the Canadian bush for the spring drives, but soon it was obvious they would need more time than had originally been estimated to get to Khartoum. The British offered a raise in pay and new clothes if they extended their commitment. They said they'd take the men to London before heading home and they could experience the delights of the world's most famous city. But few were interested. Only eighty-nine said they'd stay on for another six months.

Meanwhile, the situation in Khartoum was worsening. Gordon felt that it was only a matter of weeks, even days, before the iron grip of the Mahdi closed in on him. He sent a message out with Major Herbert Kitchener, who dressed as an Arab and concealed a poison vial in his flowing clothes in case he was apprehended. Kitchener made it through, but the message he delivered from Gordon was far from encouraging: "We are besieged on three sides. Fighting goes on day and night. Enemy cannot take us except by starving us out. Do not scatter your troops. Enemy are numerous. Bring plenty of troops if you can."

Wolseley's grand scheme of using Canadian voyageurs to slip up the Nile and rescue Chinese Gordon was now in shambles. It was taking far too long. In an attempt to reach Gordon more quickly, a decision, rather boneheaded, was made to travel by camel cross-country. Not enough camels could be found to carry the fourteen hundred troops in the Desert Column, under command of Sir Herbert Stewart. Nor were there enough saddles for the camels that were available. Perhaps it was all just as well, as the soldiers had little expertise in riding the camels, an art as difficult as learning to swim or skate, and that plan, too, bogged down. At the Battle of Abu Klea, twelve thousand "dervishes" ran at the British soldiers, despite the presence of artillery and a Gardner machine gun, and the famous British "square" broke down for a while, leaving seventy-four British soldiers dead along with more than one thousand followers of the Mahdi. The battle had lasted barely fifteen minutes.

Wolseley's faith in his old cohort was disintegrating: "Chief of Staff Sir Redvers Buller, who was responsible for logistics, had evidently failed to do the arithmetic. He had secured enough camels to carry his vital supply of Veuve Clicquot but neglected to ensure there were enough to do the job" of carrying Stewart's Desert Column to Khartoum in time. As for the soldiers advancing by camel, it was a disaster, as the saddles ordered had stirrups that irritated the camels and they endlessly tried to throw their riders. When this failed, the camels, in a display of dexterity unavailable to horses, simply turned and bit their riders.

An increasingly resigned Gordon wrote in his diary on December 13, "All that is absolutely necessary is, for fifty of the Expeditionary Force to get on board a steamer and come up . . . and thus let their presence be felt; this is not asking much, but it must happen *at once*, or it will (as usual) be too late."

It was indeed too late. The camel march had failed to reach Khartoum in time. The voyageurs, despite their best efforts, had failed to get the soldiers and their crafts past the cataracts in time. When the first vessel finally came within sight of the city on the morning of January 28, they could see no Egyptian flag flying. Colonel Sir Charles Wilson sent two spies out from his vessel, dressed as followers of the Mahdi, and they soon returned with the news that Khartoum had fallen two days earlier and Gordon was dead.

"This confirmation of the news quite finished the natives," Wilson wrote in his journal; "the dull heavy weight of despair seemed to settle down upon them, and they looked like men who no longer have an interest in life."

It was a grisly discovery the British soldiers finally came upon. As the siege had continued, the civilians had eaten everything they could find, even the skins of animals. Corpses lay in the streets. So weak had the survivors become, they couldn't even clear away the dead. Gordon had offered money for every burial but there were no takers. The Mahdi wrote several missives to Gordon, imploring him to surrender, but Gordon, ever stubborn, never answered.

Chinese Gordon sat in a window each night, the light on behind him, daring them to try and shoot him while he wrote in his journal. He would not give in. He ordered every male in the city over the age of eight to fight and fight they did, though they had neither the strength nor the numbers. Men apparently shot their wives and daughters in order to spare them the horror, and then shot themselves.

When it was over, the streets were littered with four thousand bloated corpses, soldiers and citizens hacked to death by the Mahdi followers. Gordon had been killed, it was reported, rushing down the steps to meet the charge. He had been decapitated and his severed head put on display in the fork of a tree in the dervish camp.

There is a famous painting called *General Gordon's Last Stand* by British artist George William Joy, which hangs in the Leeds Gallery. It depicts a tall (!), uniformed and defiant Gordon standing at top of a flight of steps, his dervish attackers frozen and fearful ... ing of the doomed British leader, their spears thrusting toward him as they cower lower down on the steps. It is, Terry Kirby wrote in *The Independent* in 2006, "a piece of Victorian myth-making. Iconic it may be, but the events it depicts may not have happened." Better the public had that image of their doomed hero than to leave as a last impression the general hacked to death and his head paraded about the city on the end of a pike.

No matter the truth of how Chinese Gordon met his end, the fallout from the tragedy was enormous. Britain had spent a fortune on the rescue, only to fail. And failing was not something the Empire was used to doing. Hundreds, thousands of lives had been lost. Queen Victoria fell ill on hearing the news that Khartoum had fallen. Gladstone, now derided by the people as "M.O.G." ("Murderer of Gordon"), lost his government.

Wolseley, who had come up with the voyageurs scheme and who had fool-ishly dispatched the soldiers overland on camels far too late, blamed the popular scapegoat, Gladstone, entirely for the fiasco.

"If God punishes men in the world," Wolseley wrote in his journal, "and if we are judges of right & wrong, he will send down this old hypocrite in shame to his grave & with the miseries of the nation he has misgoverned ringing in his ears dies de & hated by every good Englishman."

But again, this istorica cy. As Michael Asher wrote in his 2006 book, *Khar The Ult nperial Adventure*, "Wolseley was pathologically inc taking sibility for his own mistake. The greatest of these L p e Nile route in the first place. . . . His plan, with its a boatmen imported from Canada and west Africa, oops, its supply columns and its intricate lines of co r-elaborate. ks had been lost simply waiting for m scratch

Asher not fact, blamed offi-cially, if qu ce jobs and little further res o their own alco-holic mists.

It was, As enture of the Imperial age."

There was noth ig for m he return home. Those few who had n t vo unte d to tay on lor assist the British troops left on a train to Cairo. I must h e been a d up, as two of them died when they somehow managed to ll off and nde the wheels. They toured the pyramids, though most we e far more inter te in the city's infamous brothels. The bushmen could not believe that women in Cairo smoked cigars. They bought souvenirs, mostly turbans and spears, but some purchased small monkeys and cockatoos to take back home to the Ottawa Valley as pets.

The British troopship *Poonah* took the Canadians to Alexandria, then on to Malta and eventually to Ireland, where seven of the "voyageurs," likely with strong Irish roots, decided to disembark permanently and begin a new life. On February 20, 1885, the SS *Hanoverian* set sail from Queenstown for Halifax, crossing difficult seas in the bitter winter weather of the North Atlantic. Those who weren't sick from the tossing seas were sick from the excessive drinking.

They landed in Halifax in the ____ hours ____ 4, and the men, most wearing colourful turbans, ____ welco____ throngs eager to hear their tales of adventure. I____ wa, who ____ arrived by train on March 7, large crowds cheered ____ paraded through the streets by two bands while ____ the souvenirs—turbans, spears, shields and the ____os—the voyageurs proudly showed f.

In the mon____ follow, ____ flanked by Wolseley, Queen Victoria ____ struck and distributed, many ____ received, as there was no wa____ eds Art ____ held to honour the Ca____ ling at the ____.

But that d____ the da____ the voyageurs. "Hurrah ____ a____alized, "well and bravely h____ ____has been hard and perilous, ____ h____ faced ____ danger, and overcome it! We____ou____ cherished country which proudly salutes ____d totally ____ to honour you."

Soon enough, th____ few doz____ rem____ing voyageurs who had volunteered for further duty returned home as well. The British had decided to withdraw completely, and the unique river skills of the Canadians were no longer required. They did not leave quietly.

A report in the London *Morning Post* slammed the remaining voyageurs for their boorish behaviour before they left Egypt on their way home to Canada. The *Morning Post* claimed, "Each man carried a bottle of spirits, many were drunk and were fighting with each other, brandishing their knives, and did not pay the slightest attention to their officers."

Other correspondents signed off on the adventure with a more favourable impression of the Canadians, saying they had played an invaluable role, even if the rescue of Chinese Gordon had failed. Of the 386 who had set sail for Egypt, sixteen had given their lives, six by drowning, eight from diseases like typhoid and smallpox and, of course, the two who fell from the train to Cairo. One was said to have gone insane.

Ironically, though the Mahdi had defeated the British and evaded all British attempts to capture him, he himself died suddenly in Khartoum on June 22, 1885. The cause was said to be typhoid fever. He was in his early forties.

By the fall of 1885, all the returning "voyageurs" were back in the Ottawa Valley bush, back in Winnipeg or back on the reserve.

The greatest canoe trip in Canadian history was over.

The Canadians had been welcomed home by the *Ottawa Free Press* claiming their country was proud to salute them and delighted to honour them. And yet, as Anthony P. Michel pointed out in his 2006 article in *The Journal of Social History*, "In public memory, the expedition seemed to have left little lasting impression, winning no commemoration in statues, works of memorable Canadian fiction, history texts or school books."

Michel, who plans to publish his own comprehensive history of the expedition, has visited Egypt but said, "Sadly, it is not possible for someone in our time to see the Nile as the Canadian voyageurs would have seen it in 1884 to 1885. The river was forever changed by the Aswan High Dam, which flooded the area between the first and third cataract, and the more recent Merowe Dam in the Sudan, which flooded the land between the fourth and fifth cataracts.

"If one visited those places today, in search of the sites where the men worked, or even the makeshift graves where several were buried, one would find oneself standing on the edge of massive hydro reservoirs that have forever altered the geography, buried a great deal of human history and displaced numerous local inhabitants."

There is, however, one small reminder to be found in the Ottawa Valley, where so many of the voyageurs came from—perhaps including the mysterious relative of whom Duncan MacGregor was so proud. On the Ontario side of the Ottawa River a few kilometres upstream from Parliament Hill, at a small rise in the shoreline known as Kitchissippi Lookout, stands a small blue memorial plaque that reads:

> In 1884 the British Government decided to send a military expedition up the Nile River to relieve Major-General Charles Gordon, who was besieged in Khartoum by Mahdist tribesmen. Appointed to command the relieving force, Viscount Wolseley, who had led the expedition to the Red River in 1870, requested the recruitment of experienced Canadian voyageurs. Almost 400 volunteered, including many superb rivermen, and the largest group came from the Ottawa Valley area. Commanded by Lieutenant-Colonel Frederick C. Denison, they were largely responsible for the successful navigation of the Nile's difficult cataracts, although sixteen voyageurs died on service. The contingent returned to Canada in 1885.

On a gorgeous summer day in 2014, the plaque stood as cyclists, roller-bladers, runners and the occasional elderly stroller passed by.

And not a single one paused to read the sign.

The plaque mentions only four names, three directly (Gordon, Wolseley and Denison) and one, the Mahdi, indirectly. Only one of the four, Frederick C. Denison, was Canadian. He landed in London and was given a hero's welcome and again in Ottawa and his hometown, Toronto. He received medals and was made a Companion of the Order of St. Michael and St. George. He ran for federal office as a Conservative and won by a landslide. He died in office in 1896.

No names for the 386 voyageurs.

No mention of any Jack Carson.

And nothing at all about the canoe that had been the inspiration for Canada's strangest military expedition.

5

THE MISSION

THERE IS A SPECTACULAR RED FLOWER found almost exclusively along the Petawawa River and the Barron Canyon, two of the most popular canoe runs along the eastern boundary of Algonquin Park. The cardinal plant, *Lobelia cardinalis*, requires not one, but two visits by a humming-bird in order to procreate. The bird arrives when the flower is in early bloom and uses its long bill to sip the nectar, which lies just deep enough that the "brow" of the bird brushes against the flower and picks up pollen. Later, when the stamens of the cardinal flower no longer produce pollen, the pistil, the female part of the plant, protrudes through the spent stamens to a point where, when the flower is again visited by a hummingbird whose head has been dusted with pollen from another plant, fertilization takes place.

In other words, new life here requires a return visit.

In the late summer of 2013, the Fraser family set out on a deeply personal mission to paddle the Petawawa and right a wrong. The August weather was spectacular—days calm and warm, nights cool under a blue moon—but the water low. The Petawawa can be dangerous in high water and low, as is the case with most rivers that buck and tumble down through the Canadian Shield. It drains southeast from the Algonquin Highlands to the Ottawa River, with a forty-kilometre stretch from Lake Travers to

Lake McManus containing a number of rapids—Big and Little Thompson, Grillade, Crooked Chute, Rollway, the Natch, Schooner and Five-Mile rapids—potentially too wild to chance in the spring runoff, fabulous tests during most of the canoeing season, though sometimes too broken and shallow to run when the summer water levels approach seasonal lows. Continuing through to the Ottawa River is impossible for reasons other than whitewater and rocks: beyond Lake McManus the river enters the sprawling Petawawa military base under thick wire fencing, barbed wire and "NO TRESPASSING " signs.

In the early years following the War of 1812, when the British colonies in Upper and Lower Canada were fretting over future conflict with the ambitious Americans, a safe route was sought from the Ottawa River to Lake Huron, and the Petawawa was briefly considered a possibility. Lieutenant Henry Briscoe travelled it in 1826 with a hardy group of paddlers and reported back that the river is "nearly one entire rapid." Not only that, Briscoe told his superiors, but the banks are so steep and rocky that work to make the river more passable would be nigh impossible. The river today remains, happily, much as Briscoe and his men found it.

One hundred and eighty-seven years after Briscoe's journey, Graham Fraser was on the second-to-last set of rapids before the Petawawa quiets and eases gently into McManus Lake. His mission was almost completed.

Tall and lean, Fraser looked fit for sixty-seven. He paddled well but in fact had never before travelled down a whitewater river, which can be a profoundly different experience for even the most practised of flatwater paddlers. He had approached this deeply personal quest with considerable determination and some understandable trepidation. He was still learning when, suddenly, an unseen twist in the surging water sent the canoe carrying him and his son Malcolm into a large boulder, the strong current pinning the vessel fast and instantly dumping the two men.

Graham had been paddling stern, Malcolm bow. Graham had carefully tucked his size-thirteen runners in under the seat and his feet caught as the canoe turned and sent Malcolm, paddles, water bottles and everything else that had not been secured, into the white foam. Graham felt trapped as he wiggled one foot free of the seat but the other seemed to be stuck, a sense of panic quickly rising in him.

"Well," he said to himself, "this just may be the way that it ends."

Only it did not.

And it was not his own life that flashed before Graham Fraser's eyes—it was his father's.

Graham Fraser had plenty to recall from his own lifetime as an accomplished journalist and foreign correspondent. His impressive CV included reporting for several national publications, including *The Globe and Mail*, the *Toronto Star* and *Maclean's*, which is where I had come to know him well some thirty years earlier. He had written well-received books on national politics and bilingualism and, for the past seven years, had held one of the most prestigious civil service posts in the land: commissioner of official languages.

This trip, however, had never been about him.

The Frasers—Graham, Malcolm, a thirty-nine-year-old writer and film critic from Montreal, Nick, a thirty-seven-year-old professional musician from Toronto, and Nick's thirteen-year-old son, Owen Heathcote-Fraser—had come to the Petawawa during this week of a rare blue moon to avenge a misguided insult to the family name and to pay their respects to a grandfather and great-grandfather the younger ones in the family had never known.

Forty-five years earlier, on May 12, 1968, Blair Fraser had died in these same waters—thrown from his canoe on the sometimes-treacherous Rollway Rapids, smashed into rocks and hurtled down the long jumble of rushing water and jagged granite to drown in the deep pool at the end of the run.

Blair Fraser had been fifty-nine and in the prime of his life and career, as the Ottawa editor of *Maclean's*, and known throughout the country, most particularly in the small towns and more rural areas, for his reasoned and rational "Blair Fraser Reports." He was a familiar face on television, a friendly voice on radio. He had reported from around the world, and yet felt that the most precious place in that world was the Canadian wilderness. He had interviewed prime ministers and presidents and maharajahs, yet preferred a workplace where the only position worth holding was steady against the current.

Blair Fraser was born in Sydney, Nova Scotia, on April 17, 1909. The lantern-jawed transplanted Cape Bretoner had, as his decades in Ottawa passed, become a great champion of the Canadian landscape, particularly the Far North. Out of a 1951 dinner party, a small group of public servants and journalists became a vanguard for what developed into a continuing national passion for summer canoe adventure and would have a profound effect on wilderness paddling in the North.

At the party, the Ottawa group had proposed to a few foreign diplomats that you had to get out and really experience a country to understand it. Eric Morse, the national director of the Canadian Clubs, was the main proponent—he had read Harold Innis's *The Fur Trade in Canada* and had long wished to retrace the footsteps and paddle strokes of the likes of Mackenzie, Thompson, La Vérendrye and Samuel Hearne.

The core group called themselves "Les Voyageurs" after the original paddlers, mostly French and Metis, that opened up North America to European exploration. The core of the Ottawa group numbered seven: scientist Omond Solandt, who was chair of the Defence Research Board, Elliot Rodger, a retired army general who became chair of the Manitoba Liquor Commission, Tony Lovink, Netherlands ambassador to Canada, Denis Coolican, head of the Canadian Bank Note Company, Tyler Thompson, a U.S. diplomat, Fraser and Morse. It was a flexible club, however, in that others were often included and the core seven could not take in every trek.

The famous American nature writer Sigurd F. Olson became a member after they sought advice from him on a good route through the Quetico-Superior area of northern Minnesota and Northwestern Ontario. Olson decided to meet up with them and found he enjoyed their company enough to become one of Les Voyageurs himself.

Olson, author of *The Singing Wilderness* back in 1956 and president of the Wilderness Society, was a major American voice in nature protection. He was also an avid paddler who once wrote, "The movement of a canoe is like a reed in the wind. Silence is part of it, and the sounds of lapping water, bird songs and wind in the trees. It is a part of the medium through which it floats, the sky, the water, the shores. . . . There is magic in the feel of a paddle and the movement of a canoe, a magic compounded of distance, adventure, solitude, and peace. The way of a canoe is the way of the wilderness, and of a freedom almost forgotten. It is an antidote to insecurity, the open door to waterways of ages past and a way of life with profound and abiding satisfactions. When a man is part of his canoe, he is part of all that canoes have ever known."

The 1950s were glory years for recreational canoeing. Railways had attempted in earlier decades to promote it with posters that suggested people transport their canoes by rail to wilderness areas finally accessible by the many tracks spreading across North America. But it was the end of the Second World War that really saw the canoes return to prominence in the land where it had been born centuries earlier. And, ironically, these peaceful recreations came in no small way out of the war itself.

"The war," historian James Raffan wrote, "had forced the Grumman aircraft company to perfect aluminum fabrication techniques that were transferred almost instantly to canoes in 1945. And the Aircraft Division of Canadian Vickers in east-end Montreal, which had turned the science of wood lamination into an art form during the wartime production of Mosquito bombers and other wooden aircraft, did the same."

Vickers, as Raffan points out, was sold to the American Electric Boat Company, which was soon mass-producing hardy canoes constructed of aluminum for the general population. The 1950s brought an explosion of children's camps. Canoeists like Omer Stringer were spreading both love of canoeing and sophisticated paddling skills to younger generations. Families were camping, and from camping out of cars many moved easily into short tripping along well-marked routes.

"There is no doubt, however," Raffan wrote, "that it was the Ottawa Voyageurs, led by the irrepressible Eric Morse and his wife, Pamela, who pointed the way north from the mid-1950s onward, proving again and again that it was not only possible to travel the remote routes of the original voyageurs and gentlemen adventurers, but that one could live to tell the tale."

The impact of Les Voyageurs was immediate and lasting. Morse wrote about paddling in the Barrens, published a book on the fur trade routes, with a foreword by Pierre Elliott Trudeau, who had himself written years earlier about the canoe as a metaphor for life. It was after Trudeau became prime minister in 1968 that, finally, the country launched its Wild River Survey, leading to the creation of dozens of organizations dedicated to wilderness adventures. As Kirk Wipper, the "godfather" of the Canadian Canoe Museum, put it: "It was as if the canoe had just been invented."

Morse wrote a memoir, *Freshwater Saga*, which was published after his death in 1986 at age eighty-two. In the book, he recounts how a life of adventure grew out of that evening dinner party in Ottawa: "After dinner, in a spirit of gentle banter, some of the Canadians were asking the diplomats how they could possibly learn much of the true Canada on the cocktail circuit. They should experience what it was like to paddle the Canadian lakes and rivers, trudge over portages, feel the spray of rapids, camp among pines and face the insects. In the end the diplomats said, 'Okay, show us.'"

And so they did. Morse, Solandt and Fraser—who, surprisingly, had no experience with canoeing—took three of the diplomats down the

Gatineau River, and the diplomats were so taken with the experience that one of them, Netherlands ambassador Tony Lovink, became a permanent member of the canoeing group.

Michael Peake, the editor of *Che-Mun*, has long been a passionate chronicler of Les Voyageurs' adventures and influence. By Peake's tally, they undertook eleven major trips, beginning in 1951 with that relatively easy trip down the nearby Gatineau River, which empties into the Ottawa across from Parliament Hill. In 1952 and 1953 they went to Quetico Provincial Park in Northwestern Ontario, where Olson first joined them. They then moved on to increasingly challenging adventures. They took on the incredibly gruelling Grand Portage, a carry of nearly fourteen kilometres, during a trip to the Fort Frances area of Northwestern Ontario. They took on the challenging Churchill River that runs into Hudson Bay. Driven by Morse's interest in old fur trade routes, they paddled through northern Saskatchewan and Manitoba and deep into the Northwest Territories. Always a new river, always new challenges.

Peake believes it was Les Voyageurs Olson was thinking about when the American naturalist wrote in *Reflections from the North Country* that "I know now as men accept the timeclock of the wilderness, their lives become entirely different. It is one of the great compensations of primitive experience, and when one finally reaches the point where days are governed by daylight and dark, rather than by schedules, where one eats if hungry and sleeps when tired, and becomes completely immersed in the ancient rhythms, then one begins to live."

Following the second Quetico trip, Olson had become a permanent member of the group. The others called him "Bourgeois," the fur trade moniker for the one leading the expedition and, appropriately, their trips invariably retraced routes that the original voyageurs and their bourgeois leaders would have travelled. In 1955, without the use of guides, they reached Cumberland House, the Hudson's Bay Company post established on the Saskatchewan River by Samuel Hearne in 1774. Olson wrote the story of the trip in *The Lonely Land.*

Some of their northern trips were costly and, at times, there were complaints about the rising expense, but each summer found a half dozen or so of them setting out in pursuit of something they came to believe had value beyond money. One paddler who occasionally joined them, and who could easily afford any trip, was the young Montreal academic Pierre Trudeau, already well known to the group for his passionate writing on the joys of canoe tripping.

Blair Fraser was rather less poetic but more to the point when, as Les Voyageurs were passing through Edmonton following a northern trek, he was asked by a local newspaperman the most basic of questions: *Why?*

"Most people might think we are touched," Fraser answered, "but if you work on a job where tension is the only cause of fatigue, you can't really relax because your troubles stay with you. But if you're paddling down some river toward dusk looking for a place to camp after a long day of rapids, portages, and fighting the wind, there is no time to worry about anything else and the tension just works out of you."

Jean Fraser, Blair's wife, came to appreciate what her husband meant. She had worried terribly about these dangerous trips to the northern wild, but as she explained to *Maclean's* following his death, "Then I saw those refreshed and rejuvenated faces that returned, and I remembered the white, pinched faces that had left, and I didn't worry anymore."

Fraser was a beloved character on the trips, always willing to do his share and more, always singing, often at the top of his voice over the sound of rapids, a variety of shanty songs he somehow knew, and always with a good stash of brandy for evenings around the campfire. Les Voyageurs were also partial to a drink called "falernum," which Charles Dickens once described as "a curious liqueur composed from rum and lime-juice."

In springtime, Les Voyageurs came to treasure the nearby Petawawa River as a tune-up. The river is hardly the most difficult in the country, but it requires a lot of technique and is considered a jewel by whitewater advocates such as filmmaker Bill Mason. It behaves like a different river each time it is run. As the Greek philosopher Heraclitus said 2,500 years before the Kevlar canoe was invented, "You cannot step into the same river twice."

That most assuredly applies to the wondrous Petawawa.

A year before the tragedy, Trudeau had flipped in the Little Thompson Rapids above Rollway and emerged unharmed, if a bit wet and embarrassed. That same year, Canada's 1967 Centennial, a gorgeous photograph had been taken by the other paddlers of Blair, paddling bow, and Omond in the stern of their canoe. They are paddling away from the bottom of tumbling Rollway, exactly where, one year later, Blair Fraser's body would be recovered.

On that sad spring day in 1968, the group had no intention of running Rollway. The water was high and cold, the familiar stretch a jumble of white water cascading off large rocks both below and above the water line. The group broke camp in the morning and set out. Blair, paddling stern, was with Elliot Rodger.

Les Voyageurs had invited two young newcomers along on the Petawawa trip: a lawyer, Peter Blaikie, later to co-found the prestigious Heenan-Blaikie Montreal firm, and teacher Tom Lawson. Blaikie had just celebrated his thirty-first birthday. He and Lawson were "on trial"—invited to paddle the nearby river so that Morse could check them out as possible invitees to that summer's trip to the Arctic. Blaikie had whitewater experience but had never been on the Petawawa—and would never return. Blaikie and Lawson had followed Fraser and Rodger from the campsite and intended to take their cues from the experienced men as to when they should eddy out for the Rollway portage.

When the two newcomers reached the anticipated pull-off, they noticed that Fraser and Rodger had continued to the top of the rapids. Their canoe was turned around and they were paddling upstream, trying to breach the current and gain the calm water again. Had they miscalculated?

Were they showing off their expertise to the newcomers following them? Had they actually thought of trying to run the rapids and then, too late, had a change of heart? No matter the reason, the result was unavoidable given how far they had ventured into the foaming top of the rapids.

"It was almost like a hallucination," Blaikie told me in early 2014. "We got there and saw this canoe backwards at the top of the rapids. It didn't look 'fatally' close or anything. The paddlers didn't have a sense of panic or anything. There was no frantic paddling. We shouted to them, but with the roar of the water I don't think they could hear us. They just sort of slowly slipped back into a standing wave."

And then they were gone, Blaikie and Lawson watching helplessly as the other canoe seemed to be lassoed and hauled from behind into the current.

"Tom and I beached the canoe," Blaikie wrote in a private letter to Graham Fraser forty-five years after his father's accident, "and ran down the portage which, as I recall, was four or five hundred yards long. When we got to the bottom, we saw the upturned, damaged canoe and, a few seconds later, Elliot scrambling to shore a bit further downstream. There was no sign of your dad. Tom and I spent several minutes diving into the bottom of Rollway but, obviously, without success . . . "

Blaikie believed Fraser had been trapped in a hydraulic, a dangerous situation where water drops over a ledge into deeper water, causing water on the surface to be drawn back toward the ledge. Such a "sous hole" can be impossible to escape and is one of the great hazards of running high water rapids. The two fit young men were cautious about themselves getting caught and trapped, and the water was frigid, but they dove until they were certain Blair Fraser could not possibly be alive. There was nothing the group could do but leave him there and notify the police when they got out, so that professional divers could be sent in to retrieve the body.

"It was the most bizarre experience," Blaikie said in 2014. "Surreal, really. We had no cell phones, of course, no radio, no way of contacting anyone. We had no choice but to continue our trip. The weather was lovely and the scenery absolutely beautiful. We had two more days' paddling to put in. We couldn't talk endlessly about what had happened, so for the most part we just paddled on in silence, knowing we had just left a terrible, terrible scene."

At the time of the drowning, Graham Fraser, then twenty-two, had just started his first job in journalism. He had graduated from the University of Toronto and had been hired on as a summer student at the *Toronto Star*. By coincidence, Graham was also canoeing in Algonquin Park that weekend, but under very different circumstances. He and his then girlfriend, Barbara Uteck, now his wife, had gone for a long drive north of Toronto to talk about their relationship and future commitments. They had driven into the park through the West Gate and, at Canoe Lake, had rented a canoe from the Portage Store and gone for a quiet paddle on calm waters. They passed the memorial to painter Tom Thomson at Hayhurst Point and, naturally, discussed the mysterious disappearance back in the summer of 1917—completely unaware that another park drowning, one that would also become famous, had just taken place.

Graham called back to Toronto, and his friend Bob Rae, who would go on to be premier of Ontario and, briefly, leader of the Liberal Party of Canada, was the one who had to break the terrible news. John Fraser, Graham's older brother, was then an up-and-comer in foreign affairs and had been posted to the Canadian embassy in Warsaw, Poland. John flew home immediately. Jean Fraser had been in Paris, visiting friends, when the call came about her husband. It was during the 1968 student riots and getting to the Paris airports was impossible. Instead, friends spirited her out of the French capital and drove her to Amsterdam, where she caught the first flight to Canada.

"We have lost a great Canadian," *The Ottawa Journal* said in an editorial the day after the tragedy became known. "His objective was the pursuit of truth, fairness and the giving of a better break in life to the underdog and the misunderstood. He was a vigorous fighter: fought sham, vanity, and deceit, arrogance and half truth. He loved hard work, hard sport, hard argument, hard principles. He loved the out of doors, youth, literature, laughter, his family and friends."

In the tribute *Maclean's* printed that summer, "The Last Journey of Blair Fraser, Canadian," staff writer Douglas Marshall called Fraser "a gentleman journalist" and argued, "No individual did more to create and sustain this country's international reputation for superior journalism than Blair Fraser." The canoe story, tragic as it was, said Marshall, also "explains how one man, grappling with the problem of his own and his nation's identity, found the solution where he least expected it—on the sparse granite banks of half-forgotten northern rivers."

The magazine went on to quote from Fraser's book (unfortunately his only one), *The Search for Identity*, which had come out a year earlier, during the country's Centennial celebrations:

> "'Development' continues. Canada's standard of living, second highest in the world, is in no danger of losing that proud position. Washing machines and television sets abound, as in no other nation save one. . . . Ugly little towns prosper, all calling themselves cities and all looking like faithful copies of Omaha, Nebraska.
>
> "This is not a Canada to call forth any man's love. But just north of it lies a different kind of land—too barren ever to be thickly settled, too bleak to be popular like Blackpool or Miami. There is no reason to doubt it will always be there, and so long as it is there Canada will not die."

Pierre Trudeau, who six weeks after the drowning would win the election that made him prime minister, later wrote to the head of the Quetico Foundation, which was putting together a book on wilderness writing dedicated to Blair Fraser's memory. "In two activities in which we shared an enthusiasm," the new prime minister wrote, "political analysis and canoeing, I came to admire Blair's exceptional skill and judgment. We respected him for what he could do, but we cherished him for what he was, a wise and generous man with a gift for un-demanding friendship."

The tragedy shattered the Fraser family and deeply rocked Blair Fraser's fellow paddlers, who had always seen their friend as a sensible, safe canoeist, never one to take foolish chances and, they knew, never for a moment intending to risk Rollway in the spring high water.

That fall, with the full blessing of the park authorities, Les Voyageurs decided to erect a small, discreet cross at the rapids in his memory. They arranged for the Fraser family to be driven in using the logging roads that cobwebbed through the eastern park.

Sig Olson, unable to make the cross ceremony, wrote a letter to Jean Fraser:

> When you gather on the Petawawa a week from Sunday I will be thinking of you and of Blair. To tell you how I feel is difficult, for Blair is much to us all, his gay and indomitable spirit, and his love of the lakes and the rivers of the Canadian Shield. When he left us he took something away that can never be replaced. We will go on without him, but it will never be quite the same again. The first to go of our group makes us more conscious of the strong bonds of love and loyalty that have been welded through our experiences together. Though he can no longer be with us, we know his spirit will be at every campfire, and when we run the rapids of the future, or fight the big waves on the lakes or struggle across the portages, he will be there, too.
>
> So Jean, when Sunday comes and your heart is heavy, try and remember when his cross is erected above Rollway Rapids, some part of all of us is left there with him and know that we are all proud we knew him as we did and better for having shared with him and know what 'His Search for Identity' really meant.

Les Voyageurs purchased their cross from a small company in Milton, Ontario, for the grand sum of $84.67, taxes included. Its simple message read, "In Memory of Blair Fraser, 1909–1968. Erected by his Fellow Voyageurs."

For forty years the little bronze cross stood there, a silent legacy to a man who, largely by accident, did a great deal to revive and promote recreational canoe tripping in a country only made possible by the canoe.

Right up until someone tore it down and threw it away.

In the fall of 2008, *Che-Mun* ran a story about Blair Fraser's cross being torn down. Editor Michael Peake was furious, calling it "the ignorant act of an ignorant person."

The self-righteous perpetrator had subsequently written to various officials and environmentalists to boast of his service to nature. He had ripped out this blight on the wilderness, he smugly claimed, and had placed it harmlessly in an out-of-the-way place. Then he sent an unsigned letter off to the superintendent of Algonquin Park:

> *The rollway cross was thoughtfully removed, as was its spawn: a plaque screwed to a tree in the midst of a falls campsite, and a large freshly carved marble plaque from the "Gourmet Paddlers" on behalf of one of their kin, prominently urethane foamed to a rock at a popular scenic location and adorned with a toy plastic canoe.*
>
> *Make peace with your own mortality, park your sense of self-importance and recognize immortality graffiti where you see it. Meanwhile, a small, frail, anonymous memento hides in a special spot requiring days of tripping and hiking to reach, on behalf of someone's dying wish. You can appreciate the difference . . .*
>
> *"Passing Through."*

When the Fraser family was informed of this vandalism, they did not know what to do. *Replace the cross? Look for it? Forget it?* The immediate desire was to return it to its place, if possible, but . . . *where was it?*

Graham Fraser found it difficult to think the situation through. More than forty years had passed since the cross had been erected. Times change, society changes. If the cross was lost, as seemed likely, would an appropriate memorial today be a religious cross or something more in keeping with the natural environment of that area? Was it right to put anything there? There was, after all, both a government-erected historical plaque to honour Tom Thomson at Canoe Lake and a large cairn built by his artist friends. No one ever complained; there had never been a movement to have them "thoughtfully removed." Other plaques and cairns in the park honoured park founders and several long-time park rangers; national and provincial parks throughout the country are home to innumerable plaques and monuments.

There was no doubt that the Fraser memorial mattered to canoeists. In the final canoe trip undertaken by Pierre Trudeau, he returned to the place where the weathered cross still stood in honour of the friend he had lost on the Petawawa so many years earlier. It was 1997. The former prime minister was nearly seventy-eight years old and not well. He was thin. He had been diagnosed with Parkinson's disease, and though he did not tell his friends, they could see that he was struggling.

Trudeau and his friends portaged Rollway rather than risk running it. They carried their first loads along the twisting path and soon came to where the memorial, then twenty-nine years old, still stood. "Whenever he passed the spot," CTV newsman Craig Oliver recounted in a later book, "he never failed to pause and gaze at it in silent reflection. This time Trudeau lingered a few moments longer than usual before shouldering his pack and continuing down the trail."

Michael Peake found a speech given by Robert Olson in January 1982 to commemorate the dedication of a memorial plaque raised to his father, Sigurd, in Ely, Minnesota. Robert Olson spoke, it seemed, for all of Sigurd's old paddling friends, Blair Fraser included, and it struck Peake as a pointed defence of the value in such a commemoration.

"This plaque," Robert said, "is surely more than a memorial to the 'Bourgeois' alone. Is it not, rather, a memorial to the Voyageurs themselves, to what they were, to what they stood for, to what bound them together? You were truly voyageurs of the lonely land, tracing the old trails of the frontier, reliving in our days the age of exploration and adventure; you were voyageurs of the spirit too, rediscovering the elemental things of life. In open horizons you recovered that wonderful sense of 'something lost behind the ranges.' You travelled with beauty in the flowing water and the starry nights. In the silences of the North, you knew again some of the basic truths and realities which Omond once said, helped to 'iron out the wrinkles in his soul.'

"But, above all I think, you were Voyageurs of comradeship and camaraderie. You knew again what it meant to be men, to work and play, to strive together, to share the burdens and the laughter of the trail. And you forged, in those days, bonds that go beyond friendship and memories which can never fade. . . . When in future days we might wander down to this spot and see this plaque now firmly and forever set in the living rock, we shall think of those things, of all of you, of the Voyageurs and their exploits now passing into legend, but especially of their spirit which lives on and which has already enriched immeasurably the lives of us all."

The attitude expressed by "Passing Through," the self-appointed vigilante, is not one widely shared by other dedicated trippers. Kevin Callan, who has written numerous guide books on canoe tripping in Canada, says, "When I come to a memorial in the woods I always feel a sense of empathy to the one who died and the family they've left behind. More strongly, however, I sense the connection the deceased had with nature and how they felt about being in the wilderness. By placing the memorial—beyond helping the ones closest to the deceased deal with the death in a remote and uncommon setting—it gives a strong message to strangers passing by. It reminds them of how we all are a part of nature, not detached from it."

Owen Heathcote-Fraser, a Grade 8 student who would learn to run rapids and fly-fish on this trip to honour the great-grandfather he never knew, said it all in a single word.

"Disrespectful."

In August of 2012, my friend Phil Chester, the rock-'n'-roll-singing retired high school teacher from Deep River, suggested we paddle the Petawawa and see what we could find out about the missing cross. We were accompanied by our daughters, Holly Chester, a professional guide on the Ottawa River, and Jocelyn MacGregor, who was then working as a naturalist in Fairmont Hot Springs, British Columbia.

The water was high enough that we easily shot Rollway Rapids and then retraced our steps in search of the cross. We found a watch, still ticking, but no sign of the uprooted monument as we walked the banks of the river. Having run the rapids we had no reason to walk the portage trail deeper in the woods. We knew the cross had been ripped from its moorings, but we had no idea where it had been placed, thrown or taken. What we did not know was that, earlier that same summer, it had already been found—by members of the Wilderness Adventurers of Ontario. One of the group had seen the glint of something shiny in the then very shallow water, and they were able to retrieve the bronze cross and carry it back up the portage to lay it, no longer anchored, against the rock from which it had been torn.

The supposed crusading environmental avenger had simply tossed the cross into the river.

With the cross found, the remaining members of Blair Fraser's family were anxious to repair the base. A number of friends and interested paddlers offered whatever help they could. Park authorities were open to the family going in by logging roads and trails—as they had decades earlier—but a fierce July storm had swept through the area, and downed trees had made such passage impossible.

The only way to do it was to paddle in.

For all his experience canoeing flatwater, Graham Fraser was uncertain about taking on any whitewater challenge. It wasn't so much his age and fitness as it was an understandable trepidation: the Petawawa, after all, had taken his father's life.

Malcolm Fraser had canoed little, and Nick and Owen were also inexperienced, but game. Phil Chester and I would go along, as well as another area guide, Dan Caldwell, who knew the tricks of the Petawawa as well as Chester. The group, seven in four canoes (Caldwell paddled solo), put in at Lake Travers on a day when the water was black and smooth as obsidian stone. It was just the sort of day, sunny, warm, quiet, when you realize why so many consider the Petawawa one of the world's most beautiful rivers.

Tom Thomson went down parts of the Petawawa twice in 1916 with fire ranger Ed Godin. Thomson had taken on summer work as a fire ranger based at Grand Lake and took advantage of the spectacular scenery of the eastern part of the park to do some of his best-known paintings. *Jack Pine* was painted not far from today's Achray Campground. He painted high rocks along the Petawawa, the majestic gorge downstream from Rollway Rapids and was fascinated by the red pointer boats built in nearby Pembroke by John Cockburn for J.R. Booth's timber operations. He twice used the distinctive boats as subjects, sketching *Bateaux* and *The Pointers*, the latter of which he turned into a large canvas over the winter and today hangs in the University of Toronto's Hart House.

The trip was not hurried. The group spent time diving off the rocks and swimming in the clear, cold waters as the flow slowed near the various campsites. Owen learned how to fly-fish and soon was catching and releasing on his own. Blair Fraser's son and two grandsons were given a crash course in what it was about this sprawling, unknowable country that so inspired the man they had come to honour.

Blair Fraser himself had had what he'd called a "fairy-tale romance" with the rugged and difficult Canadian Shield. He wrote about it once in *Maclean's*, calling it "Canada's ugly duckling," despite its making up more than half the land mass of the nation. "The hardiest of fairy tale themes," he wrote, "have always to do with the finding of treasure in the commonplace, the scorned and the rejected. In these classic stories, ugly ducklings turn into swans . . .

> One of the things that make our country what it is a little different from most other countries however similar or however friendly, is the awareness that the wilderness is not far away. However urban we become, however soft and civilized, we still have the cleansing wild within a hundred miles more or less. It is good to know that no matter how much richer and stronger we may grow, Canada will still be the same kind of country.

He came to believe, at a time of great internal dissension, even violence, in the country over Quebec separatism, that his "Ugly Duckling" was, in fact, what held this tortured confederation together. "Never in their history have Canadians demonstrated any warm affection for each other," he had written a year before his death in *The Search for Identity*.

> Loyalties have always been parochial, mutual hostilities chronic.
> No separatist of the 1960s spoke more bitterly than had Joseph Howe, the "Tribune of the People" whom Nova Scotia still regards as her greatest son, in his campaign of the 1860s against alliance with "three million frost-bound Canadians" in their alien fastness a thousand miles away. No French Canadian has used stronger language against *les anglais* than was commonplace among western wheat farmers about the money barons of Bay Street and the tyrants of the CPR. (An old story, still current on the prairies, tells of the farmer who woke one morning

to find his ripe crop ruined by blight. After a long silence he said to his wife: "Well, God damn the CPR.")

Suspicions reigned not only among but within the regions. The historian A.R.M. Lowers quotes the prayers of a Presbyterian minister in the nineteenth century, on Cape Breton Island, the eastern tip of Nova Scotia:

"And most especially do we thank Thee, Lord, for the Gut of Canso, Thine own body of water, which separateth us from the sin and wickedness on the other side thereof."

What held such people together was not love for each other, it was love of the land itself, the vast empty land in which, for more than three centuries, a certain kind of man has found himself uniquely at home.

What Blair Fraser found there for himself was a sense of awe, a size and space in which "a man can still enjoy the illusion of solitude."

The group paddled hard each morning, hard after a shore lunch. They took instruction on eddying and different strokes and how to read the current. Clearly nervous, the Frasers were taken down the relatively easy Big Thompson and Little Thompson rapids one by one and then began shooting some of the rapids in pairs. No one tipped. Their confidence grew. They began paddling for long, long stretches without so much as a word being spoken.

They had found "the illusion of solitude."

Time to think about where they were and where they would soon be.

On Saturday, the group reached Rollway. With the water fairly low, the rapids looked a jumble of jagged, dark granite. "Everywhere you want to go," Caldwell said as we scouted the potential routes, "there's a rock."

But the Frasers were not interested in running the rapids that had taken their patriarch. Leaving the canoes for Caldwell to dance through the rocks, the rest of the group set off down the lengthy portage until a slight fork took them into a small clearing. It is a lovely spot, high over the rapids that roar constantly, the air slightly damp and refreshing on a late summer's day.

On the rocky outcropping closest to the water, all that remained embedded in the granite was the badly bent stem of the bronze cross. Those who had found the memorial in the water the previous summer had placed it carefully upright to the side, supported by a few small stones.

For a long time, Graham Fraser just stared. He had not seen the now-corroded cross for nearly forty-five years, not since that September afternoon when the family gathered here and the memorial was newly forged, the bronze glistening in the sunlight.

Finally, he spoke: "My father often said that if he had to go, he hoped it would be right after a good winter ski down Mount Tremblant. . . . This, I have to think, would have been his second choice—if it had to be."

For the better part of two hours, Blair Fraser's son, grandsons and great-grandson worked with a trowel, water from the river and a small amount of ready-mix cement to provide a new base. When it was once again solid, they gathered stones from the area to cover up any signs of the repair work, the cross restored to a reasonable semblance of how it had stood here for more than four decades.

Phil Chester, who tries to paddle this river at least once a season, was angry when he thought about what had happened here. The vandal who had claimed the memorial had been "thoughtfully removed" had so thoughtlessly tossed it, with its sharp, jagged bottom, into the river where paddlers not keen to run the rapids and reluctant to unload to carry their packs over the portage often line their canoes down the more shallow edges of the river with ropes. The jagged cross could easily have tripped someone or badly cut someone's foot or leg.

"Did that guy ever think about how many lives might have been *saved* by this cross?" Chester wondered aloud. "How many people came here to scout the rapids and saw this and decided maybe it might be a wise idea to portage instead?"

Graham, understandably, became sentimental. His father, he said, used to say "that he didn't know anyone who took so much pleasure out of the things that he did badly. After he died, people often wrote about him as if he were an expert canoeist, but he wasn't. He always described himself as the drudge labour on the trips."

"He was a fundamentally modest man," Graham said. "That modesty applied to both his professional work, where he had little reason to be modest, but also to sailing and skiing and canoeing. I think we've all taken a little pleasure in trying to restore this memorial to his memory with a certain amount of awkwardness, a certain amount of determination— and I hope a substantial degree of modesty, which was his most endearing characteristic.

"The last conversation I had with him, he said, 'Don't think I've been a success. I became a journalist because I didn't have the imagination to do anything else.' It was fundamentally not true, because he was extremely successful, but I think it spoke to his sense of himself as somebody who observed others doing things. He felt there were doers and there were observers, and he was an observer not a doer. And he had great admiration for those people, whether in politics or the public service, who actually did things."

The family spent a little while tidying up the area one last time and, for a considerable stretch, they all just stood silently staring at the cross until first Nick, the Toronto jazz drummer, then Malcolm, the writer, and finally Owen, the grandson, went over and collected Graham in a group hug.

After they separated, Graham had one more thing to say, his voice breaking: "Until now, I've been following in his footsteps. From now on, we'll be going where he wasn't able."

One day later, his words would prove prophetic.

We were nearing the end of the journey, working our way down Five Mile Rapids, which pales compared to the Big Chute or Rollway runs. Mostly you merely steer and enjoy the long ride.

Five Mile can still trick you, however. It happened to Pierre Trudeau in 1997 on that final trip down the Petawawa. Craig Oliver described the moment:

> We were spent by the time we reached the last rapid of the day. Trudeau and his companion, the experienced canoe guide Wally Schaber, were in the lead. They were backpaddling, stern into shore, sneaking down the edge of a fast stream swollen by recent rains. Trudeau was in the bow, reaching far over the gunnel to draw the canoe out into the current to avoid a rock outcropping. As Trudeau pulled out, the boat was caught for a moment in suspension between powerful cross-currents that he did not have the strength to counteract. The canoe flipped, sending Trudeau headfirst into the rapids.

The former prime minister was fortunate. He was travelling with one of the best paddlers in the country, the founder of Black Feather Wilderness Adventures and the Trailhead outfitting store in Ottawa, and Schaber was able to clutch the back of Trudeau's life jacket. Oliver, who had been travelling in another canoe behind, was then able to grab Schaber and help stop the two from being swept downstream. Trudeau had already slipped below the crushing waves. He was fine, though, but very quiet around the fire that evening. His dignity, thought Oliver, had been badly wounded. He had been too weak to prevent the canoe from turning over on them. Three years later, at the age of eighty, Pierre Trudeau would be dead.

It is a rare, perhaps even unique, whitewater paddler, however, who has not dumped in rapids. Tom Thomson did on his very first trip to the north country, in 1912, when he and co-worker Ben Jackson tried to shoot a small run on the Aubinadong River. Thomson lost all his photographs of the trip apart from two rolls of shot film they were able to recover from the bottom.

The first time you go over is terrifying. Hell, the next time you dump is terrifying. There is a strange sense of helplessness, of insignificance, when a turbulent river tosses you, your canoe, your packs and, usually, your paddling partner as easily as a cat cuffs a small toy. Time seems to slow and yet, even if you had all the time in the world, you can do nothing to prevent the canoe from going under or over. If the canoe hits sideways into a rock, it can "wrap" around that rock in an instant, literally throwing its cargo into the foam on both sides.

Once into the water, especially on rivers like the Petawawa where jagged rocks lurk at every depth, a dumped paddler wearing a flotation device needs to let go and turn so that the head is up and protected, the backside is down and the feet float in the lead, the theory being that it is easier to kick away from danger than chance hitting your head, the reality being that it is better to come to shore with a sore bum than a busted knee or ankle—or, worse yet, a banged head or broken shoulder. Letting the current take you until the water is still enough to allow an easy paddle or walk to shore is much preferable to trying to fight the panic that a first-timer invariably feels with that shock of cold water and the frightening, surprising strength of the current that grabs you and hurls you downstream.

Graham and Malcolm Fraser were in the final canoe coming down Five Mile Rapids. They were close enough to see the flat, calm waters ahead that would take them through a long series of twists, turns, small swifts and flatwater before reaching pullout at McManus Lake.

Perhaps they were momentarily distracted—it happens to us all—but whatever happened, they failed to turn enough to slip down through a small opening between large rocks into the line the rest had taken. Their canoe bucked in the fast-moving water, cracked off the largest rock and over they went; packs, paddles, Malcolm's jacket, water bottles and Malcolm, all bobbed to the surface—but no Graham.

In a moment of bizarre irony, on the final test of the Petawawa, he had dumped in the same waters that had taken his father's life.

His size thirteen sneakers had wedged between floor and seat as he had, as instructed, kneeled for navigating through any fast water. He could not pull free, could only fall into the roaring, surging water as panic tore hard at his mind

But then, suddenly, both feet popped loose. He turned in the water and worked his way to shore, soaked but relieved. He scrambled onto the rocks, the waters of the Petawawa falling like rain from his clothes, with a look of shock and disbelief on his face.

While the others worked to free the canoe from where the rocks had snared it and retrieve the paddles and water bottles that had floated downstream, Graham gathered himself before changing into dry clothes on a rock-strewn shore littered with bright red cardinal flowers.

"My feet were caught under the seat," he said over the roar of the water. "As I hit the water, I thought, 'Well, this may be the way that it ends.'"

Just as, forty-five years earlier, it had for his father.

"But it didn't," he said, smiling at his momentary scare. "It ended happily."

The year after Blair Fraser's death, brothers John and Graham Fraser edited a collection of their father's work, which they entitled *Blair Fraser Reports* after the column and radio show that had made him a household name in Canada. They included, curiously, a piece that had never appeared in *Maclean's* or been broadcast over the airwaves.

It was, instead, a talk he had given to a Unitarian congregation at the Church of the Messiah west of downtown Montreal. Founded in 1842, it was the church the Fraser family had attended when they lived in the city for a half dozen years in the 1940s. Blair spoke to the gathering on Sunday, July 2, 1967, the day after Canada had celebrated its one hundredth birthday. He entitled his talk "A Centennial Sermon."

He spoke about human welfare and civil rights. He talked about his world travels and the extraordinary experience, only two weeks earlier, of being in Egypt and seeing the Sphinx, "the oldest surviving artifact known to us of civilized man." And then he talked about something much older, much more precious, hopefully far more lasting: the Canadian wilderness.

"Not everyone requires or responds to this experience of the cleansing wild," he told them from the pulpit. "But in a country to which almost everyone who wants to may come, and from which anyone who wants to may go, a land whose endowment of comfort will never be better than second best but whose avenue of escape to solitude will always be open, we may expect that the people who do so respond will be the ones who want to stay here.

"In that expectation lies hope. We all, I'm sure, have many hopes for Canada on this Centennial day—that she may grow, thrive, prosper in all things. To these I would add one hope more: that Canada will not so greatly grow, and not so greatly thrive, as to destroy this heritage of solitude which makes us what we are and which our children will know perhaps better than we how to value."

Forty-six years later, forty-five years after his fatal tumble down the Petawawa River's Rollway Rapids, those children—son, grandsons and great-grandson—finally knew exactly what Blair Fraser meant.

6

"A PLACE OF POWER"

In 2012, I was asked to serve as editorial consultant on a book Prime Minister Stephen Harper was writing about hockey. It was a subject that also intrigued me—the rise of the professional game from the amateur ranks more than a century ago—and I happily agreed to work with him. On occasion I would visit Parliament Hill and we would meet in his office.

Stephen Harper is a punctual man, but he is also prime minister of Canada. Scheduled meetings don't always happen when the Peace Tower clock strikes the designated moment. As I waited in one of the chairs just outside his second-floor Centre Block office, a security guard or two would always be near. There would be some small talk, but mostly we would stare at walls and staircases and wait for the time to pass.

Hanging on the stone wall in front of me, on temporary loan from the National Gallery of Canada, was a large glass-covered painting. It is entitled *Shooting the Rapids* and dates from around 1879. The artist is Frances Anne Hopkins.

Shooting the Rapids, set on the Mattawa River, is a striking work: sixteen paddlers in a birchbark freight canoe, seven men digging hard on each side, a bow paddler attempting to draw the bow right to avoid the rocks, a helmsman standing in the stern as he deftly steers the huge canoe and its load into a black tongue of very dark and fast water that will carry them through the cascading rapids.

The painting takes a paddler's breath away.

Sitting dead centre in the canoe is a couple clearly different from those paddlers doing the work. The man and woman are wearing fashionable hats and upper-class clothes. The woman seems so calm and content that she might just as easily be sitting in church in her Easter finery rather than challenging jagged rocks and fast water, with stacks and sous holes seemingly but a stroke—either by paddle or by coronary—away.

The woman in the canoe is Frances Anne Hopkins herself. The painter is seated beside her husband, Edward Martin Hopkins, private secretary to Sir George Simpson, governor of the Hudson's Bay Company. The Hopkins family was very distinguished back in England. Edward was uncle to Gerard Manley Hopkins, who would go on to become one of Great Britain's most renowned poets. Frances came from the upper-class Beechey family and, like so many of her relatives—Sir William Beechey was a member of the Royal Academy of Arts—was a gifted and dedicated artist.

Frances married Edward Hopkins in London in 1858. He was a widower with three children, and they soon settled in Lachine, near Montreal, where the company's headquarters and warehouse were located. She would bear Hopkins five more children, two of whom would die in infancy. She was not a typical homemaker, often accompanying her husband on trips inland, going north by freight canoe up the Ottawa River, west across the Mattawa River, Lake Nipissing and the French River to the upper Great Lakes. She would sketch and later complete large canvasses, of which "Shooting the Rapids" is best known.

What sets the paintings of Frances Anne Hopkins apart is their absence of romance, or bucolic idyll, as was then the fashion among British landscape artists. Her sketches and larger works from her time in Canada seem as real as if a photographer were standing on the river rocks to capture the moment the canoe breaks over the curling rapids. Her depiction of paddle strokes is uncannily accurate, her ability to give life to faces and action to limbs remarkable. The body language is exquisite and precise.

It is fortuitous for Canadian history that Hopkins was here at just the right time to record the passing of an era. The large freighter canoes were then being phased out in favour of steamboats, horse-drawn wagons and, most significantly, the new rail lines spreading across the young Dominion.

Her work was known but hardly celebrated. She lived to the age of eighty-one, dying in relative obscurity in London in early 1919. It took another seventy-one years before any gallery thought to mount a comprehensive exhibition of her work.

But then, the combination of women and canoeing has too often been an afterthought.

Eighteen-year-old Frances Ramsay Simpson, fresh from the society salons of England, preceded Frances Anne Hopkins by more than three decades as a white woman canoeing the wilderness waterways of North America. She was the new bride of George Simpson, the imperious governor of the Hudson's Bay Company. The new Mrs. Simpson and her travelling companion, Catherine McTavish, wife of the company's chief factor, John George McTavish, left Lachine with the governor, the Simpsons' servant and two canoes, each manned by fifteen voyageurs.

"Our canoe," Mrs. Simpson wrote in a later narrative, "a most beautiful craft, airy and elegant beyond description, was thirty-five feet in length. . . . We started, the voyageurs singing, and the Canoe almost flying through the water—the motion is perfectly easy, & in fine weather it is the most delightful mode of travelling that can be imagined."

Frances Anne Hopkins put herself in several paintings, but never with a paddle in her hands. In one magnificent canvas, "Canoe Manned by Voyageurs Passing a Waterfall," painted in 1869, she holds a large white water lily on her lap, likely plucked from the water by one of the company employees. It is doubtful that she, like Mrs. Simpson, ever paddled a stroke.

Aboriginal women had been canoeing rapids—paddle in hand, paddle in water—since long before the first European set foot in North America. So gifted and experienced was a young Dene woman known as Thanadelthur, born in the Chipewyan nation in the late 1690s, that even as a teenager, she is said to have helped early Hudson's Bay Company traders by mapping out numerous rivers that she had travelled. Having once been captured by the Crees, she was also able to use her considerable language and persuasive skills to help the Hudson's Bay Company forge a peace between the Cree and Chipewyans that allowed for safe travel in the far Northwest. Thanadelthur may still have been but a teenager when she fell ill with a virus and died unexpectedly in February of 1717.

Hopkins may have left the paddling to others, but she is renowned by canoeists for the accuracy of her whitewater portrayals in oil on canvas, just as another European woman, Anna Brownell Jameson, would record the experience in words. In 1837, the year before Frances Anne Beechey was born, Jameson went down the St. Mary's Falls Rapids—but again, she did so without having a paddle in her hands.

Jameson wrote about her adventure in *Winter Studies and Summer Rambles in Canada*, an account of the nine months she spent in Canada in 1836 to 1837. She was forty-two years old when she came out to the North American colony in an effort to reconcile her disintegrating marriage to Robert Jameson, then serving as attorney-general of Upper Canada. The reconciliation failed, but she did get a bestselling book out of her trip.

Having watched native guides pick their way down the nearly mile-long rapids of St. Mary's Falls, Jameson insisted on going along for the ride. She sat on a mat—native style, as the canoes had no "seats"—and held on as her guide "danced them through" the rocks and ledges on a seven-minute run. She said the natives gave her a name after the trip, Wah-sah-ge-wha-no-qua, which meant "woman of the bright foam" in Chippewa.

"I can truly say," she wrote, "I had not even a momentary sensation of fear, but rather of giddy, breathless, delicious excitement. . . . When I reached *home*, my good friends were not less delighted at my exploits: they told me I was the first European female who had ever performed it, and assuredly I shall not be the last. I recommend it as an exercise before breakfast. Two glasses of champagne could not have made me more tipsy and self-complacent!"

Friends certainly thought Fannie Case must be drunk, given the ideas that were racing through her head like a runaway canoe in the rapids. Case was a high school teacher in Rochester, New York. She was also a trained psychologist and was convinced that the outdoor experience—canoe tripping, paddling, making decisions—was critical to the healthy mental and physical development of young people. Boys had their Scouts and camps, but girls had precious little to choose from that was physically demanding and out of doors. So she decided to start up an all-girls summer camp dedicated to, of all things, wilderness survival.

In 1906, the year she turned thirty-eight, Fannie Case brought a small number of local Rochester girls by train to the Ontario bush. They set up a summer camp on Ahmic Lake, which is part of the Magnetawan River system that carries water from the Algonquin Highlands to Georgian Bay. She didn't find the area "wild" enough, however, and in 1908 relocated the camp to Cache Lake, still along the train line but deep in the heart of the then fifteen-year-old Algonquin Park. Here she established Northway Lodge, which remains active to this day.

This was no picnic ground. She chose a high point running north and south, so there would be sunrise to one side, sunset to the other. Conditions were extremely rustic: tents, toilets in the woods, a paddle, a pail and a short hike to get water from a spring across the bay. And "Miss Case" could be a stern taskmaster, assigning the girls to jobs from clearing the land to running the kitchen tent. She made sure that campers learned how to survive in the wilderness with only canoe, paddles, tent, some supplies, essential camping equipment and their wits. She once arranged for one troublesome, whining camper to "be lost in the woods by herself for a bit," and believed the frightening experience had dramatically changed the girl for the better. Case may have taken on the title of "camp director," but she was still a psychologist.

In a short memoir she wrote not long before her death in 1955, Fannie Case recalled those early years and the philosophy behind her unique camp. "Starting our first year with emphasis on canoe trips," she wrote, "we thought best to live in much the same way at camp as on camping trips, so that the group would be better prepared for trips away. We were sure that best results would come from living the pioneer life."

Over the decades, Camp Northway for girls aged seven to sixteen—a later camp for boys, Wendigo, would follow—changed and slightly modernized. But I can recall going into the camp in the 1950s when my cousin Jake Pigeon would deliver supplies to Northway and it was nowhere near as modern and comfortable as other summer camps nearby, such as Taylor Statten or Tanamakoon. It remained rustic. Case insisted there be no cozy retreats where a young girl might tuck herself away with a book—not that she was against books: "But the open book of nature was before us all in all of its glory, to be met first-hand. How to open our eyes and ears to it is our quest."

Case began with an emphasis on canoeing and kept it there. "Canoe trips," she wrote, "are the crowning experience of camping in the country. There is a tang in the deep and lasting memories of camp that undoubtedly is derived largely from this mettle-testing experience. Camp directors in Algonquin and similar country know this to be true. The trips mean hard work, and everybody works (that is an unwritten law). Arms ache but keep on paddling. Three campers in each canoe, and two canoes. Next day arms are stronger and want to keep going into the unknown, new glimpses always ahead. They are young explorers. Every girl carries her own pack, not too heavy, twelve pounds for beginners, twenty to twenty-five later in the season for strong campers."

If the young campers complained, their protestations fell on deaf ears. There would be no shirking of duty, no stragglers, no shortcuts. But it worked, and it held such magical powers over those first young women who set out in their canoes that eventually their daughters came to Northway, then their granddaughters, and today there are campers who can trace their Northway lineage back to their great-grandmothers.

The notion that wilderness canoeing is somehow a "man's" game, some machismo, muscular, masculine enterprise that requires bulging biceps and hair on the chest has long been a challenge for women in the wilderness. When those four city-dwellers set out on a whitewater trip in *Deliverance*—a 1970 novel by American poet James Dickey and a 1972 Hollywood movie starring Burt Reynolds, among others—they were deliberately breaking contact with anything to do with domesticity. As Dickey wrote, "The flight into nature becomes a flight into a closed masculine world where a man can recover the heroic dimension normally lost to him."

Mercifully, such exclusive thinking has long and successfully been challenged by women of virtually every age.

"It is a nice thing to be a lady canoeist," E. Pauline Johnson wrote in *Saturday Night* magazine in 1891. "All the men in camp revere you, and if you are a very good paddler, they may do you the honour of imposing on you."

"If a man can do this, why, under modified conditions, cannot a woman?" Ella Walton asked in an 1899 issue of *Rod and Gun*. A good camping trip into the wilderness, she argued, was an ideal way for "weary mothers, energetic housekeepers, brain-workers and fagged-out society women" to get a break from their daily obligations and spend some healthy time free of "mental worry."

There were other women, however, who felt that "modified conditions" were not necessary. If a man can do this, they said, so, too, can we. What made men special that only they could enjoy "roughing it"? There was nothing.

"When the rivers are freed from their icy chains, the innermost depths of my being respond to the calls of the wilderness," Martha Craig wrote in 1905 about her summer outings in Labrador. "Tell me where anything comes from, and I will tell you whither it is going. Things animate and inanimate move in circles. In their course they change their identity from time to time, but each change is only a step on the journey back. I go back to nature because that is where I came from, that is where we all came from. We are all on the way back, but at different stages on the journey."

Often sexist, often nonsensical, the debate over whether canoeing was right for women went on for decades and involved everything from appropriate clothing to how girl campers should portage a canoe—three carrying together—while boy campers were expected to throw a canoe over their heads and portage like a man. Over time, however, women broke through all the preconceptions, including any notion that, at the very least, they should never head out alone.

"In the act of going out alone," Ruth Goldman of the Canadian Outward Bound Wilderness School once wrote, "we are claiming wilderness as a place for women. We are taking up space, breaking traditional stereotypes of where and how women should be confined. Wilderness can easily be a very safe place for women. There are no men (women's greatest predator)."

In the fall of 1926, a young woman named Gertrude Bernard of Mattawa, Ontario, headed up the Jumping Caribou River north of Lake Superior with a much older Englishman the twenty-year-old barely knew but believed herself so in love with she would follow him anywhere. The Englishman was Archie Belaney, who would reinvent himself as Grey Owl and, in turn, recast her as "Anahareo," drawing on her partial

Mohawk heritage. As mentioned in an earlier chapter, Belaney had no native heritage at all, but would successfully transform himself from an educated man born into a genteel family in Hastings, England, into an "Indian" who would fool the entire world right up until his death.

It was a long and arduous trip up the Jumping Caribou. No romantic evening paddle—Bernard faced day after day of Archie lecturing the young woman on how to paddle, how not to paddle, how to stay in unison with his stern paddle. He had no use for idle chatter. He insisted on doing the carrying, alone, over portages while she walked silently and obediently alongside.

Finally, she had had enough. "Archie made it clear that he felt women should not attempt what was clearly a man's job," Bernard's biographer, Kristin Gleeson, wrote. "Those sentiments were a red rag to a bull for Gertie. Impulsively she launched the canoe, headed for the rapids and plunged into them shooting each swell. It was a foolish and risky move and by mere luck she survived unharmed, with the canoe intact. . . . But Anahareo had made her point."

It was a point that Joanne Kates never had to make. She was born into a world where the canoe remains the preferred form of transportation and portages are equally peopled with working, carrying women and men. To the director of Algonquin Park's Camp Arowhon, the canoe is not just beautiful, not just functional, but a significant statement.

In a lovely essay that Kates wrote for *The Globe and Mail*, the newspaper she long served as restaurant critic, she talked about learning to paddle from the master himself, Omer Stringer. She had been a teenager, he a senior citizen, yet he had taught her the essential strokes, the pry and the inside draw, until she, too, could perform "ballet" on the waters of Teepee, Joe and Canoe lakes, all quickly accessible from her parents' camp.

Her knees creak a bit, she wrote in the year 2000, "but I celebrate that I can canoe at fifty; better, I can still canoe-trip. I can portage, I can paddle hard, I can cook outside, do my business in the treasure chest, and I can even sleep on the ground (with a little help from my Therm-a-Rest)." If it all takes a little longer, so what? What's the hurry anyway? If packs are harder to carry, then she makes two portage runs instead of one. If canoes grow heavier, there are lighter ones being produced every year.

"For me," Kates wrote, "a middle-aged woman, paddling a canoe is also a place of power. Paddling along, you know your luck as a person who is no longer young. More aggressive sporting pursuits close their doors to us as we pass 50. And indeed I am creakier, more cautious, less agile than I used to be getting in and out of canoes. But once settled in my wood and canvas canoe, I can still fly. . . . The world of the canoe is a place of beauty and grace, the most direct path I know to the home of the soul."

Olivia Chow would surely agree. In the summer of 2011, her husband, Jack Layton, federal leader of the New Democratic Party of Canada, passed away from cancer only months after leading his party to Official Opposition status in the House of Commons. Given that her fondest memories of being together had been on canoe trips down the Nahanni and Alsek rivers in the Far North, the following summer, 2012, Chow set out to remember her late husband with a journey down the Mountain River in the Northwest Territories.

It was a therapeutic experience for the then NDP Member of Parliament. She, too, wrote about it in *The Globe and Mail*. With professional guides, she paddled through seven canyons and dozens of fast-moving rapids.

"The intensity of the ride," she wrote, "the quiet yet grand splendour of the North and the material comforts in the harsh and wild environs had all succeeded in helping me look forward with renewed confidence. Would I be able to conquer the next set of rapids without capsizing?

"Over the course of 12 days of wonder on Mountain River, I survived. I know I can go on. I know I can tackle whatever comes my way."

Late in the summer of 2003 I received a small package in the mail. It contained a letter from an eighty-eight-year-old woman I had met a number of times many years earlier in Algonquin Park, though I could not claim to have known her well. The letter accompanied a small memoir Esther S. Keyser had written with her son John S. Keyser: *Paddling My Own Canoe: The Story of Algonquin Park's First Female Guide.* The sepia cover showed a canvas-covered cedar strip canoe holding a large backpack, and standing beside the canoe, laughing, an exquisitely beautiful young woman in pigtails.

Esther?

The things you don't know about people you think you know . . . To me, Esther Keyser was a Smoke Lake cottager and a much older woman from my childhood who simply got older. Her memoir certainly set me straight. Esther, it turned out, had been one of Fannie Case's early converts. She had been born in Fredonia, New York, and had come to the girls' camp at Northway Lodge the summer she was twelve years old. It changed her life—but not immediately.

She went on to college and graduated in fine arts. She married badly to a man who would rather spend his holiday on a cruise than help Esther with the rustic little cabin she insisted on building on Smoke Lake, not far from Fannie Case's camp in Algonquin Park. Her husband liked and valued nice things—clothes, cars, trips—while Esther practised one of Fannie's favourite sayings: "The experience of being without things is in itself an exciting adventure." The marriage was doomed and soon over.

Esther was able to spend the entire summer at Smoke Lake by taking on guiding jobs. She guided for six summers, charging forty-eight dollars for a two-week trip—her party usually six people in two canoes, sometimes nine in three—and was able to save enough to pay off the five-hundred-dollar loan she had taken out to build the cabin.

Esther soon found the love of her life in Joe Keyser, a fellow educator and then director of athletics at the college in Fedonia. They were a perfect match from the beginning. They married, and Joe and Esther honeymooned by taking an arduous canoe trip, without guides, down the Missinaibi River to James Bay. Early into the trip, they capsized in rapids, collected their packs safely and decided to repair the canoe in the morning—only to discover come dawn that Esther had suffered a miscarriage, not even aware that she was pregnant. Three weeks later, they paddled into Moose Factory, a bit the worse for wear, but in good spirits.

Joe Keyser would go on to become director of athletics at the State University of New York. Esther was active in the Girl Guides movement. They spent every summer at her little cabin on Smoke Lake, where they taught their three children and subsequently eleven grandchildren—there were seventeen grandchildren at the time of her death in 2005—how to paddle and camp.

Esther called Joe "Minawaska." They often shouted, *"Au large!"* at the start of a day's paddle, the phrase taken from the cry of the voyageurs—"Au large! Envoyez au large!"—which Joe had once come across in an essay and took to mean "good luck" and "good journey."

"Au large" would be the last words Esther would speak to Joe before he died, fifty-one years after that incredible first trip down the Missinaibi River.

In the summer of 2001, at the age of eighty-six, Esther Keyser, retired guide, went on what she was sure would be her final canoe trip. She knew she was getting old for such strenuous adventure. Three summers earlier, while about to land at the gorgeous, pine-scented portage that runs between North Tea Lake and Manitou Lake in the northwest corner of the park, she had fallen backwards out of her canoe and into the water. She struggled out onto the shore and stripped to the buff while unpacking dry clothes—only to be forced to quickly cover up with towels when a group from a boys' camp came paddling up to the same portage. Esther thought the scene was hilarious, but the reality was that she no longer felt completely at ease in the wild as she always had before.

"I am reaching the end of my last portage," she wrote in her charming memoir. "My body, like an old canoe, is wearing out and needs frequent repairs, patching and special handling."

And yet, her love of being in the wild, even if it meant a humiliating fall from a canoe she had once mastered, still shines through. "I am an old woman with weakening eyesight, failing hearing, slowing reaction time and diminishing stamina," she wrote. "But, in spite of the pains and discomforts, I prefer being in my canoe, sleeping on the ground, cooking over a campfire and walking over portages to anything else in the world."

In the small cabin on the western edge of Algonquin Park that my wife, Ellen, inherited from her parents, we keep a journal of what happens each summer on Camp Lake. I see that on a hot August week just before the turn of this century, we headed off on a micro-canoe trip with two of our daughters, Christine and Jocelyn, and a youngster from down the lake, Shauna Kearns. If the cabin is escape from the city, a paddle can sometimes be a welcome escape from the lake.

In two canoes and a kayak, the five of us set off on a sunny afternoon to paddle down Smoke Lake, passing by Esther Keyser's log cabin, and then portaged into the string of pretty lakes that lie south of Smoke and loop back toward Cache Lake, where Fannie Case established Northway Lodge in 1908.

It was a simple trip—short portages, easy paddles, no whitewater—in which the most memorable event was the evening the three young women spent watching a large garter snake ingest a leopard frog twice the size of the snake's own head. And yet, looking back these years, I cannot help but wonder if Shauna fell under the spell of the women adventurers who had preceded her along this very same route.

She was twelve years old when her parents, John Kearns and Alannah Campbell, sent her off to Camp Wanapitei on Northern Ontario's magnificent Lake Temagami. The camp dates back to 1931 and, under the Hodgins family, has grown over the years into the premier canoe-tripping operation in North America.

That summer, Shauna went on her first real canoe trip—she had earlier gone overnight only at another summer camp—setting out from Wanapitei and returning to it six days later. "I have very little memory of that first trip," she says today. "I remember rain and marshmallows, but nothing else."

Since then, this petite young woman from Toronto has become, in a fashion, a canoe explorer who has paddled as much of the country as any of the sixteen coureurs de bois paddling Frances Anne Hopkins and her husband down those rapids. Her first long trip was James Bay to Moosonee via the Kesagami River, a twenty-four-day trip. Two years later, she spent fifty-two days on the Rackla River, the Bonnet Plume, Peel and Mackenzie, finally stopping at Inuvik.

Shauna showed such promise as a camp paddler on those trips that Wanapitei put her on staff as a full-time group leader on subsequent outings: nineteen days paddling from Lake Temagami down the fabulous, fast Dumoine River to the Ottawa River; nineteen days taking young paddlers down the Coulonge River; twenty-four days down the Kattawagami River to James Bay and on to Moosonee; fifty-four days along the Tsichu, Keele, Natla, Ravens Throat, Redstone and Mackenzie rivers to Norman Wells; fifty-two days along the Great Bear River, across Great Bear Lake to the Camsell River, the Hepburn and Coppermine to Kugluktuk.

Shauna and Tim Leckie, her male co-leader, were responsible for a dozen young paddlers on that trip down the Coppermine. She had to calculate the food required for the entire trip, as there would be no drop-offs, no caches, no opportunities to purchase additional supplies. They carried a satellite telephone for emergency purposes only, and the sole contact the group had was an occasional satellite GPS signal to give their position so that the camp and their parents could follow the trippers' progress.

"A big part of this trip," she says, "was realizing that many southern tripping organizations are short-sighted. We often make the mistake of just sort of 'passing through' up there. Before this particular trip we would end up in a northern community and maybe buy a bunch of food there but not really make an effort to connect to the people who live there year-round.

"Watching these kids interact with the Dene people over the course of two weeks while we went up the Great Bear River and crossed Great Bear Lake was amazing. In the evening, community members would come to our sites along the river. We'd share a pot of tea or maybe a side of smoked trout they'd bring with them. We quickly realized how ignorant we'd been before—taking pride, really, in seeing no one in the North. We learned so much from the people who actually call it home."

They were invited into the village of Deline, a Dene First Nations village on Great Bear Lake where the first language is North Slavey. It may have been here where Canada's national game was first played, as the diaries of Sir John Franklin, who froze to death in search of the Northwest Passage, make reference to his men having "skated and played hockey" on nearby Little Lake. Elders in the village recount a tale of white men "floating on ice with sticks in their hands while hitting at a rock."

The Wanapitei paddlers were welcomed with a village feast and some were taught "hand games"—a complicated entertainment, actually a gambling game, in which teams of eight attempt to determine in which hand an opponent is holding a small object. Once the paddlers had moved on to their next camping spot, "sailing" several kilometres down the lake by holding makeshift sails up to catch the prevailing wind, they were surprised to see that they were being "chased" by villagers in boats with large Canadian flags streaming behind them. For the better part of two weeks—as the campers completed their strategic point-to-point crossing of the vast inland lake and headed up the river—the people of Deline made evening treks to join the campers over campfires and meals, an extraordinary cultural exchange the likes of which Shauna Kearns had never before experienced. The campers came from a world where food comes from the grocery store and were now in a world where food comes from the land. The Dene, it turned out, were also noticing the cultural differences.

"They kept asking us, 'So, why were these children chosen to go on this great adventure?'" Shauna remembers. "And we had to say, 'Well, actually, they weren't chosen . . .'"

The cost to the parents of the children "chosen" to paddle the Coppermine was approximately eight thousand dollars. This, in fact, touches on one of the awkward truths of canoeing. Those who get to enjoy life at its simplest, its most basic, a life without electricity, running water, television, motorized vehicles, cellphones and Internet, without even a roof over their heads, tend to come from privilege. It costs a great deal to paddle the Nahanni; it costs a great deal to send your child to a summer camp where love of canoeing might be ingrained for life. Those who would argue, as this writer has so often, that each child in Canada should, at some point, be sent on a mandatory canoe trip in the Canadian wilderness to learn teamwork, sharing and co-operation and develop a lifelong love of nature, never get around to what it might cost. We are fools to think schools or government might provide such an adventure, but we are well-meaning fools who truly believe in what we preach.

This matter of privilege is something Shauna has often considered while leading groups of young paddlers born to fortunate circumstance. "I recently heard someone say that kids these days don't really have enough grit," she says. "And it made me think about my high school experience and how lucky I was. I attended a fantastic private school and felt deeply supported by my teachers. I was made to feel I could achieve great things. I feel very lucky that I lived in such a supportive environment at school and at home. As odd as it may sound, canoe tripping made me realize that I'm not special, an awareness I feel equally grateful for.

"You get on a canoe trip and realize, 'Whoa, this is really *hard!*' Everyone works hard and nobody is getting any kind of recognition. It's just expected that you pull your weight. And you're not going to be told that you're special. The environment around you is what's special and that's what is to be respected. You can't control it, because you aren't as powerful an individual as you might think. You're just a part of it—and you feel so totally small."

There were times when that smallness hit home. There was the reality of bears. The Dene visitors had asked one evening where the paddlers kept their gun. When told they had no weapons, the Dene returned the next day with a magnificent rifle, its stock ornately carved, and handed the rifle and a box of shells over to the two guides. They never used it and, at trip's end, shipped it back to Deline.

The Dene also taught them to have an even greater respect for their surroundings. "They emphasized that in order for us to have a successful trip," Shauna says, "that we'd have to make offerings to the river. They said if you take a fish, you have to give something back. We became much more spiritual on the trip than we had been before. We made tobacco offerings. If we caught fish, we would leave a piece of bread on the water. I don't really know what to say about it, but tapping into that made us feel a sense of protection."

The fifteen-kilometre crossing of a wide bay on Great Bear Lake—the fourth-largest body of water in North America, eighth-largest lake in the world—proved an enormous challenge, as once the group began the crossing, they were committed. Weather can shift quickly and dramatically in the North, and they had to wait for calm, determine that the calm would last the several hours required for the crossing of the bay, and then strike out, never slacking the pace until, together, they reached their destination. As the Dene had taught them, they made a tobacco offering before setting out, moving swiftly and safely across the immense bay to a campsite on the other side.

If there was some sort of mystical protection, real or imagined, it came again when the group reached the Rocky Defile Rapids along the Coppermine, a rumpled stretch of whitewater that runs and twists for nearly two kilometres through high canyon walls. Shauna and her co-leader scouted the rapids from high above and thought the run looked doable. When they reached the end of the portage, however, they came upon a memorial for a couple who had died there in the summer of 1972.

The tragic couple had drowned on the same August day the paddlers from Wanapitei would be chancing the rapids. In the morning, their tents were covered in frost. They did not feel right and decided, instead, to portage around Rocky Defile.

"The water was so cold and it was so remote," Shauna concluded. "Rapids we would just shoot in Ontario or Quebec we couldn't take the risk of running up there."

The paddlers returned safely, without incident. Following Wanapitei tradition, they did not drive into the camp after their long flight back but instead once again piled themselves and equipment into canoes on the shores of Lake Temagami and paddled back to camp, parents, staff and other campers cheering and applauding as they passed under the bridge that joins the shore to a nearby island. After fifty-two days of paddling through the Northwest Territories, they were returning as different people, changed forever by the experience.

"There's something you see on those long trips that you don't see on younger trips," Shauna says. "I don't know if it has to do with age. Maybe a combination of age and the longevity of the trip. They bring home a maturity that is hard to believe. Every kid there has a difficult dynamic or history with someone else. They come on this trip, and they somehow make it work."

Tempers are shorter on short outings, she has found. People snap easily and are more impatient if there is a sense that you must be somewhere this day rather than, as happens in the north, you just make camp wherever you happen to be when the day is done.

As for romance, it sometimes happens, but at times love has its own different dynamic. "When we did the Mackenzie trip in 2011," Shauna says, "my co-guide, Toban, and I knew two of the kids were getting pretty close. But they came to us separately, on different occasions, and told us, 'We really like each other but we don't want to compromise any others on the trip—so we'll just wait." Two years later the young couple was still together.

Shauna says there is solitude with the group as well as solitude alone—no cellphones or tablets to lose oneself in or hide in. "It ties in with the whole stripping away of materialism," she adds. "I have always found it important to find time to be alone, even when you're out there with a group. We often have shorter days on the water just so the kids can have some time off and get away and think by themselves."

The end of a long trip is always emotional: "Time always passes faster than you think it will. They've been waiting for years for this trip—and now it's done. I remember going off to school right after my first long one, when I was eighteen. It's done and most depart for college or university and it's a feeling like a rite of passage. *Now what? Life after this trip—what does it hold?*"

This concept of "a rite of passage" is apt. One of the young paddlers cried herself to sleep each night for the first twelve days, yet by the end of the trip was telling her parents she had an "incredible" time. For most such paddlers, a trip ends and there is calmness, there is fulfillment, there is confidence. You are at peace with yourself and, equally important, at peace with your surroundings.

"How to hold on to that?" Shauna wonders. "Even on shorter trips there is this feeling that you get. How do you hold on to that when you go back to the city, because I enjoy the city, too. But how do you keep it with you?"

"I don't know the answer to that."

A decade or so ago, Carleton University in Ottawa asked me to serve as a casual adviser in a student-mentoring program. One arts student, Kristina Leidums, was eager for any advice she could get on what she hoped would be her future career: writing. But I suspected that may not have been the main reason she had connected with me: she could also hitch a ride home once in a while to her little hometown, Huntsville, where we, too, had roots and family.

First impressions, as Lemony Snicket has said, are often entirely wrong. I met a very soft-spoken young woman who said she hoped one day to be a published poet. With her long brown hair, slim arms and quiet demeanour, she seemed perfectly constructed for the coffee-house circuit and a life where adventure enough would be found in the alphabet. I simply did not, at first, see the daring voyageur that lay hidden beyond that erroneous first impression.

That she was interested in canoeing was quickly evident on a ride back to Huntsville that took us through Algonquin Park and included a stop for ice cream at the Portage Store at Canoe Lake. There, while looking at the historic plaque erected in memory of Tom Thomson, who died there in the summer of 1917, she told me that she and her brother Erich were thinking of travelling by canoe from their home in Huntsville to Georgian Bay.

"I've always loved reading about the explorers," she says. "The voyageur lifestyle always put dreamy notions in my head, for some odd reason, about life in the bush and travelling on the water. I've sometimes said that I might have actually been a short, stout Frenchman in a past life!"

She devoured books on modern-day homesteaders while growing up, dreaming of one day living in a remote cabin in the deep woods. She discovered canoeing at the age of ten when the Huntsville Youth Club went on a small outing in Haliburton, where they camped on an island. She paddled the club's canoes at Mary Lake and paddled the family's red fibreglass canoe at nearby Arrowhead Provincial Park. With a group of high school friends, she began exploring other parks—Algonquin and Killarney—and was soon a confident tripper in search of greater adventure.

"At some point in high school," she says, "my bedroom started to look like an outfitter's, as I preferred to store boxes of camping dishes, bundles of ropes, packs, maps and assorted camping necessities there, rather than in the basement. I wasn't a 'gearhead,' but just loved to dream about the next trip and having all those gritty, campfire-smelling reminders around me in between trips sure helped."

Canoeing fed something inside her. It was something she craved, something she came to consider almost spiritual. "I know of no other feeling," she says, "that is so great as having the time to drift in a canoe alone on a warm day, puttering around the end of a lake and watching . . . noticing birds, bugs, waves, ridges of maples and birches in the distance. I can be sitting, in body, on a mountainside in B.C., with my mind canoeing on a dark Ontario lake surrounded by hardwood ridges. I feel totally at peace and in my element sitting at a campsite after a long day of canoeing, watching crayfish in the shallows, fire crackling, sun setting . . ."

Once in university, she began looking for summer jobs that would involve canoe tripping. The first one she landed involved taking twelve- to fifteen-year-olds on a five-day trek down the French River. She misread her map, leading the kids into a small outlet that dead-ended in a bay, forcing the youngsters to spend the night with their tents haphazardly set up on a rocky island and regroup the next day. "It was a reality check," she laughed.

Kristina and her brother Erich set out in the summer of 2006 from Huntsville. They paddled down the Muskoka River that splits the town of Huntsville, over the Port Sydney Rapids and across Lake Muskoka to the Moon River and on down to Georgian Bay. It took them nine days and involved thirty-one portages, the most unusual among them when brother and sister carried the family's red fibreglass canoe up Manitoba Street, the main throughway of Bracebridge, holding up traffic as they crossed roads to avoid the power dam.

Within a few years, Kristina was heading out on trips—both alone and with paddling and life partner Karl Sommerfeld, with whom in 2013 she would have a baby boy, Markus—that she began writing about in magazines such as *Explore*.

This young woman with the slim arms paddled down the Pigeon River and carried canoe and pack over Minnesota's nearly fourteen-kilometre Grand Portage to Lake Superior, the famous fur trade highway that even the hardy voyageurs found gruelling. In fact, she portaged forty-two kilometres, given that canoe and equipment could not all be carried at once. The carrying and walking, however, was but a small portion of the

2,400 kilometres she covered that summer from Alberta to Lake Superior, 500 kilometres canoed and portaged entirely on her own.

"I've never professed to like portaging," she wrote of that trip, "but I am bubbling over with excitement as the metres fall way. It's late August and I'm revelling in a strength I hadn't known I'd possessed."

She had not intended to do so much of the trip on her own. The woman friend she started out paddling with unfortunately had to bow out after six hundred kilometres when a nagging back injury worsened. Nine days into the trip, it seemed it was already over, but Kristina's family back in Huntsville encouraged her to press on, even if it would have to be solo.

"I've always been fascinated by the tales of adventurers and explorers like David Thompson," she wrote in an account of the trip for *Explore*, "wondering how it felt to cross the country by canoe—and now at age 26, with eight weeks of canoe travel ahead of me, I'm about to find out. There's no-one to carry the vision of this iconic Canadian dream through but myself.

"I have butterflies in my stomach as I push off into the North Saskatchewan River alone, feeling small and vulnerable in the stern of my 17.5 foot canoe. . . . I take my first tentative strokes as a solo paddler, noting how the boat responds to my steering. Questions race around my head, doing nothing to ease the jittery feeling. Can I do this? Do I even want to? The river is widening, the winds worsening. Is my body strong enough to keep up the necessary 60 km/day average? I've paddled alone many times, I remind myself. I have to try, or I'll always look back on this moment and wonder."

While she paddled, she pondered the *why* of her journey. What were other people her age doing? Jobs, careers, socializing, worrying about what to wear that night rather than where they might find flat, clear ground on which to pitch a tent, reading restaurant menus rather than the instructions on the packages of freeze-dried food, young women going with the flow rather than against the current.

She had long known she was different from others her age. Friends and family talk about her "Next Corner Syndrome" and how a simple chat or the opening of a map can set off her imagination. If others wish to call it "eccentric," so be it.

"When I was going solo on the North Saskatchewan," she says," I spent one night in North Battleford in a hotel. I pulled my canoe up into the bushes, stashed my bags and hiked a couple of kilometres through a water treatment complex and into the city. The next day I got a ride back to that spot with a couple I'd met, and they literally dropped me off and watched me disappear into the bush towards the riverbank. I felt like a ghost, and always wondered what they thought about this strange girl!"

She crossed the North Saskatchewan, then took the train around the unpredictable brown waters of Lake Winnipeg. Running short on time, she felt she could not afford to wait out the steadily high winds on the sprawling, dangerous lake. From the town of Powerview-Pine Falls, she paddled down the Winnipeg River and through the chain of lakes across the international border and into the state of Minnesota.

"I began to realize the power of acting on a dream," she wrote. "I felt like I could take on the world."

She had acted on her dream but still had to come to terms with her nightmare. Being alone in the wilderness is far different by day than by night. She did have a cellphone, but often the towers were out of range and, besides, she had limited battery backup. Her family and friends were able to track her only by GPS postings.

Kristina had limited experience travelling alone. In her early twenties she had taken a three-day solo trip into nearby Algonquin Park—but this would be profoundly different. It would be for a very long time and, on occasion, in isolated and dangerous situations. She could have done with the wisdom of Bill Mason the day she set out. "All my life people have been telling me you should never travel alone," Mason would say. "But it's interesting I've never been told that by anybody who's ever done it."

Kristina had her fears, as anyone heading out alone would, and grew increasingly concerned about an incident with wildlife. Not bears, though there is always the threat of them nosing about a camp and creating havoc. Not the deer she might startle as they drank along the riverbanks, their white tails flagging as they crashed back into the woods on seeing her canoe round the bend. Not the many curious and stubborn cattle she encountered as she paddled through what seemed like endless farmland and had to search out a quiet campsite where they would not intrude.

Her fear had to do with . . . beavers.

She had heard stories of beavers clawing through the bottom of a canoe and of beavers successfully counterattacking wolves trying to make off with a kit. She worried about a beaver dragging off her paddles. She fretted while hauling her canoe and equipment over beaver dams. Fortunately she was still a couple of years away from hearing the story of the sixty-year-old fisherman in Belarus who tried to get close to a beaver for a photograph, only to have the animal attack when he came too close. The beaver's razor-sharp teeth sliced an artery in his leg and the fisherman bled to death before his travelling companion could get him to medical help.

Fears have a way of snowballing. One night, finding cleanly stripped white-as-bone aspen and alder branches cached near her campsite, she could not sleep for her "beaver paranoia." At one point she wrote, "I realize I'm being just as stubborn as those cows by not letting anyone at home know that I'm scared at night and not sleeping well . . . my tough-girl facade is crumbling."

Months later, she was able to reflect on her moments of panic. "I think I just let myself be scared," she said in an email. "When I spent 8 nights camped out alone on the North Saskatchewan River, I was afraid at night of bears, beavers, strange people. But the days were so wonderful, paddling alone, stopping on sandbars to eat and watch animals, that it made the long nights worth it.

"Storms and wind have always scared me, and I definitely get anxious. On a Prairie section by myself, the wind once got so bad I thought I was going to lose control of the boat and swamp. It was really scary. I managed to get control and get to shore, where I sat in a tiny, sweltering pump shed for a few hours waiting for the storm to pass."

Kristina had the advantage of knowing where she was. There is great comfort in that, so long as you feel safe from the storm itself, as she had in that handy pump shed. There is, on the other hand, no comfort to be found in the rising fear and consuming panic that can come with getting lost.

Justine Kerfoot knew that terror first-hand. Kerfoot, who passed away in the spring of 2001, ran Gunflint Lodge in Minnesota for half a century. She often guided, and in her 1986 memoir, *Woman of the Boundary Waters: Canoeing, Guiding, Mushing, and Surviving*, she recalled a time when she had taken a group of women tripping and told them to wait by their canoes while she scouted for the familiar blaze marks that would guide them through to the next lake. Regrettably, she set off without compass or map, certain that she remembered the trail from previous trips.

"I found a path which could be the portage," Kerfoot wrote. "It seemed familiar and yet a little different from the one I remembered. I went further and came to a large pond, which didn't look right either. Thinking the trail was further to my left, I searched in that direction. Then I turned to head back to the canoe. I found myself hopelessly lost in unfamiliar country, on an overcast day, without a compass.

"Momentarily I was overcome with utter panic. I felt nauseated as thoughts whizzed through my mind. No compass, no matches, no protection from the elements. Gone for a week and no one would make a search for several days, plus the unpredictable reaction of two novice canoeists for whom I was responsible. It took all my will power to calm down."

Desperate, Kerfoot climbed pine trees in the hope that she might see the shoreline. She whistled and, eventually, her call for help was heard and voices guided her back, safe and sound. Never again did she set out, even for the shortest trail check, without a compass.

Kristina Leidums had no such experience on her long journey, as the portages were well marked and unmistakable. Two months after setting out near the Rocky Mountains, she made it to her destination, having travelled for weeks alone and with three different partners at various times: the woman who had to quit due to back problems, her brother, who joined her for long stretches, and, for the final leg, Karl.

The sweetest moment of all, she says, was coming down the Grand Portage in Minnesota to Lake Superior. Karl let her carry the canoe alone for that final, last symbolic leg, portaging through the old fort and taking the canoe right to the edge of the water.

"I can remember smelling the cool Superior air," she recalls, "and feeling so excited to finally see the lake. But the strangest, and best, feeling was actually knowing that I didn't want to stop. After two months in a canoe (and a month solid of no days off), I had the biggest urge to keep going, to see what was around the next bay, what the next beach looked like, what it would feel like to paddle on that huge lake, ending up in Montreal, maybe the Gaspé . . . "

A child changes everything, they say. One day you are free to do as you wish, the next day you can no longer recall what freedom once was. It is as if one door slams behind you and another door opens—excitingly, filled with promise—before you. You step through as a family, not quite sure when that canoe that was so important to your very being will once again find a place.

Kristina and Karl became parents to young Markus in June of 2013. They soon found their dreams of parenthood running cross current to their dreams of continuing on from Thunder Bay to Montreal, which would be the last leg of their voyageur route. They had started their incredible journey as a couple; they would have to finish it as a family.

"I'm certain our child will be along for lots of canoe trips at an early age," said the young mother. "The idea of paddling the north shore of Superior excites me and terrifies me. I don't know if I could do that with a small child."

But it has been done.

In the summer of 2013, it had been six years since Geoff and Pam MacDonald of Calgary had set out to paddle across Canada. They began their great adventure in March 2007, from Victoria, paddled up the B.C. coastline, portaged to the Nechako River, on to the Fraser, then the Columbia. With ropes and their dog harnessed to the canoe, they dragged it and their packs up three ranges, covering more than one hundred kilometres of "mountain portaging" until they reached the Continental Divide along the B.C.-Alberta border, whereupon they cracked open a bottle of champagne, raised a toast, did a little dance and then stared east into the great unknown.

By Canada Day 2013, having paddled the north shore of Superior, which so concerned Kristina Leidums, they were travelling the calm and easy Trent-Severn Waterway, which would take them from Lake Huron to Lake Ontario. It seemed then like an eternity looking back. "The Incredible Journey" doesn't quite do it justice. Better descriptives might include: sensational, daunting, breathtaking, exhausting, obsessive, ridiculous, *insane* . . .

"Sometimes I wonder!" Pamela said over the phone that early July day.

It was not as if they had been paddling forever. The MacDonalds had stopped to have Jude three-and-a-half years earlier, and Rane two winters past. The pair of children were instantly every bit as much participants on the trip as Taq, the MacDonalds' seven-year-old 109-pound Alaskan malamute, who has chased black bears, stared down a grizzly and more than met his comeuppance when a Rocky Mountain porcupine left fifty-odd quills in his curious snout.

Time moves far more quickly than a canoe. It had never been the MacDonalds' plan to complete their trip with children, but then, what family can truly claim that everything in their lives has gone exactly according to a master plan.

"We didn't think this would take six or seven years," Geoff said. "We thought two years. When it wasn't going to be that, we thought we might as well go ahead and start a family."

"We weren't getting any younger," added Pam. "We figured we could do it."

"But until you have a baby, you just have no idea," said Geoff. "We thought we'd just work him into the trip. Not so simple."

There was not only the tent, safety equipment and packs for the paddlers, but packs required for a preschooler and then a baby. Before setting out each spring, the family would check in with a doctor who specializes in travel care. They packed certain medications as well as adult and child Epi-Pens in case of severe allergic reactions. They carried special equipment to send out their location each night for family and friends to follow, and they kept a satellite telephone for emergencies. They periodically updated their website, canoeacrosscanada.ca, with photographs and stories on the various legs of their amazing trip.

The two adults, two children, large dog and equipment were carried across the country in the family's twenty-foot Quebec-made Esquif Miramichi canoe, named the *Suzy Jack* after the boat in Stompin' Tom Connors's ode to lobster fishing, "Gumboot Cloggeroo."

Of the children, Jude was obviously the veteran, by then on his fourth straight summer of paddling across the country. He had his Matchbox toys and his Goldfish crackers and had, by this point of his life, slept almost as many nights in a tent as he had under a roof.

Rane, the baby, had no idea what a schedule was, yet he controlled it.

Their dad, Geoff MacDonald, a thirty-eight-year-old geologist, was born in Trail, British Columbia, but grew up near Orillia, Ontario. At twelve, he was sent to summer camp in Ontario but ran into a young Quebecer whose parents had sent him there deliberately in order to learn the other official language. Geoff talked his parents into giving him a similar opportunity, and after three summers at Camp-école Kéno, located in Saint-Augustin-De-Desmaures, Quebec, had become fairly proficient in French and completely proficient in canoeing.

Pamela Harrison was born in Whitehorse, Yukon, thirty-seven years ago but grew up in Fort McMurray and Provost, Alberta. Her family might well have seen this coming: when her parents tried to put her into ballet, she insisted, instead, on martial arts and today has a black belt in tae kwon do.

It was Geoff who got Pam into canoeing after they met at a volunteer ski-patrol course in 1997. Geoff had a wild dream of paddling from Rocky Mountain House to James Bay, but she extended the plan to something even wilder: crossing the country itself.

Pam was already well into her love for the wilderness, having once lived in a self-made shelter for a year to practise survival skills, but did not have Geoff's canoeing expertise. They originally sought two others to join them—there's safety in numbers—but eventually decided, on their first big whitewater adventure together (the East Pukaskwa River in Northwestern Ontario, 2003) that they could do it alone.

"He showed me how to draw and cross draw," Pam remembered of her five-minute whitewater lesson. "He said to keep an eye out for the white waves that don't move. That's where the rocks are. Don't hit any."

Married, they eventually settled in Calgary, where Geoff was able to strike a deal with a company in which he would have a significant leave in good weather. They had long been dedicating their savings and spare time to planning what would grow into a "Grand Tour" the likes of which are rarely imagined, let alone taken. They would work each winter and paddle each summer. Inspired in part by Terry Fox's iconic run in 1980 and in part by Stompin' Tom's songs of Canadian travels, they set out to see the country as the explorers first saw it.

The young couple decided they would do it on their own, financing it all and counting on a generous system of family and friends to help with flights, delivering vehicles and supplies to isolated locations, helping out and, at times, putting up.

"We didn't have a specific cause we were supporting or a sponsor," said Geoff. "Maybe we were being a bit selfish—but we wanted it to be our trip completely."

They did not see the multitude of hurdles they would face: stranded by weather and wind for a week while trying to make it around Cape

Caution north of Queen Charlotte Strait; the agonies of paddling upstream through the Fraser and Columbia; the unbelievable effort to crawl over the mountains; the winds of Lake Winnipeg, which would force them to change their planned route and instead head down the swollen Assiniboine River to the Forks of Winnipeg; the gusts that kept them windbound for two weeks on Lake Superior . . .

"The weather has been unstable at times," Pam said over the phone. But she also remembered how nature had helped, in particular after they had crested the mountains and were heading down the Bow River toward Calgary.

"We were finally going with the current."

Both said they are cautious to the extreme, especially when testing winds, waves or whitewater with children on board. Fortunately, Pam added, "We work incredibly well together in the bush."

Their one constant wildlife concern had been bears, though Taq delighted in nothing more than chasing off the more timid black bears that often haunt campsites in search of an easy meal. Grizzly bears are another matter altogether. "We yelled 'Hey Bear!' until we were hoarse," said Pam of their long, difficult portages over the mountain ranges.

One night, while camping at B.C.'s Cheslatta Lake, a grizzly came into their camp. "I thought it was Pam snoring," laughed Geoff. "Then I looked for Taq and he was just sitting there staring at the grizzly. The bear stayed around about ten minutes and then just left."

Once on the Trent system, they knew they would reach Lake Ontario. From there it would be up the Rideau Canal and River system to Ottawa, down the Ottawa River to Montreal and the St. Lawrence River and then continue through to Quebec City, where once they reached tidewaters, they would be able to say they paddled *a Mari usque ad Mare*, from sea to sea.

"This is really the last year," said Geoff. "It's time."

"It's been really hard, but it's been really rewarding," added Pam.

On August 30, 2013, the MacDonald family—parents, two youngsters, dog—paddled into Quebec City and, in the dark, docked at the Yacht Club de Québec. Family and friends hurried to greet them, talking a shocked security guard into letting them uncork champagne for a toast.

They had paddled 9,500 kilometres, from Victoria to Quebec City, Pacific saltwater to where the St. Lawrence first meets Atlantic saltwater. They had set out more than six years earlier to see the country and ended up meeting the people. People along the way invited them in, invited them to camp on their property, even sleep in their beds. One man lent them the keys to his truck. A woman in Le Pas gave them "the best gift ever"—two jars of wild strawberry jam.

"When we started out," said Pam MacDonald, "the plan was to more or less avoid people, see the landscape. But now it's almost as if we reach out for the populated places—because it's the people who make you understand and appreciate the landscape."

They had been told it could not be done and most certainly could not be done with infants and toddlers in tow—but they had done it.

"We don't know what our next adventure will be," Pam posted on their website when it was over.

"However, we do know that we aren't going to stop exploring Canada by canoe."

7

THE MAN WHO MEASURED CANADA

IF THIS WERE THE CALGARY STAMPEDE and not the Kootenay River, I would be expected to stay in the saddle for only eight seconds. But this is British Columbia's bucking bronco of a river that falls down from the Rocky Mountains a few hours to the west of Calgary, and while I am indeed seated on what looks and feels like a saddle—paddling, for the first time ever, a Tomahawk solo canoe—the count is not in seconds but in hours, the delight immeasurable.

The Kootenay is a glacial river that drops two kilometres over nearly eight hundred kilometres while running north to south, then north and south again, twice crossing the Canada-U.S. border between the Kootenay mountain range and the small city of Castlegar, at which point it then joins the mighty Columbia River.

That the Kootenay travels so incredibly far before meeting with the Columbia is surprising; in the mountains above the pulp town of Canal Flats, B.C., these two major rivers pass within a mere kilometre of each other. The name "Canal Flats" even comes from an ambitious scheme by William Adolphe Baillie-Grohman, an Austrian-born English adventurer, promoter and author of books on hunting big game, to join the two rivers.

Late in the nineteenth century, Baillie-Grohman came up with a scheme to develop the rich and temperate Columbia Valley. He and his financial backers raised money to have Chinese labourers build a canal that would join the Kootenay to the Columbia some seven hundred kilometres ahead of nature's design. If they could divert enough of the Kootenay into the Columbia, it would drain vast areas around Creston and open up new farmland. Fortunately, Baillie-Grohman's grand idea ran into complications—such as a boat getting so tightly jammed in one of the locks that that it had to be blasted free—and the project quickly fell apart, allowing the Kootenay to tumble on intact.

There is a great difference between the rivers of the east and the west. A paddler's first impression might even be that the water of each must be a different element. In the wilder rivers of the east, the water—often tea-coloured—boils white, yellow and black through rapids, where the canoeist's great fear is being thrown by the shoulder of an unseen boulder into dangerous, jagged rocks. In the west, the water is clear as polished windows and rolls and bobs over rounded boulders that form a bottom that is often so visible the paddler feels as if he or she is flying through thin air. Here, the fear lies in the water more than the rocks, the worry less about blood flowing than blood freezing.

We had come here on whim, the best excuse for any paddle. Ellen and I had been visiting daughter Jocelyn, then a naturalist with the Fairmont Hot Springs Resort in the Rockies, and Jocelyn and her partner (now husband), Andi Dzilums, along with lifelong river runner Vern Irvine and his wife, Joanne, decided to take us for a long run along the nearby Kootenay on a gorgeous late-summer day when the poplar was just beginning to blush.

Vern outfitted Andi and me with the strange-looking—think of a dugout banana—Tomahawks. Instead of kneeling close to the middle, with your butt hard against the front rim of the seat, the paddler sits almost dead centre on a saddle-like seat, knees set into foam forms along the bottom. As snowboards are to skis, the banana canoe is to regular canoes, seeming to run as well sideways or backwards as they do straight on. Andi was first to discover you could turn sideways while entering a dark tongue—a move all-but-guaranteed to dump you when in another canoe—and you could just let go, heading sideways into the boil or, if you had the nerve, using the paddle to spin through it like a top. Like those stubby dolphin-nose whitewater kayaks, Tomahawks are made for water play.

We came down the Kootenay fast, the current so quick that it might be possible to travel all day without so much as a single stroke of the paddle. All you needed really to do was use the paddle as a rudder. Paddle hard, though, and dancing through the clear white rolling rapids becomes all the more fun.

While the water boiled and roiled always, there were times on sharp turns the river became more of a challenge. At one point, Ellen and Jocelyn, who were paddling a more- traditional canoe just in front of me, simply vanished before my eyes. All I heard was a scream and then, moments later, screeches of laughter as their canoe appeared to have been shot out of the water by cannon.

In an instant I was into the hole myself, paddling furiously to punch through—only to be spit out like a watermelon seed of so little consequence the powerful river had barely noticed.

When the great map-maker first paddled the Kootenay River in 1808, he believed he was already on the Columbia. Early explorers had long believed, thanks to conversations with area natives, that the Columbia River might be the long-sought navigable passage through the obstreperous mountain ranges to the Pacific Ocean and new trading opportunities.

An American sea captain named Robert Gray had come across the gaping mouth of the river in 1792 while sailing up the coast of what would one day become Oregon. Gray named the river Columbia after his ship, the *Columbia Rediviva*, and he sailed upstream a while but did not explore further. He knew the river was large but had no idea it was the largest river in the Pacific Northwest. He did not know where it went or where the source might be found, though it was not long before speculation began that it might well link up with the Missouri, or perhaps even the rivers draining into Hudson Bay.

"The river would not only be long and mighty," Canadian author D'Arcy Jenish wrote in his biography of Thompson. "It would be navigable. They would be able to put their canoes in near the headwaters and ride its waters, allowing for portages around rapids and waterfalls, all the way to the sea, where they would meet a ship that would take their furs to the Orient and leave behind goods from China or Britain."

Thompson was then a "Nor'Wester," an agent in the service of the North West Trading Company. His job was to find new routes into the interior and to the west and to map those routes for future trade. The fur dealers were most anxious to find a route that would allow them to dominate the West Coast and compete with the arch-rival Hudson's Bay Company, Thompson's initial employer.

In early May 1807, Thompson set out from Rocky Mountain House, the North West Company's trading post on the North Saskatchewan River within easy sight and reach of the Rockies. It was a main trading centre for both fur companies, the Hudson's Bay Company having established Acton House nearby (when the two rivals merged in 1821, the name Rocky Mountain House was kept). Thompson's assignment was simple: find the Columbia River, establish a trading post and, if possible, descend all the way to the sea. The trading companies knew where it ended, but had no idea where it began—or whether it would provide safe passage.

The party travelled by canoe and included Thompson's wife, Charlotte Small, and three of their children, six-year-old Fanny, two-year-old Samuel and little Emma, who was but fourteen months old. One of the voyageurs travelling with Thompson also brought his wife and three children. Travel was difficult because game was scarce and they often went hungry, but by late June the group had reached a large river that flowed north through the first great valley beyond the most easterly range. This river was, though he had no way of knowing, the Columbia they had been seeking—but it seemed to Thompson and his fellow travellers that it flowed in the wrong direction and, therefore, could not possibly be the river they sought. The other river nearby flowed south and west—to their minds rather in the direction of where Captain Gray had established the mouth of the Columbia River lay. Their thinking seemed logical at the time, but this river that appeared to be heading in the right direction was, in fact, the Kootenay, not the Columbia.

Thompson was carrying all available navigational equipment—sextant, astrolabe, sounding line—but unfortunately no TomTom GPS to tell him to "*Turn around at your first opportunity.*"

Canada has any number of poignant statues—Terry Fox just outside Thunder Bay, Evangeline at Grand-Prée, Nova Scotia, Samuel de Champlain doffing his hat in Quebec City—but the finest statue may well be found in a small park at the entrance to Invermere, British Columbia.

The monument is in honour of David Thompson, dressed in bucksin, which he rarely, if ever, wore. It is, however, a good likeness. He stands holding his sextant and looking out toward the Rocky Mountain range and Windermere Lake, which is near the head of the actual Columbia River. Yet he does not stand alone. Beside him, staring into the same distance, is Charlotte Small, Thompson's wife of fifty-eight years.

It is unusual to honour a couple together, though there are good arguments for doing so. Lester Pearson, who won the Nobel Peace Prize as a diplomat and, as Canada's fourteenth prime minister, was responsible for such pivotal legislation as medicare, the national pension plan and the flag, sits alone looking out over Parliament Hill in Ottawa. Nowhere is there any evidence of Maryon Pearson, who was very much a power behind the "throne" and who is famous in her own right for once saying, "Behind every successful man, there stands a surprised woman."

The surprise Charlotte Small would have felt, however, would have been how *un*-successful her husband was—at least in the long latter years of their remarkable partnership. Together, they had thirteen children. Together, they paddled vast amounts of this land during her husband's explorations, including the trip in which he became the first white man to travel the length of the Columbia. In his lifetime, decades before mechanized transportation, Thompson undoubtedly saw more of this land than any other person—and yet claimed to have seen but a small, small fraction of the sprawling territory that, a decade after his death, would form the Dominion of Canada.

When the town of Invermere decided to raise this lovely stature in honour of Thompson's achievements, the sculptor, Rich Roenisch of Longview, Alberta, insisted that Charlotte be included. It was a valid demand. Charlotte Small, married to the young Hudson's Bay Company trader when she was but thirteen years of age, would travel herself more than three times as far as the renowned American explorers Lewis and Clark, who had completed their expedition to map the western United States the year before the Thompsons set out from Rocky Mountain House. She was with her husband in the wilds, enduring incredible hardships, and she stayed with him for life even though that life dwindled into obscurity, his bouts of blindness and abject poverty.

When David Thompson died, friends say that seventy-two-year-old Charlotte lay on his Mount Royal grave throughout the night, staring up at the stars that had guided them their entire lives. Three months later she passed away.

It is as much a monument to love as it is to accomplishment.

In the spring of 1784, when he was only fourteen years of age, David Thompson left London to become "a reluctant, unhappy apprentice in the service of the Hudson's Bay Company." He would never return to England. He would, however, come to love his new life, and, in the employ of HBC and later the North West Company, he would spend the next twenty-eight years exploring the west.

Thompson was not an impressive figure. Relatively short and fairly stocky, he was plain looking and wore his hair as if cutting it was merely a case of keeping it clear of his eyes. He put on no airs and did not brag. Perhaps if he had been more full of himself, as so many of his exploring contemporaries were, he might not have been forgotten for decades.

The quest for the Columbia would become the crowning achievement of Thompson's attempt to map the west from Lake Superior and Hudson Bay to the Pacific Ocean. The bitter experience of another famed explorer had already proven the effort would be difficult. Alexander Mackenzie, five years Thompson's elder, had set out to find the long-talked-about route to the Pacific Ocean back in 1789 but ended up paddling down a long, wide river that took him instead to the Arctic Ocean. He called it "River Disappointment"—the very river that, ironically, would one day be re-named the Mackenzie to honour his memory.

Three years later—the same year Captain Gray found the mouth of the Columbia—Mackenzie tried again, paddling up the Peace River with a half dozen voyageurs, two native guides and his dog, and eventually reached the dangerous and all-but-impossible Fraser River. Mackenzie and his men persevered and eventually reached Dean Channel, where, on a large rock where they had camped, he mixed some vermilion colour in melted grease and wrote: "Alexander Mackenzie, from Canada, by land, the twenty-second of July, one thousand seven hundred and ninety-three." He had reached the Pacific, but he had done so over a route so difficult that it was immediately deemed not economically feasible for trade.

Thompson's assignment from his superiors at the North West Company, fourteen years later, was to cross the Continental Divide and establish trade with native tribes west of the Rockies. He and his party passed the winter of 1807 to 1808 at "Kootenae House," the trading post they built by a creek that ran into the Columbia, though Thompson was then unaware that these waters flowed north and west for some 3,200 kilometres, growing in size, and at the northern reach of the Selkirk Mountain range turned abruptly south, heading toward the northwest of the United States.

It was a tough time, with game still scarce and the threat of attack from Peigans who were concerned that the traders might arm their enemies in that territory. Throughout 1808 and 1809 Thompson mapped out the area and established trading posts on tributaries to the Columbia: Salish House and Kullyspell House in 1809 and Spokane House in 1810. In the summer of 1810 he was headed back east over Howse Pass but found the route blocked by the Peigans. It turned out to be a fortuitous turn of events in that it forced him to consider looking north. And north, of course, would take him along the Columbia River.

In October, Thompson's entourage—twenty-three men, their wives and children, and twenty-four horses—set out for the Athabasca Pass and reached it in late December. They wintered over at a ramshackle cabin and, come spring, crossed the pass to end up on the Columbia at Boat Encampment, at the mouth of Canoe River, where the growing river bends sharply and turns southward. From here Thompson, with only three men accompanying him, went along the Columbia and then down the Kootenay to the portage leading to Clark's Fork. He travelled to Salish House thinking more of his men would be there to meet him. When none were found, he moved on, first leaving a note for others who might pass by that they should be aware of the Peigan threat. At Kullispell House he again failed to meet up with his men. He travelled to the Pend Oreille River and finally did meet up with them. Arrangements were made to transport trade goods to the posts and Thompson then travelled by horseback to Spokane House before travelling overland to Kettle Falls on the Columbia. Back on the huge river, he then made for the sea. He reached the Pacific Ocean on July 15—only to discover the Americans were already there and had established a trading post at Fort Astoria.

He had found the headwaters of the Columbia River, had travelled its incredible length and he had found, finally, a navigable passage through the mountains to the Pacific Ocean. The trade route he established across the Rockies would be used for decades. He might not have been first, but he had certainly been best.

Thompson's lasting accomplishments were his maps. His explorations were impressive. Despite treacherous rapids, near starvation, illnesses and winter blizzards, he never lost a man. He refused to trade alcohol for fur, provisions and guiding services, having seen first-hand the ravages liquor was causing on the other side of the Rockies. But all this counted for nothing in the history books. Had he been first to establish that trading post on the coast—as opposed to the several he did establish along the Columbia and its tributaries—he might never have died in obscurity, but it was not to be so.

Thompson had worked painstakingly on his journals during his final years in the vain hope that he might earn some money from his writings. Eventually they would save his reputation, but not until long after he passed on. He was a gifted writer, once describing the northern lights as "a tremendous motion in immense sheets, slightly tinged with the colours of the Rainbow," but writing nonetheless proved a most difficult task for him. He continued to document his journeys despite being nearly blind and so poor that often he would have to beg paper or ink.

On the eve of his seventy-third birthday, he wrote that he had not the "wherewith to buy a loaf of bread. May the pity of the Almighty be on us." Were he and Charlotte not taken in by their daughters in the final years, they might well have starved. After his death his family sold the massive manuscript to a Toronto newspaper editor who eventually turned them over to Joseph Burr Tyrrell of the Geological Survey of Canada and, in 1916, nearly six decades after Thompson's death, *David Thompson's Narrative* was published by the Champlain Society, a Toronto-based charity founded in 1905 and devoted to the promotion of Canadian history.

Tyrrell called Thompson "the greatest land geographer the world has produced." In his introduction to the memoirs, he claimed that Thompson had led "the white flower of a blameless life." Blame, however, was not long in coming. Thompson was soon being attacked as "a bungler and coward whose observations couldn't be trusted."

Thompson's detractors said he moved too slowly, too cautiously, even that he was cowardly when faced with the Peigan threat. Historians noted that despite Thompson's fastidious journal-keeping, there are three months of missing information in the late summer and fall of

1810. Was he lost? Was he hiding from the Peigans? And if not from the Peigans, from the truth?

In a 1936 article in *The Canadian Historical Review*, historian Arthur Silver Morton accused Thompson of poor judgment and of mishandling relations with the natives. Compared to Simon Fraser, Morton argued, Thompson was a colossal failure as an adventurer-explorer. Fraser, a Scot who also worked for the North West Company, had charted much of the area that would become British Columbia, established the first trading posts in the area, built excellent relations with several native groups and had descended the river now called the Fraser, which others had deemed an impossibility. By comparison, Morton believed, Thompson was a dawdler and politically inept. Another attack in the same review, this one by historian Richard Glover in 1950, said it was time to peel away "the hagiographic myth that has long hidden the real man." Glover even argued that Thompson's mind was slipping when he was into his eighties and still struggling with his manuscript.

Hagiographic myth or brilliant explorer? There is no doubt where the people of Invermere, British Columbia, stand. All that a visitor needs to do is read the two-part plaque that graces the statue to David and Charlotte Thompson:

DAVID THOMPSON
The man who measured Canada
Born - 1770 London, England
Died - 1857 Longueuil, Quebec

In June 1807, Thompson crossed the Rocky Mountains,
and descended along the Blaeberry River reaching the
upper part of the Columbia River.

On July 18, 1807 he arrived on Lake Windermere.
Thompson established the first post on the Columbia

near Wilmer, Kootenai House, and discovered the source of the Columbia.

In 1811 he reached the mouth of the Columbia on the shores of the Pacific Ocean—the first white man to travel the Columbia's entire length.

Surveyor, astronomer, geographer, fur trader . . . Thompson travelled more than 55,000 miles over Canada and the U.S. by foot, canoe and horse, mapping more than one and a half million miles of uncharted country.

CHARLOTTE SMALL
Born - 1785 Isle à la Crosse, Saskatchewan
Died - 1857 Longueuil, Quebec

Charlotte, and their first three children, accompanied Thompson on his historic crossing of the Rockies and arrival in the Columbia Valley in 1807. She wintered with him at Kootenai House before returning to Rocky Mountain House.

Her Scottish and Cree ancestry provided her with an education far beyond the times and gave her the skills to be a companion, helper and interpreter for Thompson during much of his travel.

David and Charlotte were married 58 years and had thirteen children. They died within three months of each other and are buried in Montreal, Quebec.

ARTIST - Rich Roenisch, Longview, Alberta

At the base of the sculpture are four panels depicting four major events in the lives and journeys of David Thompson and Charlotte Small. There is the winter of 1787, when he lived with the Peigans; the year 1807, when they finally found the source of the Columbia River; July 1811, when they reached the mouth of the Columbia; and the winter of 1811, when they crossed the formidable Athabasca Pass.

Nothing, however, to mark that day when a very old David Thompson, half-blind and desperately in need of work, passed through Algonquin Park and offered his own significant contribution to the evolution of the canoe.

Thompson was sixty-seven when he took on the task of seeking a possible canal route between the Ottawa River and Georgian Bay. It was 1837, hardly a generation removed from the 1812–14 war with the United States, and two generations since full revolution south of the border. The governments of Upper and Lower Canada wanted a route that would allow military and goods to be transported from Montreal and the Ottawa River to the Great Lakes without coming within gunshot of America, as was the case for any travel through Lake Ontario and Lake Erie into Lake Huron and Lake Superior. If, say, the Muskoka River could be linked to the Madawaska River, both running through the heart of Upper Canada, any potential American threat would be eliminated.

Thompson was desperate for work. He and Charlotte were victims of terrible business ventures by several of their children. He decided to apply in person for the job and, in early June 1837, Thompson and son Henry left the family farm at Williamstown, took the stagecoach to Kingston and then boarded a steamboat to Toronto to meet with the governor of the colony. Thompson was virtually blind in one eye and his vision in the other eye was debatable. He may even have been suffering tunnel vision from mercury poisoning from his lifelong habit of carrying and working with the mysterious liquid element each day as he took his location readings with an old-fashioned sextant. At one point in his upcoming journey across Upper Canada, his bottle of mercury would shatter, causing Thompson to panic and spend considerable time salvaging as much of the precious liquid as possible and placing what he could save in a liquor flask.

Thompson's motives for taking on the assignment immediately aroused suspicion. Captain Baddeley, Upper Canada's commanding royal engineer, wrote to the official in charge of the survey, John Macauley, claiming that David Thompson was simply no longer "trustworthy as to the reporting of facts." The fear was that the legendary but impoverished explorer would simply report back what he thought his employer wished to hear.

Baddeley's concerns were unfounded. Thompson had no intention of painting a pretty picture. He found the land he entered via the Muskoka River "very rude and without Soil." It was tough slogging with a single, large canoe. They travelled upstream for much of the journey, paddling from Georgian Bay along the Moon, Musquash and Muskoka rivers to the Algonquin Highlands. Thompson counted forty-two portages in the space of 246 kilometres. There were dangerous rapids, powerful waterfalls and, of course, endless "musketoes." He wasn't impressed with the lakes he found, noting how barren the shorelines were and calling current Lake Muskoka "Swampy Ground Lake"—a name hardly in keeping with the $10-million real estate listings found there today.

Thompson was not amused. He complained about scarce game and found that his crew's wide-mesh net harvested too few fish—perhaps because the large, delicious lake trout of the area flee to the deepest waters in summer.

With so many portages, the men found the carrying tough. Little wonder, too, as they had to haul a huge, unwieldy canoe, heavy twilled-cotton tents that never dried out and a list of supplies that would sink a modern tripper:

> 450 lbs salted pork
> 100 lbs beef
> 300 lbs bisquit

two bushels peas
one lb tea
8.5 lbs butter
5 gal. whisky
five lbs nails
2 yds towelling
tin mugs
7 lbs tobacco
tea kettle
50 fathom net of five-inch mesh

After leaving the Muskoka behind, Thompson found the travelling so difficult that he finally determined to do something about it. On Wednesday, September 13, 1837, he came to a lake in dense fog after a difficult upstream paddle along the Oxtongue River. His journals tell the story:

> As we are now at the first lake of the height of land, I resolved to do what I have long seen necessary from the shoal waters, Rapids, etc. The necessity of exploring the country to know what it is according to my instructions, etc., our large canoes being too heavy for shoal water, and also that with one canoe we cannot separate ourselves to examine two rivers at the same time, etc., I determined to make two small canoes which should be able to take all our provisions, Baggage, etc. For this purpose we crossed to the north side where we had seen cedar trees, and examining the ground and in a deep sandy bay, thank God, we found on a bank of about twenty-five feet high sufficient good cedar for our purposes.

This may well have been a pivotal moment in the development of the modern canoe. Thompson, for the second time in his journeys—the first had been in early 1811, when he was in the mountains—elected to construct canoes using cedar rather than birchbark. Unlike his improvisation out West a quarter century earlier, Thompson this time could have sought out birchbark but elected not to, going instead once again with more readily available cedar. He also made note of what he considered to be the advantages of these smaller canoes, considerably shorter than the traditional Montreal canoe (*canot de maître*) used along the Ottawa River and the Great Lakes, or the north canoe (*canot du nord*) used largely west of Lake Superior.

Using crooked knives and axes, Thompson had the men split nearly three dozen timbers. The following day, Thursday, he set three men to cut more timber while Thompson and two others went to work splitting cedar gunwales. They then split out forty more timbers for a second canoe, modelled on the first. On Friday they turned the split timbers into boards, eighty-eight in all. Each canoe would be about eighteen feet long. On Saturday they let the boards dry out and sought out young cedars with curved roots they could use for stems.

September 18, Monday . . . cleaned a place for the building of the canoes. I put the bars in the gunwales, got the stems partly ready, etc. etc. Heavy showers at times.

September 19, Tuesday . . . heavy showers . . . Put the bottom and stem on the canoe bed and by 1 pm got in the necessary timber. Put one round of boards along the gunwales, cut logs for the canoes to rest on, and put one round on each side of the bottom . . .

September 20, Wednesday . . . Ice about one-tenth of an inch thick in a kettle . . . Two men collecting gum for the canoe, put all the boards about the canoe, took it off the bed, and gave it to Baptiste to finish. Cut down two cedars, seven split out fourteen boards. We have employed more time for want of nails . . .

September 23, Saturday . . . Early got the canoe finally boarded in and set to work on getting the rest of the timbers in etc. etc., which occupied

all day with the two canoes. Pegs instead of nails—we have not one-third
enough of nails. Picked an old piece of oakum to help the stopping the
seams of the canoes . . .

September 24, Sunday . . . Men employed on the canoes running gum
into the seams, caulking slightly, etc. etc. . . . 32-degrees and water frozen
to ice. The woods in all their foliage have suddenly changed and assumed
all the vivid tints of October, and begin to fall freely, one cannot help a
sigh at such a quick change. . . .

Thompson's sigh of admiration must have been accompanied by a sigh of relief. The canoes were ready and they floated and they were perfect for the shallow waters. The company travelled farther east, located the source of the southeast bound Madawaska and found the paddling easier. They were now in the middle of what would one day become Algonquin Park and approximately halfway through the journey to the Ottawa River. The hard part, however, was now behind them. As Thompson wrote in that day's journal, "Current going with us, thank God."

The sandy beach where Thompson and his men had built their smaller, sleeker cedar canoes was the current site of Camp Tamakwa, where more than a century later Omer Stringer would do things with a cedar canoe—walking fully around the gunwales without tipping, performing headstands using the yoke—that David Thompson could never have imagined.

Camp Tamakwa is found on what campers today call Tea Lake, in Algonquin Park, but Thompson chose another, obvious, name for the place where he camped for more than a week and reconsidered the means of his final journey.

Canoe Lake.

David Thompson seemed to have invented the cedar strip canoe, but can he truly take credit for that contribution to the story? Like all explorers, he used his vessel without considering where it had come from and where it might go, beyond the next bend in the river. According to biographer D'Arcy Jenish, the explorer "appears to have been one of the first people on record at least to build cedar strip canoes."

Following his retirement from the fur trade, David and Charlotte Thompson settled in Terrebonne, outside of Montreal, and he attempted to start a small business building such watercraft. He joined the Terrebonne voyageur battalion during the War of 1812 and apparently built some canoes to order for it. Yet, like so many of Thompson's business investments, it went nowhere. The cedar canoes he built in Quebec were not watertight and the venture failed.

Jenish believes Thompson was certainly an innovator, "but it may be a stretch to say that he was pivotal in the development of the canoe." Though he was indeed a great map-maker, he was indeed a bungler when it came to enterprise—his failure to publish the narrative of his many travels the prime example. "Had his Terrebonne canoe business flourished," Jenish believes, "he may have gone down as the father of the cedar strip canoe. It failed, and inevitably others did build and manufacture them successfully."

Sean T. Peake, the Toronto paddler and scholar who edited the massive two-volume edition of *The Travels of David Thompson 1784–1812*, which was published in 2011, believes Thompson was certainly the first to build a wooden canoe west of the Rockies. In Thompson's journal of March, 1811, the explorer wrote,

> We had to turn our thoughts to some other material, and Cedar wood being the lightest and most pliable for a Canoe, we split out thin boards of Cedar wood of about six inches in breadth and builded a Canoe of twenty-five feet in length by fifty inches in breadth, of the same form of a common Canoe, using cedar boards instead of Birch Rind, which proved to be equally light and much stronger than Birch Rind, the greatest difficulty we had was sewing the boards to each round the timbers.

Thompson instructed his men to build the Kootenay canoe from the bottom up, as was the birchbark method used by Aboriginal builders. There are not enough details in the journals, Peake says, to determine whether or not this canoe was built more like a skiff or whether the men had smoothed the planking so that it was more like a common cedar strip. Thompson solved his problem of having no nails by having the men fasten the boards all together with *wattap* (split black spruce roots).

Peake speculates that the cedar strip canoes Thompson built at "Canoe Lake" may well have been the precursor of the famous Peterborough canoe. He had been pushed to use a tin canoe for the journey from Georgian Bay to the Ottawa River, but Thompson was adamant that he would always be able to find natural materials in the woods to fix his large cedar canoe if necessary. He had no idea then that he'd be building two more cedar canoes from scratch halfway through his journey. Peake thinks it quite possible that those canoes, built out of necessity, would have influenced the later cedar strip and cedar can-vas-covered canoes that would soon be widely produced in the east.

The Canadian Canoe Museum located in Peterborough, Ontario, tends to agree. In one display entitled "Who invented the board canoe?" various claims are made from journals and letters, most having to do with the pro-duction of cedar and cedar-canvas canoes produced locally around Peterborough and Lakefield and Rice Lake in the 1840s and 1850s. The declared winner, however, is David Thompson with his 1811 canoe built out west and the two smaller, sleeker cedar canoes he had his men build in 1837.

"Thompson's method was marvellous," says Jeremy Ward, curator of the museum, "and very likely the antecedent to the wood canoes we know today."

There can, however, be no question regarding David Thompson's con-tributions in another important area: the romance of the canoe. Each year, dozens, sometimes hundreds, of modern-day "explorers" set out across Canada, often taking several summers to retrace the old routes first followed by Aboriginal people and later by the likes of Thompson,

Fraser, Samuel Hearne, Alexander Mackenzie, Samuel de Champlain, Étienne Brûlé, Radisson and La Verendrye, Robert Bylot, even Lady Jane Franklin, who, in search of an answer to her husband's Sir John Franklin's tragic demise, may have contributed more to the exploration of the Far North than any man or woman.

Canadian literature is filled with tributes to their kind—inspiring adventurers who, centuries later, capture the imaginations of today's paddler. Often, the accounts are by those who have travelled the explorers' routes alone, something that the likes of Thompson and Mackenzie never did.

Hap Wilson, a modern Canadian "explorer," spent many months alone mapping out the Trans Canada Trail between Lake Superior and Lake Winnipeg, including the arduous fourteen-kilometre Grand Portage. Wilson was even struck by lightning during his journeys, yet took on and completed the task in late 2012 because he believes in the value of such a challenge. "These ancient water trails can lead today's paddlers not only to an understanding of our shared history," he wrote in *Canadian Geographic* magazine, "but also to a realization of what these waterways can mean for our shared future."

The late John Donaldson, a Scottish-born medical researcher from Montreal, set out at the age of sixty-three to replicate Mackenzie's voyages to the Pacific and Arctic oceans. A holiday paddler, he somehow completed his twelve-thousand-kilometre quest five years later, despite having to fend off storms, high winds, being "shipwrecked" on Lake Winnipeg, terrifying rapids on the Fraser River and endless run-ins with bears. For Donaldson, it was as much an internal voyage as external, as he was trying to find out who he was after a lifetime of academia and research had come to an abrupt end. He had been terrified, moved to tears by nature, overwhelmed with compassion for the Aboriginal people he met along the way and baffled to realize that in the four years it took him to reach the West Coast, he had never tipped. Best of all, though, was the letter from his six grandchildren that he received when he reached Bella Coola. "Your spirit and determination are an inspiration to all those you have met along the voyage and especially to us, your loving family."

An inspiration, just as Mackenzie was to Donaldson.

Many of the old fur trade routes have been changed by dams and encroachment, but the loss is not, happily, a total one. "It is quite a thrill to stand on, say, Frog Portage, linking the Churchill to the Sturgeon-Weir, and think of the ghosts on that trail that's been hard-packed by countless feet over centuries," said Sean Peake, who has retraced so much of Thompson's journeys. "And to read the accounts of Franklin or Mackenzie, Simon Fraser or Thompson and know you're on the same piece of ground makes it that much more special. In Quetico I remember stopping at a broad and flat rock shelf (called Mill Stone camp by Thompson) just below Mackenzie's Rock of Arrows that was a favourite camp site for the voyageurs, and it was not hard to imagine the twenty or so canoes of a brigade camped out like a Frances Hopkins painting.

"Nothing has really changed at these places because their remoteness has protected them. I find it uplifting that some of these wild and famous portages that everyone, and I mean *everyone*, travelling to the West from Lake Superior had to use are still there. And when you drop your packs and canoe at the end of one of them, all sweaty and out of breath, you can experience just some of what earlier generations did—so shut up, stop whining, and go get the other load!"

There is a timelessness and a beauty to such exertion. As Sigurd Olson once so lovingly put it: "In a canoe a man changes and the life he has lived seems strangely remote. Time is no longer of moment, for he has become part of space and freedom. What matters is that he is heading down the misty trail of explorers and *voyageurs*, with a fair wind and a chance for a good camp somewhere ahead."

These modern paddlers travel across the country every year as soon as the snow melts and the rivers start to flow again. They paddle up the Ottawa as Champlain and Brûlé did. They run the Dumoine and the Ashuapmushuan, just as the fur traders and loggers once did. They paddle the Rupert and Broadback where the James Bay Crees have trapped for ten thousand years. They paddle against the flow up the Mattawa as the Jesuits had to on their way to their mission at Huronia. They travel the French River to the Great Lakes. They challenge the Fraser as Mackenzie and Fraser did. They canoe the Peace, the Mackenzie, the Nahanni, the Coppermine. When they are on the mighty Columbia River, they may even stop to visit the statue to David Thompson and Charlotte Small at little Windermere.

And, of course, they tumble down the clear, fast and very cold waters of the Kootenay, knowing that David Thompson and Charlotte Small had also travelled it—though certainly not in a banana-shaped canoe.

Blair Fraser at camp.

Graham Fraser cleans
the cross where his father
succumbed to the rapids.

The mission assembles on the water in Petawawa Gorge.

Kristina Leidums finds perfection on Lake of the Woods.

Anahareo looks back at her life with Grey Owl.

Aunt Mary on Brule Lake.

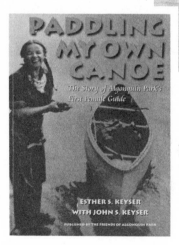

Esther Keyser's words of wisdom.

"Shooting the Rapids" by Frances Anne Hopkins.

Jocelyn MacGregor in the search for David Thompson's route to the sea.

David Thompson and Charlotte Small, commemorated in Invermere, B.C.

Adventurer-explorer
Simon Fraser.

Rollin Thurlow and his
handcrafted 17.5-foot
"Atkinson Traveler."

Birchbark-canoe
builder Daniel
"Pinock" Smith.

The Cree-Yamaha freighter canoe on the shore of James Bay.

Chief Billy
Diamond.

Doug Sprott and Lawrence
Katapatuk on Obedjiwan Island.

As innocent as it looks? Courting in a canoe.

Tom Thomson and Arthur Lismer, feeling right at home.

8

━━━∼∼∼━━━

THE CRAFT

New York State highway 30 runs south from the town of Malone to Saranac Lake, the scenery growing ever more green and wild as the road rises steadily into the Adirondack Mountains. If it weren't for the occasional vehicle encountered along the way, it would be difficult to determine what decade it is by staring out the windshield alone.

Head off the road and into the woods and tracking of time becomes even more difficult. In this heavily forested place, the closest thing to a calendar is the leaves, which is what appealed most to William Chapman White. White was a foreign correspondent for *The New York Times* and *New York Herald Tribune* in the chaotic years between the two world wars. When White would return from difficult assignments in such places as Russia, China and Germany, he would escape to his wife Ruth's family cabin on nearby Lake Colby. Here he found something in the mixed forests of upstate New York that he could find nowhere else in the world: peace . . . and perspective.

White wrote many books on world affairs, but, curiously, the one that survives long after his death in 1955 is *Adirondack Country*, in which he sought to explain what it was that drew him back here again and again and again.

"As a man tramps the woods to the lake," White wrote, "he knows he will find pines and lilies, blue herons and golden shiners, shadows on the rocks and the glint of light on the wavelets, just as they were in the summer of 1354, as they will be in 2054 and beyond. He can stand on a rock by the shore and be in a past he could not have known, in a future he will never see. He can be a part of time that was and time yet to come."

Part of time that was and time yet to come . . . An unchanging world. And what an ideal place, then, to hold the thirty-fifth anniversary annual assembly of the Wooden Canoe Heritage Association.

A few kilometres short of Saranac Lake, there is a break in the dark green corridors of pine and cedar, and a sharp turn to the right opens the forest curtain to reveal Paul Smith's College, an exclusive one-thousand-student higher education facility that, during the school year, offers courses on ecology and forestry, winter sports such as snowshoeing and cross-country skiing and, in summer, a gorgeous beach complete with lifeguard.

Here, during a sunny week in July of 2014, the grounds up from the beach that might otherwise be occupied with an impromptu game of touch football are filled instead with dozens of exquisite wooden canoes. They were all built during the last century, a few even before, and are on display courtesy of three hundred or so canoe aficionados who are as passionate about varnish and trim as other canoeists are about whitewater or finding the ideal camping spot.

They are, indeed, different. Many have stayed with the 1960s and 1970s hippie fashions of loose, flowing and brightly coloured cloth, tie-dye T-shirts, braided hair, head bands. If the people seem somewhat out of sync with the times, the canoes they have brought with them seem from a distant century, not just a past decade.

Paul Smith's College gets its name from Apollos Smith, a hotelier who in 1858 built a rustic resort here on the shore of Lower St. Regis Lake. He named his new lodge the Saint Regis House, but everyone just called it "Paul Smith's Hotel." It was one of the first wilderness resorts in the Adirondacks, and Smith, the proprietor, was one of the earliest and strongest proponents of protecting the surrounding mountainous area, an effort that finally came to fruition in 1892. Today,

Adirondack Park—larger than Yellowstone, Yosemite, Grand Canyon, Glacier and Great Smoky Mountains national parks combined—covers some six million acres and is split about equally between private and public ownership.

Paul Smith's Hotel burned down in 1930, but at one point it had grown to include 255 guest rooms, a bowling alley, casino, stable and, eventually, its own railway. Smith, who died in Montreal in 1912, knew how to attract clientele, building even his own hydroelectric plant and installing a stock ticker wired directly to the New York Stock Exchange. Not surprisingly, the resort became most fashionable, attracting celebrities such as P.T. Barnum and even U.S. presidents Benjamin Harrison, Grover Cleveland, Theodore Roosevelt and Calvin Coolidge.

The heyday of this resort in the Adirondacks, and the rise of other "wilderness" retreats throughout North America, coincided with such matters as new railway access, the rise of "muscular Christianity," the celebration of the outdoor life by such eminent personalities as Teddy Roosevelt and Lord Baden-Powell and, of course, the popularity of the canoe as something other than a tool for hunting and fishing.

James Raffan marks the year 1797 as the birth of the canoe in the style and shape being celebrated at Paul Smith's College. That year, Raffan says, the "Hudson's Bay Company began replacing the thirty-six-foot birchbark *canot de maître* and the twenty-six-foot *canot du nord* with larger, more durable York boats that could be rowed and sailed, and at this point in history marks the beginning of the evolution of the modern-day canoe."

It was, of course, a slow evolution. The larger paddling vessels were being replaced by steamers. The phasing out of birchbark canoes was largely happenstance caused by circumstance. Explorers like David Thompson found birchbark hard to come by, especially when travelling in mountain areas where birch was rarely found. And his smaller, sleeker canoes suited the rivers that flowed through the Canadian Shield area that would one day become Algonquin Park.

By the middle of the nineteenth century, the Hudson's Bay Company was also straying from the native birchbark traditions and starting to use waterproof canvas over cedar. Builders in Maine, New Brunswick and central Ontario were all building new-style canoes using wood, usually cedar, in place of birchbark. Times were obviously changing, but no one really knew what would become of the continent's original form of travel.

The American naturalist and philosopher Henry David Thoreau, who considered sitting in canoes pure "torture," was among the many who believed the vessel had seen its best days and would soon be consigned, like the bow and arrow, to history.

"The canoe implies a long antiquity in which its manufacture has been gradually perfected," Thoreau wrote in his journal. "It will ere long, perhaps, be ranked among the lost arts."

Thoreau could hardly have been more wrong, but it certainly didn't seem so at the time. The art of birchbark canoe construction might well have been forever lost but for Tappan Adney, an eccentric obsessive who was born in Athens, Ohio, in 1868 but spent most of his life in eastern Canada.

Adney was a brilliant scholar and spoke multiple languages, including the difficult Maliseet, which he learned while living in New Brunswick. He was a writer who covered the Klondike gold rush for *Harper's Weekly* and signed up with the Canadian army more than a year before America entered the Great War. He lived next in Montreal and researched the North American bark canoe through McGill University, spending more than sixty years travelling the continent to record various canoe styles and learning how to construct the different designs.

Adney never did complete his long-promised book on the art and ended up destitute and desperate, forced to sell his collection of 110 bark canoes to the Mariners' Museum in Newport News, Virginia. In exchange, the museum paid off a $1,400 loan Adney had taken out from McGill, gave $1,000 to Adney's son, Glenn, to pay back family loans, and paid a $100 monthly stipend to Adney so he could complete his book, though he never did.

"It is a shame that your model canoes cannot stay in Canada," Diamond Jenness, the New Zealand–born Canadian anthropologist wrote to Adney after the deal was struck. "I would give a good deal to be allowed to purchase them for our museum here [National Museum of Canada] but we operate on a shoe-string. . . . Some day, when it is too late perhaps, the Canadian people will wake up and decide they want a real museum in the capital city."

The bark canoe did survive, in no small part thanks to Adney's dedication. Rather than become a lost art, it became an evolving craft. And a surprising number of people came to share Adney's fascination with the bark canoe, if not quite his fanatical obsession.

Critical to the tradition's survival in Canada was William Commanda of the Kitigan Zibi Anishinabeg First Nation in western Quebec. Commanda, a much-respected Algonquin elder who went by the affectionate nickname of "Grandfather" in his later years, was a band chief, spiritual leader and named an Officer of the Order of Canada. He became known internationally for his peace pipe ceremonies at the Rio Earth Summit in 1991 and was a founder of Elders Without Borders, a gathering of Aboriginal spiritual leaders from both Americas. He was also a master craftsman of birchbark canoes.

Commanda built birchbark canoes at Montreal's Expo 67. He built a commissioned canoe for new prime minister Pierre Trudeau and one for Queen Margrethe of Denmark, each vessel constructed entirely of natural materials and signed, simply, "W.C." followed by the year of its construction.

"Grandfather" Commanda died in 2011, three months short of his ninety-eighth birthday, but his canoe-building legacy has been carried on by others from Kitigan Zibi. One of the more-celebrated birchbark builders is his nephew Daniel "Pinock" Smith, who works almost exclusively with an old curved knife salvaged from the garbage to construct his exquisite canoes. He sews their birchbark together with shaved spruce root and waterproofs them with spruce pitch.

"I could build you a birchbark canoe if I only had a stone and bone to work with," claims the builder, who goes only by "Pinock." "I harvest my own material and I get an appreciation for nature and what nature has supplied for my people. When I go out I can appreciate what the Creator gave to us."

He also has a great appreciation for what "Grandfather," the man who married Pinock's aunt Mary Smith, did for the canoe.

"Birchbark canoes kind of dropped out of sight before William started making them," he says. "He was one of the people who kept the canoe alive. He got the reputation for building canoes, but everyone had the knowledge. When I was young, a lot of people on the reserve were making canoes. It was a poor community, so whatever people needed they had to build their own.

It changed in the 1950s and 1960s, though. "People started going 'out' to work. Men were leaving to work in the bush, to guide, drive trucks, work on the pipelines. They were making money and when they came home they bought their canoes and boats. But there were still people like my grandfather, Charlie Smith, and William Commanda making canoes the old way. Most of my family built canoes. I quit work twenty-five years ago to spend a year making my own canoe and I've never stopped making them since."

That the birchbark canoe could survive, and should survive, is not a puzzle to Pinock. "It's my ancestors who invented the canoe," he says. "And if you take a look at any canoe, no matter what it's made of, you will appreciate the ingenuity of the original canoes. It's such a simple design and it works—the birchbark canoe is the forerunner of all the canoes that follow. It's something that came from nature and will go back to nature. It's not going to pollute things. It's going to rot and go back to the earth.

"The canoe served our purposes so well. But it also served the purpose of the people who came to this country. There would have been no fur trade without the canoe. The settlers could never have come inland if it weren't for the canoe. The canoe has played a very important part in both our cultures—so it's no wonder that the birchbark canoe is still alive and well."

The great John McPhee, author of such literary classics as *Levels of the Game*, *Coming into the Country* and *The Pine Barrens*, devoted an entire book, *The Survival of the Bark Canoe*, to the work of Henri Vaillancourt, a birchbark canoe builder in Greenville, New Hampshire. McPhee became as wrapped up in early canoe construction as he ever did in New Jersey folklore or the allure of elite tennis competition.

McPhee came to understand how the first white explorers must have looked upon these canoes with such wonder. There was no comparable vessel in Europe. The Europeans made land in North American, lowered their great and cumbersome longboats and assigned the men to take to the oars and row. "The Indians, two to a canoe, indolently whisked their narrow paddles and easily drew away," wrote McPhee. "In their wake they left a stunning impression. Not only were they faster. They could see where they were going."

A few centuries later, where the canoe itself was going was inevitably toward new materials. It wasn't just that birchbark was scarce in many parts of the country. Other materials became available that were more resilient, as the Hudson's Bay Company had found with waterproof canvas. In some quarters, a certain disdain grew for the birchbark canoe, as if it were somehow uncivilized. When a query arrived at *Forest and Stream* magazine in 1874 asking for information on bark canoes, the answer was dismissive: "We are reluctant to inform our anxious inquirer that the birchbark canoe is not named or known in the category of civilized craft which our modern canoemen paddle and sail. It is the peculiar toy and vehicle of the aboriginal redskin and although it is light and buoyant and full of poetry and well adapted to his requirements, the palefaces are conceited enough to believe that they can manufacture something better in all respects."

Canvas-covered wooden canoes were beginning to appear widely by the 1870s, though even they were dismissed by the establishment as "rag" canoes. The American Canoe Association (ACA), which had been founded in 1880 and strangely considered "canoeing" as the sailing of small craft, did not recognize canvas canoes as worthy of any designation. By 1910, the ACA caved somewhat and began speaking of open canoes as "Canadian" canoes. But it took the organization until 1934 to finally recognize the wood-and-canvas canoe.

It was in one of these evolving "Canadian" canoes that the earlier mentioned Scot John MacGregor first paddled on the Ottawa River in 1859. MacGregor then returned to London where he built his "Rob Roy"—more kayak than canoe, really—and in 1865 set off on that three-month, one-thousand-mile trek through France, Switzerland and Germany that would, on the publication of his book *A Thousand Miles in the Rob Roy Canoe*, so popularize and romanticize the canoe.

When MacGregor's book came out in 1866, it caused a swell of enthusiasm for the new sport and led to the founding of the Royal Canoe Club, the first such organization of its kind anywhere. Queen Victoria's eldest son, the Prince of Wales, who only a few years earlier had seen a voyageurs' regatta while on his royal visit to the North American colonies, became the club's first commodore and a passionate paddler in his own right.

By the turn of the twentieth century, canvas-covered cedar canoes were being manufactured throughout North America. Old Town and E.M. White canoes from Maine were (and still are) revered for their styling and manoeuvrability. In Canada, the Chestnut family in Fredericton, New Brunswick, turned their hardware store into a factory and began turning out canoes that would be renowned across Canada. Bill Mason's canoe was a Chestnut, as was Tom Thomson's, as was the old ranger's canoe I first paddled at Lake of Two Rivers in Algonquin Park. The Chestnut became the model for the famous Peterborough canoes manufactured by the Canadian Canoe Company. And if all these legendary canoes look somewhat similar, it is hardly by accident. The Chestnut canoe design was stolen, Maine builders claimed, from them; the Peterborough was obviously modelled on the Chestnut.

The Craft

The history of the canoe's evolution is filled with lawsuits, counter-claims and takeovers, but in the end the victory belonged to the new idea of working from a moulded form and building either a pure cedar strip canoe or a canvas-covered cedar canoe. Canvas proved most popular, as it was lightweight, durable, flexible and had a remarkable ability to hold colour. As Ontario canoe builder and author Roger MacGregor (also no relation) so perfectly put it in his meticulously detailed history of the Chestnut canoe: "Canvas has old connections with the continent. When strangers first came here on the winds over the Atlantic, canvas brought them. When they went inland on the rivers, canvas duffel went with them. When they went overland on such trails as there were, canvas covered them. It seems to satisfy something like a first principle that canvas would be the material to replace bark on what otherwise remained the ageless canoe of the aboriginal woodland people."

The turn of the twentieth century has often been called "the Golden Age" of the canoe. Those renowned manufacturers, and others, were selling exquisite crafts for under one hundred dollars. The canoe became inextricably linked with romance and courting; increasingly perceived as a healthy, harmless recreation, it allowed a young man and woman to spend time away from the dreaded chaperone.

The canoe was the perfect place to "pop the question." One early writer speculated that so many proposals took place in them because "a woman reclining in the bow of a canoe presented the image of maximum desirability and the fact of minimum accessibility, which momentarily flummoxed the suitor."

But more of that in a chapter to come.

For most canoeists, the enduring romance is with the vessel itself. People simply love their canoes. When Roger MacGregor was researching his history of the Chestnut Canoe Company, he found a 1950s letter from renowned outdoors writer Greg Clark of the *Toronto Star* comparing the canoe they had built for him to "a pair of good-fitting shoes."

Another happy customer, the Reverend. A.J. Lajeunesse of the University of Ottawa, wrote in the spring of 1927 to say he believed he might have used his eighteen-year-old Cruiser model "more than anyone ever used a canoe before." He had paddled from Ottawa to Quebec City, Ottawa to Montreal, Ottawa to the northern headwaters of the Ottawa River and throughout Northern Ontario and Quebec. He had taken as many as ten children at a time for afternoon picnics, and students off to learn about survival in the wilderness.

"I shall never sell it," Lajeunesse vowed to the Chestnut Canoe Company. "When it becomes useless, I shall burn it and keep its ashes in an urn which I shall place over my fireplace as a souvenir of beautiful and happy days."

The three hundred wooden canoe fanatics who gathered at Paul Smith's College—they have previously met in Canada at Peterborough's Trent University and in Dorset, Ontario—would understand the passion of Reverend Lajeunesse. They came for five days of celebrating "classics" from a century ago but also to marvel over "Tomorrow's Classics," exquisite, highly polished and gleaming cedar strip and cedar-canvas canoes that might have been finished only weeks and days before the annual gathering.

They talked about the great companies of the past and of great builders past and present. One name often invoked was that of Walter Walker, who spent a long and productive life building wooden canoes in the Peterborough and Lakefield area. It was Walter Walker who was chosen to build the royal canoe for Prince Andrew, a graduate of nearby Lakefield College and still a regular visitor to the Canadian North on paddling expeditions.

Ted Moores, whose *Canoecraft* is considered by many the Bible of canoe building, remembered Walker, whom Moores visited when the old man was ninety-one, as "a small man with a gentle demeanor, sparkling eyes and precious little to say to the casual visitor. The man is painfully understated, but his hands—big, rough hands for a person of his slight frame—do the talking. They are callused and scarred from sixty-five years of steady boatbulding. . . . They build what many consider to be the finest

The Craft

canoes and skiffs known today—works of art. When these hands are finally folded, there will be none to replace them."

I interviewed Walter Walker myself when he reached the century mark. He said if he could have one wish, he would like to be five years younger. "More would be good," he said, "but five will do." If he were ninety-five, he said, he'd know he had at least one more good canoe in him.

He talked about being born at roughly the same time Ole Evinrude came out with the first outboard engine, something that Walter thought hurt human beings more than it ever hurt the canoe. "People just got lazy," he told me. "They just started roarin' about—not paddling at all." To him, there was no comparison: "With a canoe you can go wherever you want to. You can't with a boat and motor."

Walter Walker never intended to become a canoe builder. He had set out to become a tool maker, but the Depression came along and he took what he could find, signing on as a "helper" at the local canoe manufacturer in Lakefield. He moved from "helper" to "master" and eventually became the builder most often connected to the famous Peterborough canoe.

Walter died in the fall of 2009, just two weeks short of turning 102. For his one-hundredth birthday, friends held a gathering for him and asked him to make a speech. He did, sort of. He carried his tool box to the front of the room and held it up. Then he held up his hands to show his proudest accomplishment: all ten fingers still intact.

I asked Walter about yokes and he surprised me by saying he had never bothered with one. How could that be? I asked.

"I've never portaged," he told me. "Except maybe from the boathouse to the water."

For five days the members of the Wooden Canoe Heritage Association attended lectures and slide shows. They took part in construction forums and classes in everything from the art of caning seats to paddle carving. They derided chemical epoxy as "frozen snot," even when forced to use it, but whenever they could, they stuck to the old methods—the way Chestnut and Old Town and Peterborough believed a canoe must be made.

Canoeing is a sport and recreation that has, to an intriguing degree, denied the Nike-*ization* of sports and recreation. Nike is hardly alone, but its "swoosh" is surely the most recognizable symbol of the multitude of businesses that make it their business to endlessly reinvent the wheel—as well as the ski, skate, club, stick, broom and, perhaps most absurdly, the very apparel one wears to engage with these items.

There was, believe it or not, a world before spandex and Lycra, before branding, before middle-aged men began dressing like NASCAR drivers just to take a spin through the park on their two-wheelers.

Some will argue, with ample evidence, that today's bicycles are faster, today's skates sharper, today's drivers hit golf balls longer, today's curling brooms clean the ice better, even that today's cross-country skis glide more effortlessly across the snow. Yet one key recreational toy—the canoe—has all but defied both marketing and composite design when it comes to the actual experience of the sport.

When Bill Mason, Canada's best-known paddler, said, "There is nothing that is so aesthetically pleasing and yet so functional and versatile as the canoe," he was talking about his own beloved red canvas Chestnut—a canoe that was being manufactured just like his long before he was even born. Mason, we recall, also believed that God first created the canoe and then set about to conceive a land in which it could flourish—Canada—so it is not much of a stretch to see how he came to believe there could be no improving on the original.

Indeed, there are lovely Kevlar and carbon composite canoes that are lighter to portage yet can carry the same load. There are thick fibreglass canoes—often called "bangers" by those who use them—that will bump and grind down whitewater and through rock gardens with barely a mark to show for it. There are aluminum canoes that can be folded around a rock and, with luck, folded right back again. All have plusses; but none has the feel of the traditional birchbark or cedar strip canoe.

When the CBC announced the canoe as among the Seven Wonders of Canada, Canadians were not responding to a trend in sports or a well-marketed way in which to spend their recreational dollars, but to something deeper that transcends generations and, in its own way, defines what it is to "be" Canadian. The response tapped into a long-recognized brilliance of a simple machine of perfect design—one ideally suited to the needs of those who originally lived on this land and those who later came along.

"You often hear people making snide remarks about natives never inventing the wheel," says Will Ruch, a traditional builder from Bancroft, Ontario, who had several lovingly constructed canoes on display at Paul Smith's College. "Well, they didn't need the wheel. The wheel required all this infrastructure in order for it to work. They had to have trails built so the wheel could travel. But all the infrastructure needed was already there for the canoe."

It was Samuel de Champlain who realized that the native-built birchbark canoe had enormous advantages in the New World. Champlain first came in 1603 on an expedition led by François Gravé Du Pont, and he was keen to know more about the inland trading routes leading west. He made a few small trips north and west of Hochelaga (Montreal), but when he reached the ferocious Lachine Rapids, the ship's heavy rowboats proved cumbersome and useless in the whitewater. At one point he and his men had to abandon their skiff, though he noted, "The savages' canoe passed easily."

Champlain realized he could go no farther by land either, so dense was the tangle they would have to cut through to form a trail. Where rapids proved impossible for the native canoes, on the other hand, their paddlers merely threw the birchbark vessels over their heads and walked into the bush. Champlain was amazed by how much the canoes could carry—and amazed again by how easily the canoes themselves could be carried.

Will Ruch, like so many at this gathering, is a traditionalist—though his reverence for tradition does not extend all the way back to the canoes Champlain saw working the Lachine Rapids. He loves the idea of the birchbark canoe but reserves his greatest passion for the cedar and the cedar-canvas canoes that replaced them. Ruch does concede that more modern canoes perform well, even better in certain conditions—but, he argues, they are just not the same.

"Synthetic canoes don't have the look," says Ruch. "Below the water-line you basically have the same thing. But you can find a Lakefield canoe built 120 years ago and it's still equal to the task."

These paddlers are purists. They deplore the destruction of old wooden canoes to make novelty bookcases. They consider today's paddleboard craze a sub-canoe experience. They know that kayaks now seriously outsell canoes and that many former canoeists are now avid kayakers—but that doesn't mean they will abandon their thwarts and gunwales and cedar ribs. Loyalty is another part of the wooden canoe mystique that they treasure. Larry Reid, writing in the summer 2014 issue of *Canoeroots* magazine, bemoans the "Red Bull–sponsored water-fall drops, a certain dirtbag mystique and adrenaline-infused sex-appeal," but keeps the faith.

"Canoeing isn't dead," he writes. "It's just taking a well-deserved breather after being the watercraft of choice for thousands of years."

Purists, yes, but it would be wrong to think of them as "collectors" who merely look, admire and lust after the objects of their passion. In the morning, a gleaming, lovingly restored Old Town or Chestnut from the early 1900s might be on display in the field, admirers reluctant to so much as touch its gunwales for fear of leaving prints, yet come evening this same canoe would be out on Lower St. Regis Lake, perhaps taking part in the group's annual "Paddle By & Salute," in which more than one hundred canoes pass the site.

That such canoes are still used, not merely admired, was underlined by the presence of Rollin Thurlow. A sixty-six-year-old former marine and former hippie from Atkinson, Maine, Thurlow has reached legend-ary status as a builder of fine canoes and is co-author of one of the best-known instruction manuals for building wood and canvas canoes.

The Craft

Over the winter of 2013–14, Thurlow had built the one thousandth canoe of his long career, a 17.5-foot Northwoods canoe, an "Atkinson Traveler," which he'd made with white cedar ribs and a white oak stem, and covered with a canvas then painted a rich, deep blue. Several times during construction he had signed his name, mostly in secret places where the signature might never be seen, and then had attached a name-plate that read: "Custom built for Rollin Thurlow. Someone else may end up owning the canoe, but it was built for me."

Thurlow had made a decision to bring his landmark canoe to the assembly and offer it up, free of charge, to the person who could convince him, in three hundred written words or less, that they would be an appropriate receiver of such a fabulous gift.

On a seat in the new canoe he had placed a binder in which to display the entries. But on the first page he had included a short personal essay for potential entrants to read before submitting their own efforts. In this short essay, Thurlow first thanked his wife, Andrea, whom he said has "supported me and the canoe company even during the times it was obvious to everyone else that wooden canvas was dead."

And then Rollin Thurlow had spelled out the rules—or, more precisely, the rule: "The only requirement is that they must use the canoe in the manner which it was designed for; canoe tripping on rivers, lakes, class III rapids, carrying loads, carrying kids, going places the owner hasn't been before, enjoying quiet ponds and beautiful sunsets as well as cold, rainy days. In short, it was designed to be used, get dirty, scruff up its paint and even crack a rib or two in pursuit of the owner's canoeing dreams."

"If I sold this canoe," he told me as people lined up to submit their essays, "the customer would be picky. It would be the customer's boat, not my boat. I built this for myself and now I want someone to use it."

His contempt for any other style of canoe was hard to miss. "You might as well be in a can when you're in an aluminum boat," he said. "And plastic canoes are like opaque oil tanks. Sit in a wooden canoe and you are instantly relaxed. You can *feel* the canoe when you go over fast water. You can see the ribs move like it's breathing. You cringe that they're going to snap but they're okay. They give. It's like it's *alive*."

Thurlow is hardly alone in thinking along such lines. Bill Mason said in *Path of the Paddle* that "the canoe is not a lifeless, inanimate object; it feels very much alive, alive with the life of the river."

Attributing personality to a wooden canoe is common among builders. At Camp Lake, where we summer, there is a master carpenter called Lanny Watts, who, in his retirement years, builds exquisite cedar strip and cedar-and-canvas canoes for a hobby when he isn't fishing. Lanny once finished a lovely cedar strip and announced to friends: "This is a nervous canoe. You can't even part your hair slightly to one side or over she'll go. You have to part your hair exactly down the middle to paddle this canoe. And then you're fine."

Some of the submissions to win Thurlow's one thousandth work of art spoke extraordinarily of canoes. "How many doors can one expect to open with, of all things, a canoe?" asked "Zip" Kellogg of Portland, Maine. "A canoe will teach you about a thousand things—maps, boat building, camping, philosophy, history, your backyard, watersheds, water balance, art, first-aid, even politics. All you have to do is have an open mind and the continuing sense of wonder that many children have. . . . If I've learned anything over these 40 years of paddling, it's that canoes need exercise. No, do not look to me for putting ANY canoe on my mantelpiece."

Rist Bonnefond of Fayette, Maine, wrote Thurlow to say he had been "messing about in boats" since he was three years old. Now he is a grandfather and battling Parkinson's disease—"but I can still paddle!"—and he would like nothing better than to introduce those grandchildren to the love of paddling a wooden canoe.

John Connell of Underhill, Vermont, wrote about how, as a boy, he once took off in the family canoe on a silent moonlit night. He had become a teacher, for twenty years working with troubled youth on what he called the Wood Canoe Restoration Project, in which he had helped inner-city youth restore more than thirty canoes. "Bringing a neglected broken canoe back to life may offer some notion of hope," he wrote. And at the end of his short essay he returned to that first moment of his own with a canoe: "Sitting there years ago, in the moonlight, rocking gently in this beautiful boat, gave me a lasting kind of grounding."

Steve Ambrose, a canoe builder himself from Stahlstown, Pennsylvania, promised if he were given Thurlow's canoe, "It would live on the truck, be splattered with bugs, kissed by granite and logs, covered with bog slime and lovingly marked up inside by kids and grandchildren, nieces and nephews."

"Every boat is a mystery," Ted Huffman of Rapid City, South Dakota, argued in his essay. "When it is constructed, the builder does not know where its journey will lead. It is only potential when it is in the shop. A boat comes alive when it is in the water. . . . No other craft can match the elegance of a canoe. A canoe can teach the harmony of muscle and water and balance and efficient motion. A canoe teaches how to encounter the wilderness without footprints. . . . The basics of paddle strokes are simple to learn, but mastery of any stroke takes a lifetime."

After sorting through more than one hundred essays, Thurlow made his decision: his one thousandth canoe was headed to Canada. Mark Dagenais and Anne Swiderski of Chelsea, Quebec, had come to Paul Smith's with their restored Old Town, which had been constructed in Reading, Pennsylvania, back in 1922. They knew because the man from whom they had taken over the restoration had all the original records of canoe #69254.18. They even had the old order forms that showed the original purchaser wished for "3/4 yellow tape with Greek ends lettering 'Slo-n-e-z' in breakoff stripe at right bow and left stern."

The price was seventy-eight dollars for the canoe. The stripes and Greek lettering $1.80 extra.

"A wood and canvas canoe is a living creature with personality and soul, not a product or commodity," the couple wrote in their essay. "She is a member of the family, one who is cherished and cared for. This

Traveler will be brought along to partake and share in adventures and experiences much like a child or friend.

"We will use this beautiful Atkinson Traveler to further build our 'sense of place' in the natural world. We will introduce her to the wilderness of Georgian Bay, part of an ancient native and voyageur canoe route. From there, she will go on to explore the shores of Lake Superior.

"She will also be part of many shorter journeys, to keep us connected and grounded to nature, when the demands of life prevent longer explorations.

"She will carry our storm-proof tent, our soft sleeping bags, our canvas kitchen pack and our treasured pack baskets.

"The abrasions and scratches that accumulate will be more than our memories, they will become part of her stories and myths. She will then be a Storied Traveler, one which will be lovingly passed on to our daughter Lia, and eventually, to future generations of trippers. By these journeys, we will bring honour to your Traveler's spirit, and to you, its creator.

"It is humbling that this canoe will outlive most of us who will paddle her."

9

<hr>

LOST ON JAMES BAY

SOMETIMES I FEEL SURROUNDED BY CANOES. There are two hanging in the garage, one a magnificent cedar-and-canvas model built by Albert Maw of Northland Canoes nearly forty years ago, the other an ultralight that says as much about change over those same forty years as does the original price of the canvas canoe: $715.00. Both, of course, are bright red. The canoes used by the Lands and Forests rangers in Algonquin Park were red, with a white stripe; the grandparents' canoe at Lake of Two Rivers, a Chestnut Ranger, of course, was red; the fibreglass canoe son Gordon and I have hidden under a spruce by a little speckled trout lake on the edge of the Algonquin Park border is red.

If I told you where, of course, I would unfortunately have to kill you.

On a shelf behind where I type this is a framed photograph, taken by daughter Jocelyn, of the Northland canoe sitting empty by a campsite on Burnt Island Lake, the water so calm at dawn it looks as if the canoe has been pulled up onto a mirror. On the wall in front of me is a copy of a brilliant magazine illustration by Peter Swan. It was done for the first magazine article I ever wrote, "The Great Canoe Lake Mystery," for the September 1973 issue of *Maclean's*. Peter did a perfect copy of Tom Thomson's famous *West Wind*, but then deftly added in a ghostly addition: Tom kneeling in his canoe, paddling hard against the churning whitecaps.

The most compelling photograph of a canoe that I keep in my office, however, has no canoe in it.

It is a large poster given to me by Billy Diamond, then grand chief of the Crees of James Bay. The photograph is black and white, which somehow has the effect of making everything appear colder and more threatening. It portrays high swells on what appears to be the open sea, almost as if the hands of Neptune are reaching up two storeys or more trying to claw down and drown anything or anyone who might dare try to cross.

There is a message over the churning waves, simple but effective: "The waters of James Bay are not always friendly."

Archaeologists say the dangerous waters of James Bay have been travelled by paddlers and sailors for at least ten thousand years, but it is only in the past four centuries that history has kept much of a record. It was in 1610 that Henry Hudson set out from St. Katherine's Pool, London, in the sixty-five-foot *Discovery* on a voyage he hoped would finally reveal the much-sought-after Northwest Passage. It would be Hudson's fourth, and final, journey to the frozen north of the New World.

With a crew of twenty-one, including Hudson's young son, John, the *Discovery* passed through Davis Strait and headed down through the huge saltwater bay that is named for the captain himself, then turned southward into the smaller but nonetheless formidable James Bay. Hudson probably should have stayed the course.

At the mouth of a large river entering the southeast corner of James Bay, Hudson and his men settled in to pass the winter, knowing they could not possibly sail north in time to beat the ice and reach the stormy North Atlantic. The crew members were miserable and ill-fitted for winter survival, as they had departed England fully expecting to reach the South Seas. They felt deceived by their captain. Hudson had even confiscated all the navigation gear so that only he would know exactly where they were.

Where they were was stuck, frozen and increasingly desperate as weather and lack of nourishment began to take a predictable toll. There was much infighting over the clothes of the first men to die. At one point, a native man arrived with a sled carrying two deer and some beaver pelts and Hudson offered him a knife, a small mirror and some buttons in exchange—thereby initiating the fur trade that would underlie much of the James Bay story.

When late spring unlocked the *Discovery* from the ice, Captain Hudson told the sick, malnourished and angry crew he intended to continue exploring the shores of the bay. Six days later, the men mutinied, cast Hudson, his son and seven others adrift, and returned to England. The Hudsons and their presumed loyalists were never seen again.

It has been speculated that Hudson's folly was in lying to his crew about the reasons for their trip. They had sailed there, ostensibly, to find the passage to the so-called Spice Islands and the Orient, but his men were seasoned sailors who would have quickly realized they were wasting time exploring the shores and inlets of the bay. In fact, so many rivers feed into James Bay that its waters are only 10 to 15 per cent as salty as the Atlantic Ocean they had crossed to get there. They would have known from the water as well as the terrain that they were nowhere near any passage to the Pacific. American author Carl Schuster has analyzed this final voyage of *Discovery* and concluded Hudson was, in fact, in search of copper and gold for wealthy English merchants and titled members of King James I's court who had underwritten the voyage.

No matter, Hudson's final voyage would be on a frail lifeboat that was no match for the unfriendly waters of James Bay.

That great river that met the saltwater bay where the *Discovery* anchored for the winter was finally named more than half a century after Hudson's demise. In 1668 two vessels arrived from England: the *Nonsuch*, with Sieur Des Groseilliers aboard as their guide, and the *Eaglet*, bearing Des

Groseilliers's partner Pierre-Esprit Radisson. When the captain of the *Nonsuch*, Zachariah Gillam, reached the river, he named it for the king's cousin, Prince Rupert, who would become first governor of the Hudson's Bay Company.

At the mouth of the Rupert River they built Fort Charles. The following spring some three hundred native men, women and children, returning from their traplines and hunting grounds in canoes, came to the fort with their winter harvest to trade. The *Nonsuch* returned to England with such a rich haul that the king granted the collection of merchants and aristocracy that had financed the trip exclusive trading rights to all the lands that drained into Hudson Bay.

The fur trade was on. One year later, in 1670, the Hudson's Bay Company was founded—the business venture that would, in so many ways, one day become the country called Canada. And it all began at the site of the encampment the Crees called "Waskaganish" and the maps, "Rupert House."

The Eastern Crees—often referred to as the "Swampy Cree"—built "crooked canoes" using birchbark. The highly rockered canoes with more curve to the keel and higher bow and stern were also preferred by the Ungava Cree of the Labrador-Ungava Peninsula and were found with the Naskapi and Montagnais tribes as well. The design was particularly effective, though far from perfect, for the high, slow swells along the James Bay coast. The Crees did not use the heavy York boats so popular on Western rivers. They required something more nimble for the swift waters of the Rupert, the Nottaway, Harricana and Broadback rivers, all of which drained into Rupert Bay—something more manoeuvrable for running the whitewater that could be run, light enough for portaging around the impossible rapids and yet sturdy and high enough to allow the Crees to deal with the vastly different waters of James Bay.

Those Cree vessels were of great interest to A.P. Low of the Geological Survey of Canada, who mapped Northern Quebec and Labrador before the end of the nineteenth century. In 2002, two modern adventurers,

Max Finkelstein and James Stone, set out to retrace much of Low's travels and were left astounded by the breadth of his explorations. "Between 1881 and 1889," they wrote, "he spent over 2,500 days travelling by canoe and snowshoe—that's almost seven years—and describing by map and in written notes more than 200,000 square miles of the Quebec-Labrador peninsula." The two consider Low's 1893–94 trip through Quebec-Labrador—"more than 5,500 miles"—as "one of the great canoe trips of all time."

When Low reached the HBC post at Lake Mistassini in 1884, he found two dozen families living nearby, the local game all but gone and the people dealing with the scourge of measles and tuberculosis. Canoes, he realized, were their lifeline in far more ways than one. They allowed the Crees to travel and hunt, of course, but they were critical in other ways, as well.

"If it were not for the provisions supplied by the Company," Low noted, "these Indians would be unable to live. . . . In the summer, all the able-bodied men descend the Rupert River in large canoes to Rupert House, with the furs taken from the winter, and return with supplies for the ensuing year." The annual trek was called "the Rupert Brigade," and it included not only the large fur-laden canoes but many smaller craft carrying the hunters' women and children, all headed for the larger HBC post at Rupert House, where they would sell their furs, pick up supplies and, from time to time, purchase a new canoe from the little factory that had sprung up at the mouth of the Rupert River.

The early fur trade canoes—the *canots de maître* best known among them—were constructed in places like Trois-Rivières. While the builders took the basic designs from the native birchbark crafts, they were built in factories by the likes of L.A. Christopherson, who for forty years built such large and sturdy vessels for the Hudson's Bay Company, each one with the letters "HBC" stamped high on the curled stern. It was the Crees who still joked that the initials stood for "Here Before Christ" well into the twentieth century.

With birchbark scarce in the trading terrain, the Crees were quick to adapt to such modifications as iron nails rather than traditional wooden pegs, and canvas instead of bark. Rupert House soon became the natural centre for building these canoes and selling them around the vast peninsula. "The HBC had set up a canoe factory in Rupert's House at the height of long-distance transporting of goods by canoe brigades," Richard Sailisbury wrote in *A Homeland for the Crees*. "It had exported its cedar planked and canvas-covered canoes to enthusiasts for canoeing during the 1950s. But in the 1960s the decline in northern use of freighter canoes, accompanied by the change in sports canoes from wood and canvas to aluminum or fibreglass construction resulted in declining production. The Rupert House canoe factory finally closed in 1977." When I first began travelling to Waskaganish a few years later, the old building still stood, the sign "Rupert House Canoe Company" faded but still legible.

The best-known craft were designed and built by the same man, John C. Iserhoff. He built two models: "a thirty-foot canoe capable of carrying 4,000 pounds and a twenty-three-and-a-half-foot freighter capable of carrying 2,000 pounds. Of these, the smaller craft was by far the most popular."

Gradually the traditionally Cree canoe changed, particularly following the invention of the outboard motor. The Rupert House Canoe Company began making square stern canoes that could hold outboards and, soon enough, all canoes made there could accommodate the new power source. They made a sixteen-footer called the Rupert, the eighteen-foot Roberval, a twenty-foot Rupert and a twenty-three-foot Rupert. They were sold throughout the North, and many are still in use.

It is a Rupert House freighter canoe—once owned by the Cheechoo family of Moose Factory—that holds centre stage in the vast warehouse of the Canadian Canoe Museum in Peterborough. It stands with original birchbark canoes, early cedar strip canoes, even dugouts from places like Bora Bora and Fiji. While it looks wildly out of place—massive, wide, heavy, boat-like—it is still considered a canoe.

"Yes—absolutely *yes*," says Jeremy Ward to the obvious question as to whether the James Bay freighter can fairly be considered a "canoe." It did, after all, begin as a canoe everyone would recognize, even if it evolved over time into something approaching a Boston whaler. (Intriguingly, there are easy comparisons to be made between the morphing of the traditional canoe into something suitable for James Bay and those "canoes" manufactured in England in 1884 for the Nile Expedition.)

"I say 'yes'—and our collection committee says 'yes,' too," adds Ward. "It is all about 'canoe genetics' and the evolving of the craft around the world."

The Rupert House factory closed when the Crees could no longer compete with the much cheaper and more durable aluminum and fibreglass canoes that were flooding the market.

The Cree canoes were for generations as critical to survival as furs, food and fire. Boyce Richardson, the Ottawa filmmaker and author who spent much of his life among the Crees, perfectly illustrated the importance of the canoe in a tale he told about Isaiah and Willie Awashish, who in the early 1970s were conducting one final check of their set beaver traps before freeze-up.

Isaiah at the time was sixty, Willie only seventeen, and he would one day be taking over the vast territory on which the Awashish family had always trapped. The two were well used to working in concert to travel up the rivers. At a rapids, it was always the older man's job to pull the canoe up close to the fast water, the young man's task to jump out of the canoe and hold it fast to the shore.

They were about halfway through the boiling rapids, close to a small island, when Willie, who could not clearly see his father, felt the rope go slack and let go his end, thinking his father had the canoe held fast. In fact, the canoe had simply stopped in an eddy. Without Willie holding on, it slipped out of the still water and shot across the river.

"Left standing on an island in the middle of the torrential Rupert River," Richardson wrote, "they were stripped of all their equipment. The unthinkable had happened: an accident, one of the very few that had ever occurred to the old man in his lifetime as a hunter. They could not swim off the island because the waters in this part of the world are always too cold for swimming. No prudent man would plunge into a northern river in October."

The men had nothing with them for survival. Not even an axe. Everything was in that canoe. The two would have perished but for the luck of a crosswind that blew the canoe over to the shore and held it fast rather than the canoe slipping into the next set of rapids and being destroyed or, at the least, carried far downstream. Willie was panicking. Fortunately, Isaiah's decades in the bush saved them when he was able, with the help of Willie, to gather enough branches on the island, tie them into a makeshift raft using roots and then use another good-sized branch as a paddle to work his way across the water and retrieve the canoe.

Had the canoe been lost, father and son would have been doomed.

My friendship with Billy Diamond went back to a spring day in 1981 when he arrived, alone, at the *Maclean's* office on Ottawa's Wellington Street and asked if he might have a word—a first word that would spawn a constant flow of conversation over the years.

The grand chief of the James Bay Crees had a story that shook me to the core. Babies were dying in James Bay and no one was listening to the Crees' call for help. The James Bay Agreement that Billy, as a young chief, had negotiated with the Quebec and federal governments in 1975—a groundbreaking deal that was the first of the modern treaties—had included new housing and infrastructure to be provided by the two levels of government. In several villages new houses had been built and work started on sewers and water, but construction had been halted when Ottawa and Quebec City went through another of their predictable piques over responsibility.

The Crees were already moved into many of the new houses but, having unfinished water and sewer systems, were forced to build temporary outhouses in their yards. In spring, the frozen sludge had melted into the ditches and from the ditches had infected the village wells. Mothers unwittingly used the bad water when they fed their babies formula, and while older Crees were getting sick and dealing with diarrhea, several of the babies ended up with E. coli infections—the Third World scourge of gastroenteritis—and, so far, three of the babies had died.

Billy and Elizabeth Diamond's own young son, Phillip, had come down with the infection himself. They had airlifted the infant to Montreal Children's Hospital, where, at one point, he had been given the last rites and his parents told to say their farewells, only to have the child rally, almost miraculously, when Billy, tired of listening to nothing but English and French instructions and explanations, whispered in Cree to the bloated, barely breathing child that he should fight to stay, that he needed to be with his family to see what was going to happen to them and all the Crees of James Bay.

Phillip rallied slightly, causing doctors to quickly ease his parents away from the bed so they could renew efforts on the infant. Phillip ended up spending four months in hospital before finally beginning a long, and happily successful, recovery at home with his parents in Waskaganish.

At least the Diamond family had been with their sick child and were given regular updates on his prospects. Not getting proper explanations from the authorities was a more common experience for the Crees. Babies that had died previously were often taken away for autopsies and unceremoniously returned weeks later for burial. Babies had been returned in pieces, in green garbage bags, in one instance stuffed into an empty milk carton.

Disdain from authority figures was familiar to all First Nations, not just the Crees. In 1975, the same year that the James Bay Agreement had been signed, James Richardson, then minister of defence, had let his personal feelings on Aboriginals be known in a *Maclean's* interview. "What did they ever do for Canada?" he had asked. "Did they discover oil? They didn't even invent the wheel. Why, when we came here, they were still dragging things around on two sticks."

The massive James Bay hydroelectric project had been announced in 1971 by then Quebec premier Robert Bourassa at a gala gathering at the

Quebec Colisée. The people who would be most affected by the development—the 6,500 Crees who, archaeologists believe, had been living in the James Bay area for more than ten thousand years—had not been invited. Worse, the six Cree villages in the area had never even been informed, even though the announced project was so vast it would rival the building of the pyramids and the dredging of the Panama Canal. Billy Diamond, then Rupert House's newly elected twenty-one-year-old chief, had learned of the Quebec government's announcement while listening to the CBC supper-time news on his little transistor radio during the spring goose hunt.

"The world begins tomorrow," Bourassa had told the cheering crowd in Quebec City.

It certainly did for Billy Diamond up in Rupert House. He called the first meeting of the James Bay Crees that had ever been held. One of the Crees who came to the little schoolhouse in Mistassini to look at the maps and hear about the province's plans to dam up their rivers and flood their traditional hunting grounds stood up and told Billy, who chaired the meeting, that they had better go out and immediately purchase an electric typewriter. Puzzled, Billy had asked, "Why?" Equally baffled, the man had answered, "Because, Billy, none of us knows how to type." Four years later these same unorganized, forgotten Crees had an agreement the likes of which had never before been seen.

With Billy as my guide, I had travelled by airplane and helicopter to investigate the E. coli scandal for myself. *Maclean's* published a cover story on June 1, 1981, showing Billy sitting at a campfire with a rifle on his lap, a title beside his stern, unsmiling face: "Rumbles from the North—Coming to the Crunch on Land Claims." The tragedy that grew out of a silly federal-provincial conflict caused such a sensation that a motion was even tabled at the first United Nations Conference on Indigenous Peoples and Land held at Geneva, Switzerland. And it brought action: the federal cabinet announced an emergency fund of more than $60 million to bring in fresh water and medical help. Work to finish the sewers and water supplies in the villages began again immediately.

Since that time, our friendship had grown. When the Crees established their own successful airline, Air Creebec, I was there to write about it. In 1989, I published a book, *Chief: The Fearless Vision of Billy Diamond,* that told the story of the leader who had been sent crying off to residential school at age seven and who had returned to lead the Crees in the incredible court battle that ended up forcing the James Bay Agreement. It also told the heartbreaking tale of the dead babies but happily included the remarkable recovery of little Phillip Diamond—thanks in no small part to most of the village of Waskaganish volunteering to massage his limbs several hours every day—into a youngster perfectly capable of walking, running and talking, at times non-stop.

The leadership of Billy Diamond—based on economic sustainability and Cree control—earned him the moniker "Canada's northern Iacocca" from author Peter C. Newman. When Billy died far too early from heart failure in the fall of 2010, Matthew Coon Come, now grand chief of the James Bay Crees, said, "My Indian friends from India had Mahatma Gandhi. My American friends had JFK. My Afro-American friends had Martin Luther King. My South African friends had Nelson Mandela. My Cree Nation had Chief Billy Diamond."

The funeral service pamphlet listed eighty-nine pallbearers. If in Africa it takes a village to raise a child, in James Bay it took the village to bury this chief. They came by the hundreds to watch Billy Diamond's casket carried through the streets of Waskaganish, pallbearers handing off to fresh pallbearers every few hundred steps. He was buried at the little church that once stood by the Rupert House Canoe Company, under a stone that held the message he had specifically requested:

"Gone to a meeting—will return."

In late June of 1986 Billy had invited me to come up to Waskaganish—the old Anglo name "Rupert House" having been retired following the signing of the James Bay Agreement—for the launch of the new "Hudson's

Bay Canoe," which the Crees were building in a brand-new factory not far from where the old canoe factory had stood.

The Air Creebec airline was up and running. Now it was time to turn his attention to the Crees' original form of transport.

Billy had gone to Japan with several other Cree leaders and had met with the giant manufacturer Yamaha, and with Cree traditional knowledge and Yamaha modern technology, they had completely redesigned the famous Hudson's Bay freighter canoe. Far too many lives had been lost to freak storms and overloaded boats and hidden rocks. Billy Diamond wanted a new boat for the twentieth and twenty-first centuries—one that would save lives rather than cost them.

He had strategically used the known Japanese fascination with North American Aboriginals to strike an initial meeting with Yamaha executives in Toronto, then had gone to Tokyo for deeper discussions. Now, after two years of negotiation, agreements and experiment, the first Cree-Yamaha "canoes" were rolling off the Waskaganish assembly line. If they looked more like a fishing boat than a birchbark canoe or the more familiar freighter canoes of the Canadian North, so be it. Safety was the number-one issue. Already that spring, five Crees had drowned when their vessels had been swamped on the bay.

With a close Ottawa friend, Doug Sprott, I had driven the better part of a day north up through Maniwaki and La Vérendrye park to Val-d'Or, and then caught the regular Air Creebec flight north. Nearly two hours later, we bounced down onto the gravel runway and hitched a pickup ride into a village so excited it could barely contain itself. There was already a feast in progress: spring goose was being smoked in tents, the geese hanging over the smoking fires and their grease dropping into pans where it would then be used in the cooking of bannock; there were plates of beaver paws and moose nostrils, smoked whitefish and trout and huge pots of dark tea to wash it all down.

The excitement was not restricted to the shores where the Rupert River flows into James Bay. Yamaha executives were on their way by chartered jet from Tokyo. Peter Gzowski would be calling Billy the next morning so that the launch of this most unusual joint venture could be carried live on *Morningside*, CBC Radio's nationally popular morning show.

The truck carrying Doug and me and our packs in from the runway came to a gravel-crunching, dusty stop. Billy was already walking toward us, smiling.

"You're going out for the 'test drive,'" Billy laughed.

"*What?*"

"It's all set up," he said. "Lawrence and Charlie are going to take you up the coast a bit to do some fishing. It's the official 'test drive' for Cree-Yamaha."

I had mentioned fishing over the radio telephone when Billy and I had spoken earlier, but had never considered fishing a necessity. This trip was not to be sport, but work, and yet what could be a better storyline than to head out onto the waters of James Bay with precisely those who would be using the new craft? Lawrence Katapatuk—rhymes with "cut a paycheque," he liked to joke—was Billy's lifelong pal, a man who mostly kept to the bush as a trapper and hunter. Billy's older brother, Charlie Diamond, was even more old world, a strong, silent man who spoke no English at all and who lived, year-round, along his traplines and in the family's coastal goose camps.

We set out Monday around noon, the Japanese not due in until Tuesday morning, when the CBC would be calling and the boat, now officially "road" tested, would be safely back. Billy thought I would be able to go on radio with him to back up his claims about the seaworthiness of the new boats.

We would be going out in an early prototype. It was the largest model, some twenty-seven feet long—somewhere between the Rupert House Canoe Company's largest Rupert model and the thirty-foot giant designed and built by John C. Iserhoff—and it was still unfinished. Essentially, it was the "shell" of the fibreglass vessel it would become. There was no trimming, not even any seats. We were to sit on stacked boards.

I tossed my backpack into the bow. A propitious move, it would turn out, but it had nothing to do with foreboding. I had some southern fishing equipment and a fold-up rod in the pack and thought I might have a chance to make a few casts. Doug brought nothing. The two hunters had a large cooler filled with food for a shore lunch, and a single packsack. Because the boat had yet to be tested for bow spray in heavier water, Lawrence retrieved a large waterproof tarpaulin from his house, which he placed over the two packs. Another propitious move.

I thought it all a bit overly cautious. We were, after all, just headed out for a trial run for a few hours at best. We set out in calm water under sunny skies. With Charlie standing Cree-style in front of the forty-horsepower Yamaha—straight up, left hand holding the upturned throttle handle as if it were the hand of a child, wind straight into his face. We headed out into the mouth of the Rupert and soon swung north into the gentle chop of James Bay proper.

"Look at that!" Doug shouted.

I turned from where I was seated on the backpacks and followed his finger. He had sighted a most unusual rock formation, a small granite island that popped out of the water like some great prehistoric creature rising to challenge our presence.

I nodded in agreement. Charlie shook his head at Lawrence, but neither said anything. Only later would we be told that the Crees considered it bad luck to point or even glance at this dramatic rock, that to acknowledge the striking rock at the confluence of the Rupert River and James Bay was to invite the wrath of Chuentenshu, the mighty north wind. We were tempting fate, at least as the Crees saw it, but Charlie and Lawrence were much too polite to say anything to Billy's invited guests.

Chuentenshu, it would turn out, knew nothing of politeness to strangers.

The Cree-Yamaha freighter canoe rode beautifully, sliding over the light chop with grace and speed and an awesome sense of power and indestructibility. We could tell from how often the two Cree hunters changed positions—first one steering, then the other—that they, too, were marvelling over this brand-new creation.

The freighter had been designed to be deliberately wide for James Bay, where the north wind is almost always blowing and the shallow water can be so easily whipped into a frenzy. Since waves tend to be narrow and tight in such shallows, the boat was constructed long, as well, so it would crest three or four such waves at once, virtually *surfing*, the ride as smooth as a limousine on a newly paved city street.

Doug and I lay back, turning our faces to the south and the sun, and prepared to let the gentle roll of the ride and the hypnotic drone of the Yamaha outboard put us to sleep.

An hour or so out of Waskaganish, however, we were wide awake—and terrified.

The wind had not built slowly, as we were used to in the south, but appeared suddenly as if to ambush us from Hudson Bay to the north. There were instant whitecaps. The boat began to slam against them rather than cut through them.

We were no longer "surfing," but "crashing," each slam into the coming troughs and waves sending harsh jolts through the crude wooden "seats." Doug, who has always had a wonky back, was wincing in pain with every smack against the oncoming waves.

And then, even though we had set out wearing light jackets and turning our faces into the warmth of the late June sun, it began to *snow*.

Snow. At first large, rolling flakes that seemed like small birds riding above the waves and boat, but then quickly changing to icy pellets that stabbed like needles into our faces. We pulled our caps and collars tight, unfolded the large tarp that Lawrence had fortunately placed over the packs, pulled the extra plastic over our legs and bodies and hunkered down.

We were quite far from shore. It had been some time since we could see land and now, with snow blowing and low, dark clouds moving in, it was difficult to make out anything at all on the horizon, except more oncoming cloud and snow.

Every once in a while, a small island would loom in the distance and we would turn toward it in the hope of shelter. Doug and I were convinced several times that safety was within reach, only to have our hopes dashed on the rocks that a couple of times prevented us from even approaching the tiny bits of land, usually solid rock themselves.

Even if we could chance a landing, we realized the pointlessness of it. The rocky outcroppings offered no support for the feet, no shelter from the wind. We would simply perish on land rather than water. Any attempt to breach the shoals and rocks surrounding the tiny atolls was so fraught with potential disaster that the two Cree hunters decided, without so much as a word being spoken, that the only option was to keep on going, even as the going on the water got continually worse.

We carried no satellite phone so could not call to be rescued. Even if they sent out rescue parties after discovering we were missing, it might be too late. We had to get off the waters of James Bay—but we had to get off someplace where we had a chance of survival until a rescue could be mounted.

Charlie, the more experienced of the two hunters, was in control of the boat now, but he was no longer standing at the throttle. He was half kneeling, the boat rocking and banging too dangerously for him to focus on anything but keeping us from flipping in the winds and waves. He fumbled with his shirt and thin plastic rain slicker, trying, uselessly, to bundle up tighter.

The wind began to howl.

I have seen this phrase written so many times—even sang along with it at the end of Dylan's "All Along the Watchtower"—but never before had I heard wind like this. Perhaps it would be more appropriate to say the wind began to *scream*. The Crees treat such things as wind and water as living creatures, animals, and now I understood why. This scream was not human, not animal; it was the wind, alive.

Chuentenshu was in full rage.

The scream grew so loud it drowned out the Yamaha. The wind began to shear off the tops of the whitecaps, sending clips of salty water to sting our faces and run beneath our collars. Lawrence, Doug and I tied the tarp down and pulled as much of it over us as we could, the three of us trying to maintain some modicum of shelter while our fourth, Charlie, drove on into the teeth of the storm.

Doug and I had both wondered why we were not turning back, but the two hunters knew that doing so would simply keep us in the storm as it powered toward Waskaganish. Besides, to turn was to risk capsizing, no matter how skilled Charlie was. And the Cree-Yamaha, remember, was still unfamiliar to him. The hunters were impressed by what it could do, but were uncertain about what it could not do. Better to keep going.

The snow was now so thick that Doug and Lawrence and I could see no landmarks, though we squinted and stared and prayed hard. Doug and I had no idea by this point whether we were even heading toward shore and not out into the deeper bay.

Sailors know there are few dangers greater than wide expanses of shallow water and a high, unpredictable wind. The small chop that we had set out in had churned into huge, rolling waves. The freighter canoe could no longer bridge several crests, as it had been designed to do, or even two or three of the crests at once; instead, it would ride up one, teeter, the Yamaha screeching as water released its grip on shaft and propeller blade, and then the boat would collapse down into the gaping funnel.

It was as if every few seconds the boat was being pushed out a second-storey window and crashing down on the sidewalk below. The jolts were crushing, our backs so hammered that, eventually, Doug had to roll onto his side each time just before impact, and then roll back up. He was in deep pain.

Charlie, still running the outboard, stumbled once, his bare hand now so frozen it would not obey his command to grip the throttle. Lawrence jumped back, taking over the steering even though, to Doug and me, it seemed there were no directions out there on the bay but straight up and straight down.

We were soaked through. The wind was still clipping the tops of the waves and tossing saltwater into our faces. The crashing of the big boat into each coming wave was now hurling water over the bow and onto the tarp and floor. We were bailing continually, taking turns with the pail that had held some of the fishing equipment. Snow was collecting on our tarp and clothes and around the improvised seats and transom.

None of us said it, but I was certainly thinking we were going to die. Doug was thinking the same. We didn't need to share this with each other to know. Hours later, speaking in Cree, with Lawrence translating, Charlie would say it was at this precise point—his hands frozen, the saltwater washing over the bow—where Charlie Diamond, who had spent his entire life on James Bay, became quietly convinced that "We weren't going to make it."

Doug and I, privately, were preparing for the end. The screaming wind was picking up rather than calming down. The crashing was getting so forceful we had to stifle our own screams each time the boat thudded into the next valley.

Preparing to die was the strangest sensation. I had been frightened before—lost in the woods, on planes where engines have blown and caught fire, in numerous near road accidents—but nothing had ever felt like this. Near certainty, but not quite certainty. Almost peaceful, but not quite, yet certainly more peaceful than terrifying.

The boat was rising so high and falling so far now that water blew in at the top of the rise and poured in at the bottom. What was surprising—and slightly hopeful—was how well the boat itself was bearing up.

A wooden freighter would surely have split in half by now, or have taken on so much water that it would be sinking, or would have flipped long ago in the heavy waves. We were bailing, but not frantically. The Cree-Yamaha boat never even shuddered. It slammed. It crashed. It growled up the wave and the outboard whined as we crested. And it slammed down again. If we were going down, it would be because we were taking on too much water, because of the elements, not the boat. Too bad Peter Gzowski wasn't going to hear this.

I began thinking about what it was going to feel like when the inevitable came. The boat would fatten with water, and one end would surely dip down first. At various times along this now-forgotten route, we had noticed the waters so shallow that rock shoals stuck out and had to be avoided. What if the boat crashed onto one of them—*we would be saved!* For a while. Or what if the boat turned over? *Could we cling to smooth fibreglass?* Not likely. What if it went down in less than ten feet of water, which was entirely possible in this huge, shallow ocean of a bay? Could we swim until we purchased footing on some island? Could we stand on the boat until help came?

Fat chance. There was no help to come. And even if there were, no time to get here.

I came to the conclusion, cold and logical, that we were doomed.

Doug and I yanked on the tarpaulin to free it of snow and some of the surface water. It flew off in all directions, most of it staying aboard.

The boat crashed so hard into the next cliff of water that it seemed, for the moment, as if it might finally fracture and splinter and hurl us all to our timely and deserved deaths.

"*Look!*"

It was Lawrence. He was pointing off over the bow. Charlie stretched up to look. Doug and I tried to see, too, but the bow rose and fell so fast that we had to hit the floor and then, when it rose again for the next wave, we quickly shifted to our knees so we could see.

The snow had turned to sleet, the sheets of wet ice drumming on the stretched tarpaulin. The visibility was almost zero, but off through the grey-white fuzz of what should have been the horizon, there appeared the faintest hint of substance: darker, steady, solid. The prettiest sight any of us had seen in these short lives we had been on the verge of giving up on.

Lawrence, now handling the outboard, turned the boat slightly and a mighty wave, a rogue wave in the eyes of the Cree helmsman, lifted the boat and spun it sideways, tossing it hard into the next wave, which washed into us and over us.

"He almost got us, there!" Lawrence shouted.

He, the sea. Not that *he,* Lawrence, had erred by daring to change course, even slightly, but that *he,* the sea, had chosen this moment to attack, the water a full and equal personality in this stark northern world, every bit as alive and with as much right to win as the Cree hunters who were up against *him.*

We headed toward the island, but Lawrence and Charlie knew that it would be surrounded by dangerous shoals. Up ahead, we could see the waves spitting high as they broke and exploded just below the surface. There was no passageway to the leeward side. We would have to come in from the northwest side.

Lawrence turned, the motor crunched into one rock, then another, the propeller screaming as we rose over the rocks, then choking as it settled back, but the sheer pin held and the motor again kicked back in. Had it not held, we would have been lost for certain, powerless as the wind rolled us back sideways into the rolling waves.

"We're going to have to head straight out into it!" Lawrence shouted. *"Once we're beyond the rocks, we'll come back in with the wind!"*

These few moments were even more harrowing than any of the last two hours. Lawrence turned the boat, deliberately, away from the only possible salvation we had seen.

The boat bucked and dropped and rose and crashed as it cut on new angles across the fury, but Lawrence held hard to the controls and angled the boat so that it rose up onto one wave and cut across at such an angle that he was able to surf the boat from one wave to the next.

Charlie moved on his knees to the front of the boat and reached down under the gunwales to retrieve a long pole. He stood, groin and stomach pressed hard to the bow, and raised the pole over his head with both hands as if he were about to drive it into a whale. But he was not looking for game. He was checking for rocks. As Lawrence turned back, he cut the engine to half, and Charlie began prodding ahead, signalling as he detected bottom, steering Lawrence always clear of the rocks.

Finally, they seemed to have the angle Lawrence wanted. With a wrench of the throttle, he turned the boat so quickly it almost dipped sideways into the next wave. The boat turned, the wave caught, the boat lifted, the motor shrieked like a siren as it cleared the water, the boat settled, the motor settled, and we shot straight over the waves, the wind now to our backs, and flew into the sheltered approach to the back of the island.

The water was but a moderate chop here, the boat once again gliding so smoothly it seemed impossible to imagine that, moments earlier, we had all been making our peace.

Lawrence aimed the boat toward a rough beach, shutting down the throttle and reaching back to hoist the outboard as the Cree-Yamaha freighter canoe sizzled into the sand and, amazingly, the world instantly ceased to roll and rise and drop and shudder. The calm was extraordinary. The feeling when our feet first hit the shallows, then the shore, was as sweet and satisfying as any sensation we had ever known.

I knelt and kissed the beach.

We spent three days marooned on little Obedjiwan Island. They were three of the nicest days of my life.

While Doug and I walked around the schoolyard-sized island, pushing through the black spruce and the aspen, scrambling over the snow-covered rocks and lichen and watching the tides come in and out, the two Cree hunters silently went about surviving for all four of us.

Even before the snow had stopped, Lawrence and Charlie had turned spruce poles and the big tarpaulin from the boat into a makeshift tent. They had found an old forty-five-gallon drum some hunter or bush pilot had once cached his gasoline supply in, and, using knives and axe, they had turned it into as cozy a wood stove as any resort has ever advertised. They found a rusted pail and Lawrence deliberately put his foot through the bottom, instantly creating a "flue" for the top of the tarpaulin tent. We had shelter; we had heat. We took off our wet clothes and dried them, dancing nearly naked in the tent while shirts danced and dried on the ends of sticks placed in the ground just beyond the edges of the flame.

When the tide was out, Charlie and Lawrence set fishing nets they had carried in their own packs. Wearing thigh-high waders, they went out into the shallow waters off the rocky end of the island and tacked the fine nets onto poles they hammered in between the rocks. Once the tide came in and went out again, they gathered up whitefish and monkfish that had been caught by their gills and cleaned the small fish and sliced them and suspended them on sticks over the open fire, the cooked flesh so sweet and tender that it seemed to melt in our hands. We had tea. We had fresh bannock.

The more we explored the island, the more we came to realize it had once, years ago, been the site of a Cree goose camp. We even fixed up the old "outhouse" with a magnificent view of the far shore, beckoning in the distance. We slept at night, warm and happy, our sleeping bags—the Cree hunters had carried an extra one that they offered to Doug—tight to our necks as Charlie and Lawrence lay casually on top of theirs and talked in Cree and giggled, probably at us. Who could blame them?

Charlie fascinated me. He walked with me about the island and everywhere he looked he seemed to find something. A bear skull, which Lawrence said meant we would have good luck. A couple of stove pipes that, fitted together, took the smoke out of our makeshift shelter. It was almost as if he had been here before, preparing the island for a future shipwreck.

I loved to watch him walk and work. He never hurried. And when he chopped the spruce for the fire, he squatted down, knees to his side, legs back, feet splayed for balance. I had never seen anyone cut wood like this, and it struck me that he was giving up too much in power and leverage. I asked Lawrence about this. He replied that Charlie lived all the time in the bush and was usually alone on his traplines, where one little slip of a sharp axe could mean bleeding to death if there was no one there to help. The Cree hunters cut their wood this way deliberately. It was safer. How different from the likes of Doug and me, who would have had a splitting block set up and swung at the spruce as if driving home the last spike in a railroad.

When the weather partially cleared on the second day, Doug and I began searching the skies for rescue planes, but we never saw a plane, never heard an engine, never even saw a high trail of a jet headed for Asia or Europe. Nothing. When I asked Lawrence if they would be sending out anyone, he laughed.

"Who says we're lost?" he asked.

If anything, those back in Waskaganish would be wondering what was keeping us, now that the storm had passed. They would presume Lawrence and Charlie were fully capable of keeping the southern city boys safe.

True enough, on the third day the storm had passed and the chop on the bay had returned to what we had set out in. It seemed a lifetime earlier.

It was low tide, the water now a good three hundred metres from where we had beached in the storm. We had to get the freighter canoe out to where it could float and we could put down the outboard.

Lawrence and Charlie cut logs and we used them as rollers, moving each one to the front of the line after the boat passed over it, and gradually pushed the craft out toward the water. It was tough slogging. Doug ripped his boot in half. We grunted and pushed, rested, grunted, pushed. Gradually, we reached the water line and, with one last mighty heave from the four of us, had the Cree-Yamaha vessel floating in the shallows. Paddling and pushing into deeper water, we were finally able to drop the outboard's shaft down. Charlie hooked the motor to a fresh tank of gas and fired it up.

It took less than three hours to make our way back.

When we turned into the mouth of the Rupert, Charlie at the throttle, we could see that the Waskaganish dock area was thick with Crees, Billy Diamond standing in the centre.

The Japanese had come and gone.

Morningside had phoned and given up.

But Billy Diamond could not have been more pleased. The Cree-Yamaha freighter canoe had passed its test.

Lives had already been saved.

CONCLUSION

IT IS NOT WHAT ONE expects upon reaching the Canadian Canoe Museum. For one thing, the building is nowhere near water. It sits, instead, on a back street a block off Peterborough's main edge-of-town strip of fast-food outlets, car dealerships and budget motels. For a facility housing the most elegant of creations, the museum has all the style and lines of a Soviet tractor plant. Indeed, it once was a factory, manufacturing of all things the very invention that many once believed would spell the end of canoeing: outboard engines.

One would expect a serious experience inside, given the uninspired look of the building and the doors that open upon a stairway—tabbed the "Grand Portage" by staff—that leads to a display called "Origins." Nowhere near water, and beginning with a history lesson—the obvious expectation would be dry, dry, dry . . .

But what is that flickering on the wall?

The museum calls it the "Tweetwall." An image is flickering on a screen with a message that would cause a historian to blush all the way to the leather elbows of his corduroy jacket.

It's not the length. It's the girth.
#canoelove #stroke #stroke

251

Conclusion

The surprising comment is, without having to spell anything out, a wonderful example of the lasting power of the canoe. It may have been launched in the era of smoke signals and sign language, yet it remains afloat in the time of social media and hashtags.

One can only wonder if David Thompson's journals would exist had the Great Map-Maker carried an iPhone instead of a sextant and tweeted his way across the country instead of spending the rest of his life writing up his journals:

ICYMI Reached mouth of Col. Riv. – Late! LOL.
#bigbuggerofacountry

The frisky "length/girth/stroke" double entendre at the entrance of the Canadian Canoe Museum welcomes visitors to a new exhibition called "Can I Canoe You up the River?" The exhibition (which ran through the spring of 2015) tells the story of paddling, romance and the canoe's charming role in courtship. It was assembled by museum staff and features several vessels from the "social canoeing" collection of Michigan wine dealer Ken Kelly, who is also president of the Wooden Canoe Heritage Association. The title for this charming show is taken from an old Arthur Godfrey song from the early 1950s:

C'n I canoe you down the stream?
C'n I canoe you up the river?
Like I did in last night's dream?

It is the story, really, about a remarkable convergence of change. The canoe as a recreational vehicle was born, purely by coincidence, in the Victorian era of strict morals and behaviour. Yet it was also a time when the concepts of romance and marriage were taking a dramatic shift. Marriage ceased to be about necessity, convenience or arrangement and instead became—in part because of idle time, urbanization, literacy and the rise of popular romantic novels—more about two people finding each other and, over time, falling in love.

Courtship became an accepted prelude to marriage, but the Victorian era tended to treat courtship as a potentially wild animal to be caged or else. Young couples could meet in the parlour under family, usual parental, supervision. They could sit on the front porch so long as a chaperone, often an elderly aunt, was included. At later stages they might even go for a walk in the park—so long as they were accompanied by a guardian. Privacy was something reserved for marriage.

However, the human condition is such that ways around this restriction were eagerly sought. The bicycle became a popular vehicle for courtship, in no small part, surely, because older chaperones either could not ride or could not keep up. The canoe was an even better option, with no room for a chaperone and carrying, for older people, a built-in fear factor of tipping. A bicycle might take a courting couple into a park, but a canoe could allow them to slip into a hidden cove or under the curtain branches of a willow.

That image was poetically captured in 1878, the peak of Victorian times, by *Treasure Island* author Robert Louis Stevenson. Following his own travel by the Rob Roy "canoe" through France and Belgium, he penned "The Canoe Speaks":

> . . . My dipping paddle scarcely shakes
> The berry in the bramble-brakes;
> Still forth on my green way I wend
> Beside the cottage garden-end;
> And by the nested angler fare,
> And take the lovers unaware.

The rise of canoe clubs, particularly in the United States, created acceptable social settings for young men and women to meet and spend time together in canoes. Changes in women's fashion—the split skirt, bloomers—gave women far more freedom of movement, no longer forced to sit side saddle on horses and able now to peddle a bicycle or step easily into a canoe.

There was also the unspoken theory—quickly disproven, surely—that a young man and young woman could hardly get into compromising positions in something so tippy and awkward as a canoe. So canoe courtship came with convenient, if somewhat naive, approval.

Canoe manufacturers were quick to move on the possibility that their product might be useful for more than hunting, fishing and racing in regattas. Sleek vehicles known as "courting canoes" became quite fashionable. The man could paddle and the object of his desires could lounge and relax, taking in the scenery and, of course, avoiding the sun. Some canoes had fixtures in which she could stand her parasol. Others, somewhat later, came with fold-up gramophones capable of playing the popular seventy-eight-rpm vinyl records of the day. The 1960s might have had their "shag wagons," but the 1890s had their "courting canoes." No records exist of their relative success rates.

While the museum holds a number of finely polished courting canoes from the era, perhaps the most interesting aspect of the exhibition lies in the collection of illustrations and postcards tied to the phenomenon. There is a frisson of risqué-ness that increases over the years as one scans through the cards and small booklet published specially for the show. While the subtext of the postcard of a young man helping the dainty young woman aboard with the line "You'll be perfectly safe in my canoe" is perhaps a tad suggestive, the intent of another, which portrays a young couple paddling over the line "I'd like to paddle your canoe," is, well, unmistakable.

The decade following the Great War was also a time of the "New Woman" and there are also illustrations to celebrate women breaking out on their own. "I can paddle my own canoe" is a popular theme on postcards featuring single women paddling, but the current obviously flows in the other direction in most other cards. "I can paddle my own canoe," says one postcard of a sad-looking young woman contemplating nature, "but it's awful lonesome."

In the background of the show, a screen shows old clips of romantic movies featuring the canoe—Nelson Eddy as the bad-paddling Mountie and Jeanette MacDonald as the damsel in distress in 1936's *Rose-Marie*, Marilyn Monroe and another Mountie in *River of No Return*, filmed in Banff in 1953.

And then, of course, there are the songs, the canoe once as familiar in the day's popular tunes as hurtin' songs are in country music:

> *In my canoe*
> *We'll hide among the willows close by the shore where no one can see*
> *I'll cuddle you and snuggle you if you'll cuddle me . . .*

All that, obviously, is not only corny but tame. There appears a different standard between the safe, innocent songs and the suggestive postcards. There is even one cartoon found in the museum's collection of a man and a very buxom woman hanging desperately on to the sides of an overturned canoe with the line "We learned one thing—*it can't be done in a canoe!*"

But, of course, it can. Canadians don't need Pierre Berton or Phil Chester to tell them that it is possible—*who knows how many of us were "launched" in a Chestnut or Peterborough or Old Town?*—and is, for many North Americans, considered an important rite of passage among those who know that "length" and "girth" are measures in cedar, as well.

It took until 2013 before *Cosmopolitan*—the New York–based magazine noted for its sexual advice—addressed the long-established art of "canoodling." Complete with illustration, the magazine got immediately to the point:

Erotic Instructions
In a canoe or rowboat, paddle a short distance from shore. Once you're at your desired locale, stretch out on your side, resting

your head on your bottom arm for cushioning. (Bend your knees if necessary.) Have your partner spoon you from behind, keeping his top arm wrapped around your waist as he enters you and begins to thrust gently.

Why You'll Love It
This relaxing pose is perfect for slow, sensuous lovemaking. Because of the close confines, your bodies will be melded from head to toe, and the rocking motion of the boat will intensify each of his internal strokes.

Cosmo Hint
Take it nice and easy or your boat could tip over. To play it super-safe, make sure you only go out on a calm lake where you can swim to shore.

Sadly, *Cosmopolitan* magazine gives "canoodling" only three out of five hot flames for its "carnal challenge." The Canadian Canoe Museum, on the other hand, deserves a four out of five for its displays and imagination, the singular knock against it being the uninspired location in the abandoned Outboard Marine factory that once produced Evinrude and Johnson motors before the company moved operations to Mexico. A new location for the canoe museum is being actively sought on the Otonabee River that flows through Peterborough—and where many of the finest products of the Peterborough Canoe Company were built and tested. If suitable funding can be found, the museum will one day be exactly where it should be.

Up the stairs of the "Grand Portage," visitors come to the origins of the dugout and the birchbark canoe. Canoes a century and more old seem to float from the ceiling, the image coming so soon after the walk through the romantic canoe exhibition that a visitor cannot help but be reminded of *La Chasse-galerie*, the famous French-Canadian folk tale that has been celebrated everywhere from stamps to beer.

In the story known in English as "The Flying Canoe," a bunch of drunken voyageurs strike a pact with the devil in which he provides them with a "flying canoe" that transports them immediately back to their sweethearts in Montreal. All the devil asks in return is that the paddlers not touch a drop of the evil drink—a deal most voyageurs would turn down even if the trip included a castle, a princess and everlasting life at the end. But off they go, soaring high above the Ottawa Valley as they make their way home for New Year's. Returning to work the next day, their drunken *gouvernail* navigating from the stern barely avoids a church steeple before smashing *la chasse-galerie* into a snow bank and a giant white pine, knocking out everyone aboard and condemning the deal-makers to paddle forever as punishment.

There are those, it might be argued, who might confuse this with heaven.

The Canadian Canoe Museum holds canoes made of single logs of western cedar, where the builders used dried dogfish sharkskin to sand the gunwales down smooth. There are birchbark canoes that predate Confederation. There is a section for the Mi'kmaq legend of Glooscap, telling how he paddled his stone canoe in pursuit of two troublesome beavers, chased them up the St. John River in New Brunswick and hurled two stones at them: one landing and forming Grand Falls, the other hitting one of the beavers at a spot called Plaster Rock, where the clay is the colour of blood.

There are multiple displays about individuals, including the reclusive Herbert Pohl, an Austrian who was twenty years of age when he came to Canada, nearly forty when he started canoeing, and yet managed thirty major solo trips. Renowned for his sense of adventure as well as his sense of humour—"The Nahanni," he would say with a twinkle, "is a flat-water trip"—Pohl was seventy-six years old when his canoe overturned in Lake Superior near the Michipicoten River not far from the community of Wawa. He was, as usual, paddling alone. "It's not that I'm anti-social," Pohl once wrote, "I just prefer solitude to companionship and silence to conversation."

Pohl believed that there was nothing that could compare to a canoe trip when it came to giving perspective. "People are always chasing material success," he once wrote in his journal. "But out there it doesn't matter what success you have in human life. It means diddly-squat in the universe. There is some solace in that."

There is a fond tribute to Bill Mason and a special section for Pierre Trudeau, the two canoeing friends and icons side by side in comprehensive displays on the first floor. Mason's familiar red canoe is there, as is Trudeau's famous buckskin jacket. There are photographs of Tom Thomson in a canoe, but how sweet it would be if the Canadian Canoe Museum, rather than the Art Gallery of Ontario, could be where Tom's magnificent painting *The Canoe* could hang.

Phil Chester believes that there should be a special display honouring Grey Owl. I think there should be one honouring Phil. But I would also like to see a special display area devoted to the likes of Jack Hurley, canoe builder and canoe repairer extraordinaire from the tiny village of Dwight, Ontario. Jack has worked on most of the camp canoes of Algonquin Park and has himself paddled most of the routes—always in a wooden canoe, each canoe, he will tell you, having its own characteristics and personality. Jack's workshop tells its own story: wood shavings and tools everywhere, paint cans, special stores of white cedar from Ostroskie and Sons Lumber in Killaloe, paint brushes, varnish, sandpaper, old canoes getting new keels, injured canoes being patched and fibreglassed and painted to a point where they look brand new. Jack's shop is unique—an old barn with one entire wall featuring photographs of those he has admired in life, from area trappers to world leaders—and yet it is also representative of hundreds of canoe shops across the continent, each one seemingly overseen by a larger-than-life, cedar-loving canoe obsessive in need of a shave and a good bar of industrial-strength hand soap.

There is even a royal connection to be found in the museum: pictures showing the production of the last Peterborough canoe to come off the line. It was a gift sent by the government of Canada to England to celebrate the 1947 marriage of Elizabeth to Phillip. There is the canoe Trudeau commissioned as a gift for the wedding of Charles and Diana.

The largest individual display is reserved, appropriately, for Kirk Wipper, the father of the Canadian Canoe Museum. Wipper was the Manitoban who eventually took over Camp Kandalore on Lake Kabakwa near Haliburton, Ontario, and turned it into a canoe-tripping legend.

Wipper was a devoted disciple of the teachings and philosophies of Ernest Thompson Seton, the British-born naturalist who moved to Upper Canada as a boy the year before Confederation and later became an American citizen. In 1902 he began his Woodcraft Indians movement and also inspired Lord Baden-Powell to found the Boy Scouts.

Seton, like Archie Belaney a born Englishman who played tricks in the New World with his identity, had a powerful hold over Canadian campers and scouts. He was a strange one—telling people he should be addressed as "Black Wolf," requesting that his family put but a single word, "Misunderstood," on his gravestone, and so afraid of nocturnal emissions that he used to sleep on a flat board and splash his tortured private parts with ice-cold water—but he was beloved for his writings in which he gave animals human personalities, like Tito the Coyote. Seton was a classic "wannabe" and would today be dismissed. In his day, however, he was revered.

Wipper, like many other camp directors of the day, followed Seton's path by adopting "Indian" rituals by the wagonload—including wearing fancy headdresses and holding campfire war dances—long before the word "appropriation" had even been used. He, like many other camp directors, meant well by this, and the appropriations, whatever one may think of them today, were often critical to attracting young city dwellers into camp life.

Conclusion

Wipper believed that the greatest attraction his camp could offer was, in fact, to escape the camp increasingly as the youngsters returned each summer. Newcomers to camp began with cookouts and day trips but soon were off on three-day trips. By the time youngsters were fifteen years old, they were either "Pathfinders," spending a month on an extended trip, or "Explorers," tripping for the entire two months their parents paid for them to be at Kandalore. If they performed well, the next year they would be invited back as leaders in training, moving on as hired counsellors or camp staff in summers to come.

The goal of the camp, as he stated it, was to "put people into an experience where there was imagination demanded, where there was physical exertion demanded. And where older and younger campers could work together . . . we always had the teams of older and younger. Well, there was a lot of learning going on—the older campers learning about the younger ones, they forget you know, and the younger ones look up and learn from the older ones . . . it was about imagination and cooperation. . . . We have to develop a fantasy world. I believe in fantasy. I think people grow in fantasy as long as it doesn't become an obsession."

Belief in "the supremacy of the long canoe trip" helped make Wipper's camp wildly successful after years of financial ruin before he took it over. And one of the happier results of reaching the black ink side of the ledger was that it allowed Wipper to continue his growing passion for collecting canoes. At one point he owned some six hundred of them, all now treasures of the Canadian Canoe Museum.

Wipper, who died at age eighty-seven in 2011, was devoted to the canoe. To him, the canoe was "the gift of freedom." As he once told CBC Radio's *Ideas*, "The canoe is a vehicle that carries you into pretty exciting places, not only into whitewater but into the byways and off-beaten places. . . . You are removed entirely from the mundane aspects of ordinary life. You're witnessing first-hand beauty and peace and freedom—especially freedom. . . . Flirtation with the wilderness is contact with truth, because the truth is in nature. . . . I like to identify myself with something that is stable and enduring. Although [nature] is in a state of flux, it is enduring. It is where reality is. I appreciate the canoe for its gifts in that direction."

Wipper collected his hundreds of canoes—often driving cross-country to retrieve abandoned boats—simply because he loved them. "I never thought I'd be involved with a museum, a worldwide museum," he once said. "I mean that was probably furthest from my mind, but it happened." And everyone who has ever held a paddle should be grateful that it happened.

There is not only something timeless about the canoe—the ancient ones floating near the ceiling in the "Origins" section little changed from the cedar ribbed canoe under construction in the open-view shop below—but something also timeless about how those who paddle feel about its intrinsic value.

Personally, I stand with my old journalism hero on this point of intrinsic value. Bruce Hutchison died at the age of ninety-two in 1991, but more than a half century earlier had written, "The underprivileged generation of affluence, travelling in a costly automobile, may get no closer to Canada than a public roadside camp, with hot running water and firewood cut at the taxpayer's expense, and will go home in the pathetic belief that it has been camping. If I had any influence on national policy, the state would put all Canadian children in a real camp for at least a month each summer. That would be the best possible investment in health, sanity and true culture. It might even stave off a revolution against the Great Society whose beneficiaries are beginning to find its imperfections already, as any old wilderness man could have told them in advance."

And to that I would add something said by the CBC's Shelagh Rogers, who is not only an avid paddler but is ambassador-at-large for the Canadian Canoe Museum. "The canoe," Rogers says, "is a threshold vessel—a skin, a fabric, and some bark between water and sky. Floating is some kind of miracle, some kind of dream. All canoers are dreamers to a degree."

And may the dream never end. May this great wonder of Canada, the simple canoe, carry them on and on forever.

ACKNOWLEDGEMENTS

Canoe trips are difficult to do alone; canoe books are impossible.

I am deeply indebted to everyone I have ever gone tripping with—especially Ellen and our family, Kerry, Christine, Jocelyn and Gordon. Husbands Olivier Dalle, Mike Cation and Andi Dzilums have all joined in later years. Fisher Cation insisted on his very own "canoe trip," just the two of us, when he was all of four years old. He still talks about it.

My own siblings—Jim, Ann and Tom—all learned to paddle in Algonquin Park, where our mother, Helen, made sure we knew better than to scrape along the gunwales. Jim and I have chased speckled and lake trout through so many park lakes and streams we long ago lost count, even if we never stopped telling tall tales. Our mother and her sister Mary (McCormick) Pigeon as well as our older cousins, Tom and Jake Pigeon and Don McCormick, master canoeists all, led the way in giving all of us a lifetime love of paddling.

Special thanks go to Phil Chester and the late Bert Cain of Deep River, with whom I spent many wonderful hours paddling and talking canoes. Phil and his brother Lorne and the Crash Test Dummies have been the grandest company imaginable on various whitewater adventures. Phil also pushed hard to see this book completed and was encouraging in every chapter—even if the former English teacher couldn't resist

Acknowledgements

the blue pencil. Two others pushed hard and advised regularly: my friend Jack Hurley, the great canoe builder of Dwight, Ontario, and Edie Van Alstine, a treasured lifelong friend whose family shares an Algonquin Park background with ours and who has been a welcome (well, not always) wise voice and eye on so many books over the years.

I am grateful to the *Globe and Mail* for indulging my passion for canoes and rivers from time to time, and to brilliant photographer Tibor Kolley for the gift of some of the terrific photos he took at Camp Lake and Lake of Two Rivers for a 2003 special feature on Canada Day.

The families of Bill Mason and Blair Fraser were wonderfully open in talking about their patriarchs, even when the subject of their passing proved difficult. Becky Mason could not have been more generous with her time and with her sage advice. Friends who paddled with Pierre Trudeau were always willing to talk about those trips and what the canoe meant to the long-serving prime minister.

The Peake brothers, Sean and Michael, were enthusiastic and end-lessly helpful when it came to tracking down hard-to-find research on everything from the New Voyageurs to David Thompson. Michael's *Che-Mun* magazine was a great source of information, and its recent demise is sorely regretted.

I also was fortunate to have research help from Sheila Rider of the CBC, who was so helpful and cheerful during the network's contest to identify the Seven Wonders of Canada and who helped later on when I was trying to remember precisely how the voting had gone. My longtime friend Don Beauprie of Deep River and Cache Lake is an expert on the Grand Trunk Railway and put me in contact with rail historian Dennis Peters, who helped with fares from the 1920s. Ottawa researcher Jenna Nunas helped in the impossible task of finding the elusive relative who went off on the Nile Expedition in 1884–85. Ottawa historian Anthony Michel, who will publish his own book on the little-known escapade, was always there with information and suggestions.

Curator Jeremy Ward and staff of the Canadian Canoe Museum in

Acknowledgements

Peterborough were always open to visits and questions. If you have not visited, do—it's a Canadian treasure that deserves to be much better known.

Behind me there is row after row of bookshelves filled with books on the canoe and canoeing. It would take pages to mention them all but I would be remiss if I failed to mention several that were of particular help. James Raffan's biography of Bill Mason, *Fire in the Bones*, is a terrific read and filled with canoeing lore. Roy MacLaren's *Canadians on the Nile 1882-1898* is, so far, the definitive study of a most remarkable event in Canadian history. Phil Chester and Hap Wilson helped me see Grey Owl in new light, for which I am grateful. I could never have written the David Thompson chapter without the help of my long-time friend D'Arcy Jenish's *Epic Wanderer*. Sean Peake generously gave me a two-volume *The Travels of David Thompson 1784-1812*, which he had lovingly edited.

There so very many books on how and where to canoe. You cannot do better than Bill Mason's famous *Path of the Paddle*, C.E.S. Franks's *The Canoe and Whitewater*, Bruce W. Hodgins and Gwyneth Hoyle's *Canoeing North into the Unknown* and *Paddling the Boreal Forest* by Max Finkelstein and James Stone. Roger MacGregor's *When the Chestnut was in Flower* is an exhaustive history of the development of the modern recreational canoe. Nor can you do better than any of Kevin Callan's several guide books on where to go and what you'll find there.

In understanding the canoe's unique position in Canadian culture, I was greatly helped by Jamie Benidickson's *Idleness, Water, and a Canoe and by The Canoe in Canadian Cultures*, edited by John Jennings, Bruce W. Hodgins and Doreen Small. Three coffee-table publications—Jennings's *The Canoe: A Living Tradition*, Kenneth G. Roberts and Philip Shackleton's *The Canoe* and *Stories from the Bow Seat* by Don Standfield and Liz Lundell—are excellent reads as well as visual treats.

My friend and agent Bruce Westwood believed in this project from first mention. Publisher Anne Collins and senior editor Craig Pyette of Random House Canada were instantly on side and supportive throughout—especially Craig, who also acted as overall editor. Andrew

Acknowledgements

Roberts did the wonderful design of the book and Frances Bedford was, happily, once again in charge of publicity. Copy editor Stacey Cameron and proofreader Alex Schultz saved me from myself time and time again. Alex, who has served as editor on several of my books and all the Screech Owls mystery series for young readers, long ago became a dear and trusted friend. Genevieve Macintyre and Caryn Cathcart helped with the images and endnotes.

I would be honoured to paddle with any of them. As for any mistakes that may remain, they belong to only one person.

Roy MacGregor
Kanata, ON
June 2, 2015

PERMISSIONS

All photos appear courtesy of the author unless otherwise noted below.

"The author gets away . . ." Photo courtesy of Tibor Kolley.

"The icon . . ." Tom Thomson's 1912 painting "The Canoe" appears courtesy of The Art Gallery of Ontario.

"Filmmaker . . ." Photo appears courtesy of Becky Mason.

"Mason's friend . . ." Photo appears courtesy of Justin Trudeau.

"The Mahdi . . ." Frontpage of French newspaper *Le Petit Parisien*, 1896/Private Collection/Getty Images.

"'General Gordon's Last Stand' . . ." George William Joy's painting appears courtesy of Leeds Museums and Galleries (Leeds Art Gallery) U.K./Bridgeman Images.

"The Nile Expedition . . ." Detail from the "Canadian Nile Contingent" appears courtesy of Library and Archives Canada.

Permissions

"Blair Fraser . . ." Photo appears courtesy of the Blair family.

"Kristina Leidums . . ." Photo appears courtesy of Kristina Leidums.

"Anahareo . . ." Harold Barkley/Toronto Star via Getty Images.

"'Shooting the Rapids' . . ." Frances Ann Hopkins's painting appears courtesy of Library and Archives Canada.

"Jocelyn MacGregor . . ." Photo appears courtesy of Jocelyn MacGregor.

"David Thompson . . ." Photo appears courtesy of Jocelyn MacGregor.

"Adventurer-explorer . . ." Portrait of Simon Fraser (1729-1777), Brigadier General of British infantry, United Kingdom, 18th century/Getty Images.

"As innocent as it looks? . . ." Image appears courtesy of the Canadian Canoe Museum, with thanks to Jeremy Ward.

"Tom Thomson . . ." Photo of Thomson and Arthur Lismer on Canoe Lake, Algonquin Park, May 1914, appears courtesy of the McMichael Canadian Art Collection.

ENDNOTES

Introduction

5   John Jennings, "The Canadian Canoe Museum and Canada's National Symbol," in *The Canoe in Canadian Cultures*, ed. John Jennings, Bruce W. Hodgins and Doreen Small (Toronto: Natural Heritage Books, 1999), 1.

5   Ibid., 4.

7   Ray Atherton, "The Man in a Canoe," *Canadian Art*, vol. 5, no. 2 (1947–48): 57–58.

7   Ian MacLeod, "The Lost Voyageur," *Ottawa Citizen*, 15 November 2008, A3.

8   Jamie Benidickson, *Idleness, Water, and a Canoe: Reflections on Paddling for Pleasure* (Toronto: University of Toronto Press, 1997), 149.

8   Pierre Elliott Trudeau, "Exhaustion and Fulfillment: The Ascetic in a Canoe," in *Wilderness Canada*, ed. Borden Spears (Toronto: Clarke Irwin, 1970), 4.

9   Benidickson, *Idleness, Water, and a Canoe*, 30–31.

10   Max Finkelstein, "Downtown Mountain Man," in *More of Canada's Best Canoe Routes*, ed. Alister Thomas (Erin: Boston Mills Press, 2003), 235.

Chapter 1—The Old Ranger's Chestnut

20   Brûlé is considered to be the first, and only, white man devoured in a cannibal feast in Ontario. http://www.ontarioabandonedplaces.com/upload/wiki.asp?entry=2001.

Endnotes

21   Liz Lundell and Beverley Bailey, *Summer Camp: Great Camps of Algonquin Park* (Erin: Boston Mills Press, 1994), 11.

21   Correspondence with rail historian Dennis Peters, who used a Grand Trunk passenger tariff for Eastern Ontario, dated July 1, 1921, to determine the costs: "The calculations in the tables are based on a per mile charge of $0.0345 for a first class fare. Most people travelled second class, however, and by my calculations, that was about 85.4 per cent of the first class rate, or 2.94 cents per mile. Scotia junction to Brule Lake was 74.6 miles, so the one-way fare would have been $2.20, and the round trip $3.95."

21   Correspondence with Algonquin Park historian Rory MacKay and Park archivist Ron Tozer.

22   Bernard Wicksteed, *Joe Lavally and the Paleface in Algonquin Park* (Toronto: Collins, 1948), 170.

26   Michael Budman, interview by author, September 2014.

28   G.D. Garland, ed., *Glimpses of Algonquin: Thirty Personal Impressions from Earliest Times to the Present*, (Whitney: Friends of Algonquin Park, 1989), 21.

30   John McPhee, *The Survival of the Bark Canoe* (New York: Farrar, Straus and Giroux, 1975), 35.

33   John A. Murray, ed., *The Quotable Nature Lover* (New York: Lyons Press, 1999), 23.

Chapter 2—Songs along the Dumoine

41   Hap Wilson, *Rivers of the Upper Ottawa Valley: Myth, Magic and Adventure* (Erin: Boston Mills Press, 2004), 12.

45   Roy MacGregor, *Escape: In Search of the Natural Soul of Canada* (Toronto: McClelland & Stewart, 2002), xi.

45   Sigurd F. Olson, *Wilderness Days* (Minneapolis: University of Minnesota Press, 2012), 63.

46   Harry Middleton, "Midnight's Rivers," in *The River Reader*, ed. John A. Murray (New York: Lyons Press, 1998), 225.

47   C.E.S. Franks, *The Canoe and White Water: From Essential to Sport* (Toronto: University of Toronto Press, 1977), 44.

48   Craig Oliver, *Oliver's Twist: The Life and Times of an Apologetic Newshound* (Toronto: Penguin Canada, 2011), 111.

48   Ibid., 217.

Endnotes

49   Ibid., 314-15.

52   Gwyneth Hoyle, "The Dark Side of the Canoe," in *The Canoe in Canadian Cultures*, ed. John Jennings, Bruce W. Hodgins and Doreen Small (Toronto: Natural Heritage Books, 1999), 212.

53   Jeff Rennicke, letter, *Canoe*, October 1987, 17.

54   Kenneth G. Roberts and Philip Shackleton, *The Canoe: A History of the Craft from Panama to the Arctic* (Toronto: Macmillan of Canada, 1983), 232.

56   Philip Chester, "Motives for Mr. Canoehead," in *Canexus: The Canoe in Canadian Culture*, ed. James Raffan and Bert Horwood (Toronto: Betelgeuse Books, 1988), 95.

62   Grey Owl, *Pilgrims of the Wild* (Toronto: Dundurn Press, 2010), 42.

62   Ibid., 229-230.

63   Hap Wilson, *Grey Owl and Me: Stories from the Trail and Beyond* (Toronto: Natural Heritage Books, 2010) 237.

65   Bert Horwood, "The Dao of Paddling," in *The Canoe in Canadian Cultures*, ed. John Jennings, Bruce W. Hodgins and Doreen Small (Toronto: Natural Heritage Books, 1999), 69.

Chapter 3—The Two Icons

78   Nancy Southam, ed., *Pierre: Colleagues and Friends Talk about the Trudeau They Knew* (Toronto: McClelland & Stewart, 2005), 262.

78   Justin Trudeau, "The Canoe Lessons," *Cottage Life*, May 2012, 146.

79   Southam, ed., *Pierre*, 285.

80   Pierre Elliott Trudeau, *Memoirs* (Toronto: McClelland & Stewart, 1993), 254.

81   Becky Mason, interview by author, July 2014.

81   Ibid.

83   Terry Orlick, email exchanges, November 2014.

84   Southam, ed., *Pierre*, 265.

85   James Raffan, *Fire in the Bones: Bill Mason and the Canadian Canoeing Tradition* (Toronto: HarperCollins, 1996), 37.

86   Jim Dale Vickery, *Wilderness Visionaries* (Merrickville: ICS Books, 1986), 172.

86   Becky Mason, interview by author, July 2014.

87   Raffan, *Fire in the Bones*, xvii.

87   Becky Mason, interview by author, July 2014.

88   Raffan, *Fire in the Bones*, 80.

89   Benidickson, *Idleness, Water, and a Canoe*, 49.

Endnotes

89 Theodore Roosevelt, "Downriver: A Yellowstone Journey," in *The River Reader*, ed. John A. Murray (New York: Lyons Press, 1998), 160.

89 Edwin Hodder, *John MacGregor ("Rob Roy")* (London: Hodder Bros., 1894), 284.

90 Ralph Connor, *Postscript to Adventure: The Autobiography of Ralph Connor* (Toronto: McClelland & Stewart, 1975), 53.

91 Robert Collins, "God Can Bring Good Out of It," *Reader's Digest*, February 1979, 183–210.

91 Benidickson, *Idleness, Water, and a Canoe*, 52.

92 William C. James, "The Canoe Trip as Religious Quest," *Studies in Religion/Sciences religieuses*, vol. 10, no. 2 (1981): 151–166.

92 John Foster and Janet Foster, *To the Wild Country* (Toronto: Van Nostrand, 1975), 88.

93 Douglas LePan, "Canoe Trip," *Weathering It: Complete Poems, 1948–1987* (Toronto: McClelland & Stewart, 1987), 75.

94 Becky Mason, interview by author, July 2014.

94 Southam, ed., *Pierre*, 270.

94 Ibid., 285.

95 Becky Mason, interview by author, July 2014.

95 Raffan, *Fire in the Bones*, 245.

96 Becky Mason, interview by author, July 2014.

96 James Raffan, "Being There: Bill Mason and the Canadian Canoeing Tradition," in *The Canoe in Canadian Cultures*, ed. John Jennings, Bruce W. Hodgins and Doreen Small (Toronto: Natural Heritage Books, 1999), 17.

96 Becky Mason, interview by author, July 2014.

97 Ibid.

97 Becky Mason, "Canoescapes and the Creative Spirit," in *The Canoe in Canadian Cultures*, eds. John Jennings, Bruce W. Hodgins and Doreen Small (Toronto: Natural Heritage Books, 1999), 235.

98 Ibid., 237.

Chapter 4—The Nile Expedition

100 Richard Gould, *Calvin Remembers, 1887–1987* (Nipissing: Calvin Township Centennial Committee, 1987).

102 Roberts and Shackleton, *The Canoe*, 199.

104 Ian Wilson and Sally Wilson, "In the Spirit of the Voyageurs," *The Beaver*, June/July 1999, 14–15.

104 Wilson, *Rivers of the Upper Ottawa Valley*, 31.

105 Ibid., 33.

107 In the fall and winter of 2014–15, research expert Jenna Fowler of Ottawa spent many hours attempting to track down Duncan MacGregor's beloved "relative" who went off to save General Gordon. She found a vast array of Ottawa Valley relatives from both sides of Duncan's family, MacGregor/McGregor and Keenan, but could neither link them to the Carsons of Round Lake nor find another name, related, who matched one of the names on the incomplete listings of those who were known to have headed for the Nile.

110 Roy MacLaren, *Canadians on the Nile, 1882–1898* (Vancouver: University of British Columbia Press, 1978), 22.

110 Michael Asher, *Khartoum: The Ultimate Imperial Adventure* (London: Penguin, 2006), xxviii.

110 MacLaren, *Canadians on the Nile*, 22.

112 Ibid., 10–12.

112 Ibid., 27.

112 Asher, *Khartoum*, 69.

113 MacLaren, *Canadians on the Nile*, 31.

113 Asher, *Khartoum*, 134–137.

113 MacLaren, *Canadians on the Nile*, 36.

114 Asher, *Khartoum*, 92.

114 Ibid., 108.

115 MacLaren, *Canadians on the Nile*, 44.

116 John Boileau, "Voyageurs on the Nile," *Legion Magazine*, January/February 2004, 41.

116 MacLaren, *Canadians on the Nile*, 49.

117 Boileau, "Voyageurs on the Nile," 41.

118 Anthony Michel, "To Represent the Country in Egypt: Aboriginality, Britishness, Anglophone Canadian Identities, and the Nile Voyageur Contingent, 1884–85," *Social History* vol. 39, no. 77 (2006): 52–53.

119 Ibid., 63–64.

121 Ibid., 67.

121 Ibid., 70.

121 Quote taken from *Voyageurs* display at The Canadian Canoe Museum, September 2014.

121 Michel, "To Represent the Country in Egypt," 74.

Endnotes

122 Ibid., 57.

122 MacLaren, *Canadians on the Nile*, 83.

123 Boileau, "Voyageurs on the Nile," 42.

123 MacLaren, *Canadians on the Nile*, 86.

124 Asher, *Khartoum*, 185.

124 MacLaren, *Canadians on the Nile*, 99.

124 Col. Sir Charles W. Wilson, *From Korti to Khartoum: A Journal of the Desert March from Korti to Gubat, and of the Ascent of the Nile in General Gordon's Steamers* (London: The Naval & Military Press Ltd., 1885), 180-1.

125 Asher, *Khartoum*, 261.

125 MacLaren, *Canadians on the Nile*, 100.

126 Ibid., 103.

126 Asher, *Khartoum*, 279.

126 Ibid., 405.

127 Michel, "To Represent the Country in Egypt," 75.

127 Ibid., 91.

128 Ibid., 122.

128 Ibid., 75.

129 Anthony Michel, email exchanges, May 2014.

130 O.A. Cooke, "Denison, Frederick Charles," in *Dictionary of Canadian Biography*, vol. 12, University of Toronto/Université Laval, 2003, http://www.biographi.ca/en/bio/denison_frederick_charles_12E.html.

Chapter 5—The Mission

132 Wilson, *Rivers of the Upper Ottawa Valley*, 35.

135 Olson, *Wilderness Days*, 63.

136 Raffan, *Fire in the Bones*, 196-7.

136 *Ibid.*, 198.

136 Eric Morse, *Freshwater Saga: Memoirs of a Lifetime of Wilderness Canoeing in Canada* (Toronto: University of Toronto Press, 1987), 11.

137 Michael Peake, "Meet the voyageurs," *Che-Mun*, no. 69, 1993.

138 Sigurd F. Olson, "A Certain Kind of Man," *The Beaver*, Autumn 1968, 12.

142 Blair Fraser, *The Search for Identity: Canada, 1945-1967* (Toronto: Doubleday Canada, 1967), 315.

145 Oliver, *Oliver's Twist*, 310.

149 Blair Fraser, "The Fairy Romance of the Canadian Shield," *Maclean's*, December, 1955, 42-45.

150 Fraser, *The Search for Identity*, 313–14.

153 Oliver, *Oliver's Twist*, 311.

156 Blair Fraser, "A Centennial Sermon," in *Blair Fraser Reports*, ed. John Fraser and Graham Fraser (Toronto: Macmillan of Canada, 1969), 302.

Chapter 6—"A Place of Power"

159 Philip Shackleton, "Beechey, Frances Anne," in *Dictionary of Canadian Biography*, vol. 14, University of Toronto, Université Laval, 2003, http://www.biographi.ca/009004-119.01-e.php?BioId=41319.

159 Toni Harting, *French River: Canoeing the River of the Stick-Wavers*, (Erin: Boston Mills Press, 1996), 84–85.

160 Sarah Reilly, "Thanadelthur: Northern Peacemaker United Chipewyan and Cree Peoples," *Canada's History*, February/March 2015, 17.

161 Don Standfield and Liz Lundell, *Stories from the Bow Seat: The Wisdom & Waggery of Canoe Tripping* (Erin: Boston Mills Press, 1999), 49.

162 G.D. Garland, ed., "Northway Lodge is Founded, 1908," *Glimpses of Algonquin: Thirty Personal Impressions from Earliest Times to the Present* (Whitney: Friends of Algonquin Park, 1989), 71.

162 Ibid., 71.

163 Ibid., 71.

163 James Dickey, *Deliverance* (London: Pan Books, 1971), 9.

163 E. Pauline Johnson, "Striking Camp," *Saturday Night*, August 1891, 7.

163 Ella Walton, "A Woman's Views on Camping Out," *Rod and Gun*, September 1899, 72.

164 Martha Craig, "My Summer Outings in Labrador," in *The Canoe in Canadian Cultures*, eds. Bruce W. Hodgins, John Jennings and Doreen Small (Toronto: Natural Heritage Books, 1999), 72.

164 Benidickson, *Idleness, Water, and a Canoe*, 90.

165 Kristin Gleeson, *Anahareo: A Wilderness Spirit* (Tucson: Fireship Press, 2012), 41.

166 Joanne Kates, "Keen and bright, flashing with silver," *The Globe and Mail*, 9 November 2000, A30.

166 Olivia Chow, "For Olivia Chow, 12 days on river offer chance to look back, move forward," *The Globe and Mail*, 9 August 2012, A1.

168 Esther S. Keyser and John S. Keyser, *Paddling My Own Canoe: The Story of Algonquin Park's First Female Guide* (Whitney: Friends of Algonquin Park, 2003), 251.

Endnotes

169 Ibid., 1-2.

171 Ken Warren, "Senators explore hockey's birthplace," *Ottawa Citizen*, 12 November 2012, B1.

181 Justine Kerfoot, "No Compass, No Matches, No Protection from the Elements," in *Stories from the Bow Seat: The Wisdom and Waggery of Canoe Tripping*, ed. Don Standfield and Liz Lundell (Erin: Boston Mills Press, 1999), 78.

Chapter 7–The Man Who Measured Canada

191 D'Arcy Jenish, *Epic Wanderer: David Thompson and the Mapping of the Canadian West* (Toronto: Anchor Canada, 2004), 122.

193 D'Arcy Jenish, "Saving David Thompson," *Canada's History*, April/May 2010, 41-44.

195 Thompson scholar Sean Peake has contended that the "Race to the Sea" interpretation has been popular but not quite accurate. His study of Thompson's journals and writings suggest that Thompson and the Northwest Company well knew that the Americans were on their way even when Thompson set out from Rainy Lake House in 1810. The NWC strategy would be the same as they had used against the Hudson Bay Company back east—cut off the trade by establishing posts well upstream and intercepting the native trappers. Thompson's slow going, therefore, was due to his obligations to establish these trading posts. (Sean Peake, correspondence with author, March 2015.)

196 Jenish, "Saving David Thompson," 42.

197 Sean Peake says that the fourteen gaps in Thompson's journals are easily explained, as they occur when Thompson was travelling over areas already surveyed. "There was no need to do it again," Peake says. "They were not diaries but rather documents he used to create his maps and reports to his superiors and partners." (Sean Peake, correspondence with author, March 2015.)

197 Jenish, "Saving David Thompson," 42.

200 Jenish, *Epic Wanderer*, 247.

201 David Thompson, "Current Going With Us, Thank God," in *Glimpses of Algonquin: Thirty Personal Impressions from Earliest Times to the Present*, ed. G.D. Garland (Whitney: Friends of Algonquin Park, 1989), 19.

204 D'Arcy Jenish, correspondence with author, August 2014.

204 Ibid.

Endnotes

204 Ibid.

204 Sanford Osler, *Canoe Crossings: Understanding the Craft that Helped Shape British Columbia* (Vancouver: Heritage House Publishing, 2014), 20.

205 Sean Peake, correspondence with author, August 2014.

205 Jeremy Ward, interview by author, September 2014.

206 Hap Wilson, "Path of the Paddle," *Canadian Geographic*, July/August 2012, 69.

207 John Donaldson, *One Day at a Time: A Canoe Quest in the Wake of Canada's "Prince of Explorers"* (Kingston: Artful Codger Press, 2006), 245.

207 Sean Peake, correspondence with author, August 2014.

Chapter 8—The Craft

210 William Chapman White, *Adirondack Country* (New York: Knopf, 1967), xi.

211 Raffan, *Fire in the Bones*, 59.

212 McPhee, *The Survival of the Bark Canoe*, 38.

213 John Jennings, *Bark Canoes: The Art and Obsession of Tappan Adney*, (Richmond Hill: Firefly Books, 2004), 22.

215 Daniel "Pinock" Smith, interview by author, October 2014.

215 McPhee, *The Survival of the Bark Canoe*, 55.

215 Jerry Stelmok and Rollin Thurlow, *The Wood & Canvas Canoe: A Complete Guide to its History, Construction, Restoration, and Maintenance* (Gardiner: Harpswell Press/Tilbury House Publishers, 1987), 17.

216 Kenneth G. Roberts and Philip Shackleton, *The Canoe*, 240.

217 Roger MacGregor, *When the Chestnut Was in Flower* (Lansdowne: Plumsweep, 1999), 81.

217 Ted Moores, *Canoecraft: An Illustrated Guide to Fine Woodstrip Construction*, (Richmond Hill: Firefly Books, 2000), 18.

217 Roberts and Shackleton, *The Canoe*, xi.

218 Ibid., 266.

219 Moores, *Canoecraft*, 17.

221 Roberts and Shackleton, *The Canoe*, 171.

Chapter 9—Lost on James Bay

229 Peter C. Newman, *Company of Adventurers* (Toronto: Viking Books, 1985), 33.

229 Carl Schuster, "Into the Great Bay: Henry Hudson's Mysterious Final Voyage," *The Beaver*, August/September 1999: 8-15.

Endnotes

230 Max Finkelstein and James Stone, *Paddling the Boreal Forest: Rediscovering A.P. Low* (Toronto: Natural Heritage Books, 2004), 237–38.

231 Ibid., 2–3.

231 Ibid., 59.

232 Richard F. Salisbury, *A Homeland for the Crees: Regional Development in James Bay 1971–1981* (Kingston and Montreal: McGill-Queen's University Press, 1986), 25.

232 Ibid., 238.

233 Jeremy Ward, interview by author at The Canadian Canoe Museum, September 2014.

234 Boyce Richardson, *Strangers Devour the Land: The Cree Hunters of the James Bay Area versus Premier Bourassa and the James Bay Development Corporation* (Toronto: Macmillan of Canada, 1975), 5–6.

239 The tale of the Cree-Yamaha test run appears, in rather different form, in *Canadians: Portrait of a Country and Its People* (Viking, 2007). In that version, much more is made of Cree enterprise, the James Bay Agreement and historical overview. In this version, while the anecdote of the "test drive" is of course similar, the emphasis is on the vessels used by the Crees over the centuries.

Conclusion

252 John Summers, *Can I Canoe You Up the River?: The Story of Paddling and Romance* (Peterborough: The Canadian Canoe Museum, 2014), 56.

253 Paul Worrel Conway, ed., *Talking Canoes* (Peterborough: Polymath Classic Reprints, 2013), 4.

255 Ibid., 55.

256 "Canoe Canoodle," *Cosmopolitan*, http://www.cosmopolitan.com /sex-love/positions/a26854/canoe-canoodle-sex-position/

258 "Pohl died doing what he loved," *InsideHalton.com*, 21 July 2006.

260 Beverly Haun, *Becoming Kirt Wipper: The Story of the Museum's Founder* (Peterborough: The Canadian Canoe Museum, 2013), 95.

261 Ibid., 52.

262 Shelagh Rogers, foreword to *Canoe Crossings: Understanding the Craft That Helped Shape British Columbia*, by Sanford Osler (Vancouver: Heritage House Publishing, 2014), 9.

INDEX

Index

Index

Index

Index

Index

Index

Index

fur trade, 5, 8, 10, 36, 40, 19, 36, 103, 120, 121, 136, 137, 177, 191, 204, 207, 214, 221, 229, 230, 231
fur trade routes race, 40
"fuzzy wuzzies," 113

Galeairy Lake, 32
Galipeau, Annie, 63
Gardner machine gun, 124
gastroenteritis, 235
Gate of Hell, 105
Gatineau Hills, 62, 73–74, 80
Gatineau River, 40, 78, 137
General Gordon's Last Stand (painting), 125
Genie Awards, 95
genocide, 109
"geographical correctness," 4, 13
Geological Survey of Canada, 196, 230–31
George VI, King of England, 62
Georgian Bay, 18, 20, 28, 161, 177, 199, 200, 205, 226
Germany, popularity of canoeing, 89
Gibraltar, 119, 121
Gilbert & Sullivan, 114
Gillam, Zachariah, 230
Gillespie, Alastair, 78
Girl Guides, 168
girls' summer camps, 161–63, 167
Glacier National Park, 211
Gladstone, William, 112, 113, 125–26
Gleeson, Kristin, 165
Globe and Mail, 1, 133, 165, 166
Globe newspaper, 73
Glooscap (Mi'kmaq) legend, 5, 257
Glover, Richard, 197
"God Revealed" (slide show), 87
God's Lake, 51
Godfrey, Arthur, 252
Godfrey, John, 48
Godin, Ed, 148
gold rush, 47, 109, 212
Golden Lake First Nation, 61
Goldman, Ruth, 164
golfing vs canoeing, 54–55

Gordon, Charles George ("Chinese Gordon")
    "Christian hero," 114
    construction of Nile fleet, 120–21
    death of, 125
    military background of, 112
    muscular Christianity, 112
    personality of, 112
    photograph, 118
    physical appearance of, 112
    popularity of, 112–13
    relationship with women, 112
    self-image of, 113
    values of, 113–14
Gordon, Charles George—rescue mission
    camel march, 122, 123, 124, 126
    casualties, 123, 124
    commander of, 118
    Desert Column, 123, 124
    perils of travel, 123
    quality of boatmen, 122
    scouting missions, 120, 122, 124
    trip to Alexandria, 121
    trip to Gibraltar, 119
    volunteers, 117, 118–19, 120, 121, 122–23, 127–28, 129
    (*See also* Khartoum, siege of; Nile River Expedition)
gouvernail (voyageurs), 103
Governor-General's Literary Award, 93
Gracefield (QC), 84
gramophones, 254
Grand Beach (MB), 85
Grand Canyon, 211
Grand Chute, 65, 66
Grand Falls, 257
Grand Lake Victoria, 9
Grand Lake, 148
Grand Portage (MB), 137, 177, 182, 206, 256
Grand Trunk Railway, 18, 20–21, 25
Grand-Prée (NS), 192
Gray, Robert, 190–91, 192, 194
Great Bear Lake, 170, 171, 173
Great Bear River, 170, 171

Index

Index

Index

Index

Index

Index

Index

Index

Index

Index

Index

Index

Index

ROY MACGREGOR is the acclaimed and best-selling author of *Northern Light: The Enduring Mystery of Tom Thomson and the Woman Who Loved Him*; *The Home Team: Fathers, Sons and Hockey* (shortlisted for the Governor General's Literary Award); *A Life in the Bush* (winner of the U.S. Rutstrum Award for Best Wilderness Book and the CAA Award for Biography); *Canadians: A Portrait of a Country and Its People*; *Wayne Gretzky's Ghost: And Other Tales from a Lifetime in Hockey*; as well as two novels, *Canoe Lake* and *The Last Season*; and the popular Screech Owls mystery series for young readers. A long-time columnist at *The Globe and Mail*, MacGregor has won four National Magazine Awards and eight National Newspaper Award nominations. He is an Officer of the Order of Canada, and was described in the citation as one of Canada's "most gifted storytellers." He lives in Kanata, Ontario, with his wife, Ellen.

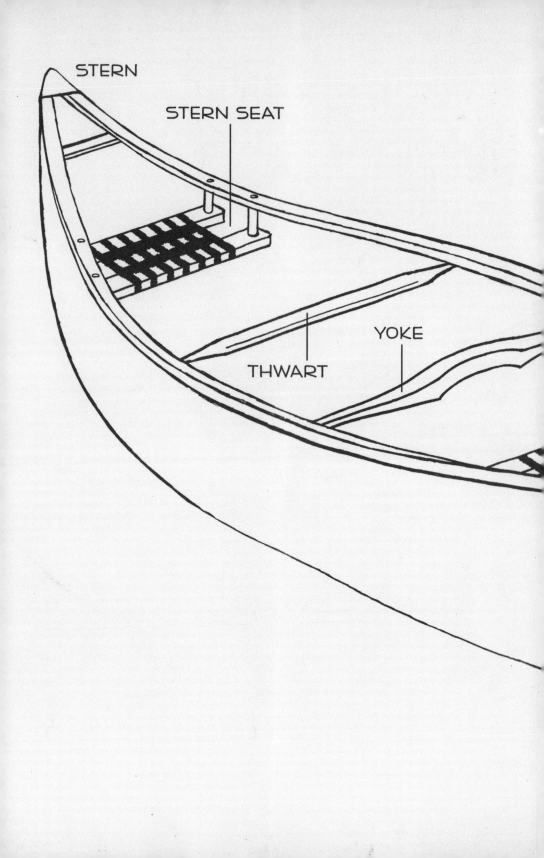

STERN

STERN SEAT

YOKE

THWART